ENGLAND AS IT IS

The Development of Industrial Society Series

William Johnston

ENGLAND AS IT IS

Political, Social and Industrial in the Middle of the Nineteenth Century

Volume 2

IRISH UNIVERSITY PRESS
Shannon   Ireland

First edition London 1851

This I U P reprint is a photolithographic facsimile of
the first edition and is unabridged, retaining the
original printer's imprint.

ⓒ *1971 Irish University Press Shannon Ireland*

All forms of micropublishing
ⓒ *Irish University Microforms Shannon Ireland*

ISBN 0 7165 1774 4 Two volumes
ISBN 0 7165 1775 2 Volume 1
ISBN 0 7165 1776 0 Volume 2

T M MacGlinchey Publisher
Irish University Press Shannon Ireland

PRINTED IN THE REPUBLIC OF IRELAND BY
ROBERT HOGG PRINTER TO IRISH UNIVERSITY PRESS

ENGLAND AS IT IS,

POLITICAL, SOCIAL, AND INDUSTRIAL,

IN THE

MIDDLE OF THE NINETEENTH CENTURY.

By WILLIAM JOHNSTON, Esq.,

BARRISTER AT LAW.

IN TWO VOLUMES.—Vol. II.

LONDON:

JOHN MURRAY, ALBEMARLE STREET.

1851.

"It behoves us ever to bear in mind that, while actions are always to be judged by the immutable standard of right and wrong, the judgment which we pass upon men must be qualified by considerations of age, country, situation, and other incidental circumstances, and it will then be found that he who is most charitable in his judgment is generally the least unjust."

SOUTHEY, *Book of the Church.*

(iii)

CONTENTS OF VOLUME II.

ENGLAND:

POLITICAL, SOCIAL, AND INDUSTRIAL.

CHAPTER XXII.

THE CHURCH OF ENGLAND.

" THE Church of England," says Southey, " has rescued us first from heathenism, then from papal idolatry and superstition ; it has saved us from temporal as well as spiritual despotism. We owe to it our moral and intellectual character as a nation—much of our private happiness, much of our public strength. Whatever should weaken it, would in the same degree injure the common weal ; whatever should overthrow it, would injure, and by immediate consequence bring down, the goodly fabric of that constitution whereof it is a constituent and necessary part." " The parochial system of the Church of England," says Dr. Arnold, " is designed to secure for every parish the greatest blessing of human society—that is, the constant residence of one individual who has no other business than to do good of every kind to every person. Men in general have their own profession or trade to follow ; and although they are useful to society, yet it is but an indirect benefit—not intended for society in the first place, but for themselves; so that no one feels obliged to them for their services, because there is nothing in them which partakes of the nature of a kindness. Those, again, who possess an independent fortune are not only raised too high to be in perfect sympathy with the majority of their neighbours, but are exposed to moral temptations of a peculiar kind, which often render them an inadequate example to others. Whereas it is impossible to conceive a man placed so favourably for attaining to the highest perfection of our nature as a parochial minister— apart from all personal and particular interests, accustomed by his education and habits to take the purest and highest views of human life, and bound by his daily business to cherish and sweeten these by the charities of the kindest social intercourse; in delicacy and liberality of feeling on a level with the highest, but in rank and fortune standing in a position high enough to ensure respect, yet not so high as to forbid sympathy; with none of the harshness of legal authority, yet with a moral influence such as no legal authority could give; ready to advise when advice is called for, but yet more useful by the indirect counsel continually afforded by his conduct, his knowledge, his temper, and his manners; he stands amid the fever and selfishness of the world, as one whom the tainted atmosphere cannot harm, although he is for ever walking about in it to abate its malignant power over its victims. Men bear impatiently the teaching of men, unless it comes with more than man's authority; the beneficial relations in which a minister stands towards his people derive much of their power from this very circumstance, that he is a minister of *religion*. And Christianity, while it fully invests him with this character, yet has provided in the strongest manner against superstition and priestcraft; for a minister can speak with no authority beyond his commission, and this commission lies open for all men to judge whether he adheres to it or no. It gives him power unspeakable, so long as he faithfully discharges it, but deserts and condemns him the very moment that he would pervert it to selfish purposes, to make his own word a law and himself an idol. But in this commission there is contained indeed the very food, and more than the food, of man's life—the remedy for all troubles and sorrows, from the simplest physical suffering of the rudest nature up to the mental conflicts which are the inevitable portion of the loftiest and most sensitive; the medicine for all moral evil, from the mere bodily appetites of the most grossly ignorant to the most delicate forms of pride or selfishness in minds of the highest intelligence; the light to clear up every perplexity of practice, strengthening the judgment through the purified affections; the most exalted hope, inseparably united with the deepest humility—because we believe in Christ crucified —because we trust in Christ risen." *

" I would not," says Canon Sidney Smith, " have the gentlemen of the money-bags, and of wheat and bean land, forget that the word Church means many other

---

* To this earnest piece of encomiastic writing Dr. Arnold appends the following note:—" I shall not be suspected of meaning this high character of the benefits of a national Christian ministry to apply in its full perfection to the actual state of the Church amongst us. The faults of human nature will always make the practice of an institution fall below its theory. But it is no less true that all the tendencies of the ministerial office, as such, are wholly beneficial; and if the actual good derived from it be not so great as it might be, this is owing to counteracting causes, some remediable—such, for instance, as faults produced by imperfect education and inefficient church discipline; others arising out of the mere weakness of human nature, admitting only of palliation, not of complete removal.

things than Thirty-nine Articles, and a discourse of five-and-twenty minutes' duration on the sabbath. It means a check to the conceited rashness of experimental reasoners—an adhesion to old moral landmarks—an attachment to the happiness we have gained from tried institutions greater than the expectation of that which is promised by novelty and change. The loud cry of ten thousand teachers of justice and worship, that cry which masters the *Borgias* and *Catilines* of the world, and guards from devastation the best works of God—

> ———— ' Magna testantur voce per orbem,
> Discite justitiam moniti et non temnere divos.' "

Many volumes might indeed be written without exhausting the topic of the general good which the Church system is calculated to impart, and without compassing the details of the practical benefit daily and hourly accomplished by the Church, in its influence upon the conduct and habits of all classes of society. The Church of England, I have no doubt, is the noblest and most valuable institution in the world—the great counteracting and counterbalancing influence which saves England from being destroyed by cupidity, worldly ambition, pride, and preposterous self-esteem. And yet they who say this, and rejoice in the confident belief that in so saying they are not mad, but speak forth the words of truth and soberness, may be mournfully conscious at the same time that not only are there very numerous imperfections in the practice of the Church, but that even in its theory and system there are defects and difficulties which occasionally give rise to the apprehensions of friends, and afford opportunity for the sarcastic attacks of enemies. They who seek the theoretical perfection of a system, rather than such approach to truth in the concerns of religion as Providence in various ways has permitted, will naturally incline rather to the Church of Rome than to that of England.   Mr. Newman persuaded himself, by an excess of the critical spirit, and an ungoverned craving for pushing every argument to its utmost limit, that there was no middle way between all Church and no Church; and, having brought his mind to this, there was no rest for him save in Rome.   It will be well if even there, his diseased activity of mind will allow him to remain at peace.   " No one," he broadly asserted, " has power over the issue of his principles: we cannot manage our argument, and have as much as we please, and no more."   Now it is true that we cannot have just as much as we please, and no more; but, as has been well observed on this very passage, there is such a thing as a morbid and irritable development of the logical faculty.   That faculty ought not to be allowed an absolute dominion to carry us whithersover it will: it is, like every other faculty, to be subdued, balanced, often overruled by our moral affections and by moral laws.   An absolute and undivided supremacy does not belong to it.

Again, they who have no respect for systems, and who join to the critical spirit a spirit of overweening confidence in their own judgment, independently of authority, will easily find matter for complaint, and even for railing, in the system of the Church of England, and especially in its connection with the State.   Mr. Baptist Noel, who for many years of his life acted as a minister of the Church of England, and of course professed adherence to its principles and vowed obedience to its rules, has now become a bitter assailant.   His book of railing accusation — which I should have thought clever enough to have effected more mischief than it appears actually to have done — is a popular and rhetorical amplification of the following bill of indictment :—

"Amongst pious Anglican pastors it is common to hear strong and even violent denunciations of Popery, which requires no courage, because the thunderer launches his bolts against a despised minority, and is echoed by admiring multitudes. But the ten thousand practical abuses within the Establishment wake no such indignant thunders : the nomination of worldly prelates— the exclusion of the Gospel from thousands of parishes in which (by the union of Church and State) ungodly ministers have the monopoly of spiritual instruction—the easy introduction of irreligious youths into the ministry—the awful desecration of baptism, especially in large civic parishes—the more awful fact that sixteen thousand Anglican pastors leave some millions of the poor, out of a population of only sixteen millions, utterly untaught— the baleful bigotry of the Canons, which excommunicate all who recognise any other Churches of Christ in England except our own — the complete confusion of the Church and the world at the Lord's Table—the obligation upon every parish minister publicly to thank God for taking to himself the soul of every wicked person in the parish who dies without being excommunicated—the almost total neglect of temporal Church discipline— the tyranny of the licence system—the sporting, dancing, and card-playing of many clergymen—the Government orders to the Churches of Christ, to preach on what topics, and to pray in what terms, the State prescribes— the loud and frequent denunciation of our brethren of other denominations as schismatics — the errors of the Articles and of the Prayer-Book, and the invasion of the regal prerogatives of Christ by the State supremacy— the total absence of self-government, and therefore of all self-reformation in the Establishment, &c. &c. : all these enormous evils are tolerated and concealed."

This explosion of concentrated dissenting enmity is worthy the zeal of a fire-new convert, though not very reconcilable with the circumstance of Mr. Noel having spent the best years of his life as a minister of that establishment which he describes as being so full of enormous evil. The accusation has in it not only bitterness of spirit, and unseemly pharisaical pride, but much error and gross exaggeration. It has, however, also enough of truth to make it dangerous, by giving a certain degree of countenance to the untruth with which it is coupled. The most ardent friends of the Church, however, do not pretend that, in its representation here on earth, it is without weak points and imperfections; but this they may say, that dissenting teachers, who have so vivid a consciousness of the defects of the Church, do not themselves succeed in producing a more practically religious community, or one which more effectually wins the confidence of the educated and thoughtful portion of mankind. The rules and forms of the Church may not perhaps in every point exactly suit the habits and circumstances of the days in which we live, but it does not appear that perfect freedom from the constraint of rules and forms is sufficient for improvement in this respect. The dissenter is successful enough in finding out some defects, and vehement enough in denouncing more than he finds; but when he endeavours to supply something better from his own resources, how lamentably he fails! How plain it then becomes that the bitterness of his fault-finding has been without consideration, and that, if he had been wise enough to seek for what is best in a world where all is imperfect, rather than to confide in his own ability to attain perfection, he would have judged with more reverential charity of the Church, and have ventured with less confident rashness into the self-flattering paths of dissent!

The virtual nomination of prelates in the Church, by the recommendation of the State, will be admitted by many churchmen as well as dissenters to be a defect. But this nomination can only be of men whom the Church has admitted to the priesthood ; and though the State nominates a man to a bishopric, it is the Church which must consecrate him a bishop. There is also the guardianship, if such it may be called, of public opinion ; and though that may sanction a political minister in choosing a bishop, for reasons which ought rather to exclude him from the episcopacy, it does not sanction the appointment of mere worldly men. There is indeed no foundation for such a reproach. It did not, however, suit Mr. Noel's position to complain that prelates of dubious orthodoxy were nominated by the State ; and, as he must have his complaint, he says they are "worldly." When he says that in thousands of parishes ungodly ministers are intruded, to the exclusion of the Gospel, one is naturally led to ask who made *him* a judge in such matters, or gave him authority to pronounce a sentence of ungodliness against those who minister in thousands of parishes ? By what right divine does *he* undertake to determine that this or that minister of the Church "excludes" the Gospel ? This is indeed a frantic outbreak of sectarian spleen. Ministers of the Church cannot exclude the Gospel if they would. They do not make the services, nor choose the portions of Scripture to be read in the churches where they minister. It cannot be pretended by any truthful man of sane mind, that the Gospel is excluded from the liturgy of the Church of England, and, until it is, it cannot be excluded from the parish church, be the minister what he may. But even if there were no security of this kind, even if the parish churches were to be contemplated as mere preaching-houses, and not as houses of prayer, it still would be, in the present state of the Church, an extravagant and calumnious exaggeration to say that the Gospel was excluded from thousands of parishes.

It may be true that one of the defects of the Church system is, that men are admitted into the ministry without having in all cases that educated training which seems to be the reasonable preparation for avocations so serious and so important ; but to complain of "the easy introduction of irreligious youths into the Ministry," is mere injustice and wanton bitterness. The examinations for Orders are in general rather severe tests of religious *knowledge* ; indeed, in some cases, the examination papers cannot be answered without very extensive Scriptural and theological erudition. Religious spirit and religious conduct are, it is true, different things from religious knowledge ; but ordination cannot be obtained without certificates of character and conduct which prove that the Church is not careless in this regard. God alone can look into men's hearts, and irreligious men may no doubt get into the Church if, upon the most solemn of all conceivable occasions, they affect to be what they are not. This, however, is no fault of the Church ; and dissenting communities are as often imposed upon in this way as bishops are. It is nonsense, however, to say that irreligious youths can easily get into the Church. Of the thousands admitted to the Ministry, some become irreligious—among the twelve chosen by our Lord there was a Judas—but that openly irreligious young men are admitted into the Church, is, as a general charge, absolutely without foundation.

The complaint of "desecration of baptism" is a very strong phrase, and expresses more than the circumstances warrant ; but it is true that the solemnity of baptism

does not appear to be felt or understood by great numbers who take part in that most important rite, and many
clergymen would probably be disposed on some occasions
to refuse baptism until sponsors more meet for the office
should present themselves, did the law permit. But it
does not. The Church is in this matter, as in several
others, subject to the tyranny of the secular law, and,
people without apparent feeling or conscience being willing to go through the forms, the Church cannot refuse its
part. But in that part there is no desecration. Language cannot achieve deeper solemnity than that of the
service of baptism as appointed by the Church.

It is not very clear what is meant by the assertion that
the Clergy leave some millions of the poor utterly untaught. If there be one thing more notorious than
another of late years, it is the great zeal of the Clergy of
the Church in respect to the education of the poor. The
dissenters on their part teach a great many, and they also
deserve much credit for their zeal in this particular: but
as it is one of their objects that the poor within their
influence should be taught by them, and not by the ministers of the Church, it is rather a stretch of the critical
disposition on the part of a dissenting teacher to reproach
the clergy of the Establishment with leaving some of the
poor untaught.

The "baleful bigotry of the Canons" is an alliterative
phrase which might answer very well for an illustration
of dissenting liberality, or platform vituperation, but it is
nothing better than scolding. The Canons were rules
made and settled when the circumstances, and the current
thoughts of mankind, were very different from what they
are at present. But they were deliberately resolved upon
by men of profounder views than any one will be likely
to attribute to their dissenting critic. They deserve to

be regarded with reverence both for their antiquity and the principles upon which they are founded. If any one demanded a bigoted adherence to their letter, there might be room to find fault; but there is a bigotry of self-opinion in serious matters, as well as of unbending and intolerant adherence to the rules of another age, and the man who rails at the Canons of the Church, after having vowed obedience to them, and who does so upon no other ground than his own opinion of their "baleful bigotry," deserves to be reminded of his own fallibility rather than to be followed as an oracle.

It is not practically true that any excommunication takes place in England of those who acknowledge other churches of Christ than that which is connected with the State. The strict letter of the Canons may regard such persons as excommunicate, but that letter is not offensively or intolerantly brought forward, except when some Dissenters do so as an occasion and opportunity for an outpouring of that bitterness which it is their misfortune to cherish. Why is the Church to be blamed for that confusion of the faithful and the worldly which takes place at the Lord's Table? if indeed it do take place. Certainly there is no want of outward decorum and solemnity on such occasions; nor does the minister fail to pronounce the warning which the Church has ordained against "unworthily" partaking of the Communion. What would the Dissenter have the Church to do? Is the minister to constitute himself an inquisitor into the lives and characters of those who presume to come to the Lord's Table? Except this, he does all that can be done, and none is left in ignorance that, if he presumes to come unworthily, he does so at his own peril. This mingling of the faithful, and of the world, upon the most solemn occasions is the inevitable result of the condition of society, and of the freedom from severity of Church discipline which is claimed as a political privilege, and chiefly asserted by that school of politicians with which Dissenters are so frequently linked.

The objection to the charitable spirit of the prayers used in the Burial Service of the Church of England scarcely deserves notice. It will be conceded, that for the benefit of the living there cannot be a more meet occasion of a religious service than that of paying the last duties to the body of a friend or familiar acquaintance whose soul has left the world. And if prayers are to be said at all, there seems no great reason to find fault with the assumption that God has taken to himself the departed soul. Take the other side, and suppose the clergyman assuming that the deceased was so wicked a person that his soul could not have gone to God, how shocking would such presumption be! and yet Mr. Noel only objects in the case of wicked persons. How can any one certainly know that this or that person is unpardonably wicked (in a religious sense) compared with another? *That* surely must be left to the Searcher of hearts. At all events, if the Church err at all in this matter, it is an error on the side of charity.

There is a foundation for the charge of neglect of Church discipline; though to say that temporal Church discipline is almost " totally neglected " is to fall into great exaggeration. This is a fault which is in rapid course of amendment, and a candid assailant would have admitted as much. It may be observed, however, that the man who has just broken loose altogether from the bonds of Church discipline, preferring the indulgence of his own will and judgment to the rule and governance of his superiors in the Church, has not much personal claim to attention when he murmurs at the neglect of discipline.

The " licence system " may be perhaps objected to, as being, in practice, too much a matter of course, but there is no just ground for calling it a tyranny. There must be a licence system, in order to preserve order and guard against abuse ; but to object to it as a tyranny, is just to hit the opposite of the real objection. It is for being too little insisted upon, rather than too much, that the licence system may perhaps be censured. Upon the whole, however, there is but little cause of complaint.

The attack on the private manners and deportment of " many clergymen " is, I think, a mistake as to the matter of fact. There are, unfortunately, instances of clergymen falling into immoralities, to the great scandal of the profession ; but this is common to all churches and all sects. As a body the clergy of the Church of England are distinguished for the decorum of their lives. I venture to affirm that it is contrary to the experience of every one conversant with English society at the present time, that " many clergymen " are in the habit of sporting, or dancing, or playing cards. Yet there seems to be no necessity, either of morals or manners, that these things should be totally abstained from even by clergymen. There are occasions where any such rigid rule would savour of mere Puritanism, which is a far worse evil, and more likely to lead to gross and abominable wickedness, than levity is, though that too is deserving of severe censure.

It is a mere misstatement to say that the State orders the Church to preach on such topics, and to pray in such terms, as the State prescribes. On rare and remarkable occasions the Privy Council points out a topic of exhortation, but leaves each clergyman to deal with it as he pleases, and never interferes beyond the suggestion. When a prayer is prescribed, the composition is intrusted

to the Ecclesiastical Head of the Church. It sometimes
appears painfully incongruous to have events which are
the common talk of the day brought into the solemn
prayers of the Church, in its public services, but no
thoughtful person will deliberately condemn this, and the
Prelate who prepares the form of prayer is responsible
for making it, in all respects, such as a Christian Church
may lawfully use.

The charge against the Church of indulging in loud
and frequent denunciation of those of other denominations
as schismatics is, I think, without foundation in fact.
The most frequent object of attack in the pulpits of the
Church of England is the Church of Rome, not as schis-
matic, but as having corrupted the true primitive faith.
But any attack at all, save on the various forms of infidelity or of vice, is in the Church of England pulpits
rather the exception than the rule. Dissenters however
seem to be always dreaming of conspiracy or of battle.
Their theology seems to be essentially antagonistic. If
there be in the Church some men whose preaching is
generally of this cast, they are the men who, while continuing to hold appointments in the Church, are favourable to some of the principles of Dissenters.

As to the errors of the Articles and of the Prayer-
Book, which Mr. Noel charges against the Church, it is
too plainly a begging of the question on his own side to
require any reply. When he can prove his right and
title to sit in judgment upon the Articles and Prayer-
Book, and not to be judged by them, his censure may be
listened to, but not till then.

When he speaks of the invasion of the regal prerogatives of Christ by the State supremacy, he falls into such
phraseology of the Dissenting pulpit as a sense of reverence
forbids one to discuss; but it is not to be denied that he

hits a real blot when he alludes to the want of self-government and self-reformation which is in some degree incident to the present constitution of the Church. His assertion about a " total absence" of self-government, &c., is but one of the forms of exaggeration which he seems to mistake for earnestness. There is enough to be sorry for, without believing the case to be so bad as this. But it does appear that in some extreme cases the Church is liable to a direction and control other than that of the Church, which ought not to be. The Privy Council of the Sovereign, generally chosen on political grounds, and not necessarily having any religious character at all, does not appear to be a fitting tribunal to determine, in the last resort, points of doctrine or discipline in the Church, which may require to be settled by authority. This however is not the fault of the Church, but the tyranny of the law—a tyranny which unfortunately the professing friends of civil, political, and religious liberty, do their best to embitter and to prolong.

It remains but to say of Mr. Noel what has been said of a much abler man—that he has always regarded the Church of England from without as an object to be criticized, improved, or moulded after a pattern of his own, not as a power to be obeyed and trusted as a parent is trusted by a child, or a master by a servant. This was said of Mr. Newman, a far more eminent traitor than Mr. Noel. I use the word advisedly, not I trust in any spirit of railing, but because, according to my judgment, no other would so truly describe Mr. Newman's conduct to the Church of England. He obtained the confidence of great numbers of those who were most loyally attached to that Church, by standing forth with great ability to show how its principles and formularies, rightly understood, developed true Christianity, avoiding the errors of

Romish extravagance and presumption on the one hand, and, on the other hand, the not very dissimilar errors of popular Protestantism. The confidence which he gained he shamefully abused, and did all he could by his personal example to draw into the Church of Rome those who had first learned to follow him from his exposure of that Church's vain pretensions, while asserting the sufficiency of the Church of England to supply those aids and that direction which were felt to be wanting in the system of popular Protestantism.

Though it must be confessed that the movement which began in 1833 and produced so much sensation in the Church of England, and such important practical effects, through the 'Tracts for the Times,' ran eventually into dangerous extravagance, yet I suppose that few who are not "Low Church" partisans will deny, that, upon the whole, the effect has been very beneficial. There is a lively interest now taken in Church principles and Church practices, and a diffusion of knowledge upon those subjects among the educated classes, which are equally remarkable and gratifying. It has been maintained by an American ecclesiastic that the benefit of the Church movement could not have been obtained without that excess which, considered by itself, cannot but be lamented. " Had not," he says, " the recent Catholicism run into a passion in England, it is very possible that the Oxford Tracts would have produced little of their good effect. Similar opinions, or many nearly such, had been held all along by no small body of English divines, but without having much influence on the clergy generally; and hence the sad condition of that Church in many respects, a century or two ago. Erastianism prevailing widely; High Churchmanship, consisting more of Toryism than of ecclesiastical principles ; and Low Churchmanship, sympathizing more with non-episcopacy than with episcopacy. From this unhappy state of things the Oxford Tracts have roused the Church of England : and I see not how, humanly speaking, they could have done so, when the divines mentioned had so long failed, had they not over-shot the mark, and not only gone for Catholicism as a principle, but carried it beyond matters of principle, and so fanned the reverence for it into a passion. This done, however, the evil must be taken with the good. The good is, that the Churchmanship of England is regene-rated ; and even in many quarters in that country, and not a few in ours also, where Church principles were lean as a skeleton ten or twelve years ago, we now find sinews and flesh at least, though not yet the fulness and beauty of their perfection. The evil is, that some of the weak-minded not only, like many of hardier intellect, run into a wild ardour on the whole subject, and defer to Catholic tradition, and to other traditions not Catholic, as they defer to Scripture, though not always as much ; they not only do this, but get beyond all control of their understanding, long for some deeper indulgence of their passion, surrender their own judgment, and so find them-selves in Rome, or not a Sabbath-day's journey from it."

This appears to be, so far as it goes, a fair account of the general effect of that awakened zeal for Church prin-ciples which has been viewed so differently by different parties ; some regarding it as nothing else than retrogres-sion to Popery, while others find in it a new religious fashion of which they are enamoured, because it is to them a fascinating novelty and a profound excitement. Again, there are the sober-minded, who, while they regret the tendency to extravagance in shows, and forms, and observances, which has grown out of the Tractarian move-ment, yet, thank God for the real and sincere revival which has taken place of old reverences, and Prayer-Book ordinances, and more frequent attendances at church, together with many other noble, and yet meek, manifestations of respect, not only for religion, but for that methodical practice of it which, hundreds of years ago, was ordained and settled by the Church of England.

Every one, familiar with libraries and the priced catalogues of booksellers, must be aware how much more extended the study of divinity has become in the last twenty years than it had previously been. The old sterling works that hung heavily on hand have mounted to double the price, and are of comparatively easy sale. True, these books may be bought in some instances, as many other kinds of books are, rather for the sake of possessing them than of studying them; but in the greater number of instances they are bought to be studied, and this appears both in the conversation and the conduct of men of education, whether divinity be or be not the profession to which they have devoted themselves. I have some reason to believe that even the medical and surgical students of London, of whom by far the greater number some years ago knew no more than Falstaff did " what the inside of a church was made of," are now found generally to attend church, because it is a shame for a man of sense and education not to do so.

And as to preaching, every one will admit that the tone of it is much changed; and certainly much for the better in some respects, though not in all. For the better, as regards more frequent introduction of Church topics, and the greater prominence given to the distinctive articles of Christian creeds, as held and interpreted from the first days. Better also, as having escaped from, and even put to flight, the laboured frigidities of the Blair school, and the whole tribe of " lean and flashy" compounds of the pompous and the commonplace. The improvement, however, is not without serious drawbacks in respect of dogmatism and mysticism, and perhaps an over-adoption and assertion of High Church views, going beyond the proper *via media* of the English Church. On the favourable side, again, we are to remember that the change has lowered the crest of *Evangelicism*, and raised the courage and strength of Catholicity.* It has drawn away many from those ministers whose disposition unfortunately led them to turn parish churches into something like conventicles, and to erect little Popedoms for themselves within the districts where they preached. In this point a change, and a very salutary one, has come over the spirit, both of the pulpit and the press. There has also been in recent years a greatly increased attention to the fabrics of churches. When we look at the unsightly church buildings, without the slightest ecclesiastical character, either

---

* Lest, perchance, any one should be offended at this word, I beg here to append a quotation from a discourse delivered at Oxford, Jan. 30, 1838, by the Rev. J. Beaven, M.A., as I find it in the introductory letter to the third edition of Miller's Bampton Lectures:—" We should be careful to avoid all ground of suspicion that we are indifferent upon the great points which form the line of separation between our Church and that of Rome. I am far from falling into the misapprehension that either here or elsewhere there are any of the upholders of primitive doctrines who are really thus indifferent. I feel in common with many others how lamentable it is that this Church should be divided from that which was the natural head of Western Christendom, and to which, for its mission to our Saxon ancestors, we owe so large a share of gratitude. But still, so long as she continues to make grievous errors terms of communion, and to keep up intrusive establishments of bishops and priests in ancient Catholic churches for the purpose of maintaining those errors, our position in regard to her is, and must be, *protesting*. Our very Catholicity must, so long as this state of things continues, render us Protestant. It seems to be the position assigned to us by Divine Providence, and I should dread that we should even appear to resign it." " These surely," says Mr. Miller, " are, in substance, wise words ;" and with this remark I most cordially agree.

externally or internally, which even but thirty years ago were erected at a great expense in London and its neighbourhood, and compare them with the really churchlike structures which are now provided at a much lower charge, we cannot but admit that in the judgment, taste, and feeling applicable to such matters, there has been a great improvement. Still there has been, even in this matter, such an over-doing, and such an excess of imitative activity, as borders upon vulgarity. The Gothic or the Tudor style of architecture must always be grand or pleasing when there is no overlaying with ornament, and when a suitable material is used ; but there is nothing either grand or impressive in the red-letter mediævality which in many instances fantastically figures upon walls that ought to be consecrated to dignity and sobriety.

Consistently, however, with this dignity and sobriety, I cannot but think that the use of symbols and emblems of Christianity is both allowable and useful. Dr. Arnold seems to me to have spoken from a just sympathy with what is natural and good in the heart of man when he expressed his wish for " the revival of many good practices which belong to the true Church no less than to the corrupt Church, and would *there* (in the true Church) be purely beneficial—daily Church services—frequent communions—memorials of our Christian calling presented to our notice in crosses and way-side oratories—commemorations to holy men of all times and countries—the doctrine of the communion of Saints practically taught—religious orders (especially of women) of different kinds and under different rules, delivered only from the snare and sin of perpetual vows :"—a society organised on these principles, says Arnold's biographer, " and with such or similar institutions, was in his judgment the true sign from Heaven, meant to be the living witness of the reality

of Christ's salvation, which should remind us daily of
God, and work upon the habits of our life as insensibly
as the air we breathe." There are many who would be
frightened at such views as these, thinking them to approach too near the views of Popery; but Arnold had
certainly no inclination that way, nor should any reasonable person decide that *all* which belongs to the devotional
practices of the Romanists is therefore wrong, or that
even what *is* wrong cannot co-exist with innocence and
sincere piety. A truly pious and devout heart, said the
philosophic Niebuhr, " finds its way to God through all
the mazes of Romish superstitions. There are many
persons who leave these matters undecided, as every man
is obliged to do in numerous cases in life, when, without
giving his positive and well-considered assent, he nevertheless does not feel called upon to reform. And not a
few of these are among the higher clergy—the Popes
themselves. But this is not what I wanted to say: I
mean there are some persons who devoutly believe every
jot even of these things, and whose hearts nevertheless
are pure as snow." Of this I have no more doubt than
I have of the pure piety and active benevolence of many
Protestants who dissent from the Church of England.
The spirit of dissent is generally carping and self-suffi-
cient, and therefore odious; but the pure Christian spirit,
it is to be hoped, may exist without assent to all the details of doctrine or discipline of any Church, and Christian
piety always demands the respect of the just, and calls
forth the admiration and sympathy of the affectionate.

Nevertheless, without presuming to judge others, or to
refuse them all credit due for such piety and virtue as
they appear to possess, let the members of the Church of
England stand fast for their own sublime and sober doctrine and discipline. And now I may conclude this part

of the Church subject with one of the most earnest and
touching passages to be met with in the whole compass
of English prose writing. "No man," says Archbishop
Bramhall, "can justly blame me for honouring my spiritual mother, the Church of England, in whose womb I
was conceived, at whose breasts I was nourished, and in
whose bosom I hope to die. Bees, by the instinct of
nature, do love their hives, and birds their nests. But
God is my witness that, according to my uttermost talent
and poor understanding, I have endeavoured to set down
the naked truth impartially, without either favour or prejudice, the two capital enemies of right judgment: the
one of which, like a false mirror, doth represent things
fairer and straighter than they are; the other, like the
tongue infected with choler, makes the sweetest meats to
taste bitter."

CHAPTER XXIII.

CHURCH REVENUES AND CHURCH EXTENSION.

In the year 1836 a digest of the Reports of the Ecclesiastical Commissioners, which had at that time been published, gave the number of beneficed incumbents in England and Wales at 7190, the number of curates employed by resident incumbents at 1006, and by non-resident incumbents at 4224, making in all 12,420. This calculation did not include the clergy belonging to cathedrals or colleges, and having no parochial employment, nor masters of schools, nor chaplains of prisons, poorhouses, and other public establishments, nor the unemployed clergy. The number then, even in 1836, may probably have been 14,000. Since that time the increase of the number of clergy has been very great, though not greater than the increase of public demand for their ministrations. In a debate of the Parliamentary Session of 1850, upon the extension of the privilege of voting for members of parliament, Mr. Page Wood, one of Her Majesty's counsel learned in the law, acquainted the House of Commons that, since the period of the Reform Act (1832), " something like 1500 new churches had been erected." This, however, is by no means the greater part of the new occupation for clergymen which the change of circumstances since 1832 has created. In thousands of places a new zeal has been awakened, and a new or augmented sense of the value of the services which a clergyman may afford to the best and most important interests of society. Where only one curate was wont to be employed, we may now often find two or three. I should think the number of clergy at present engaged in the ministration of church offices in England and Wales can scarcely be less than 16,000.*

The revenues which these clergymen derive from Church property, or from payments made in various ways, as rents of pews, or fees, or contributions of various kinds, is no doubt very considerable; but still I believe that all the money paid to the clerical members of the Church, whether as incumbents or stipendiaries, falls far short of the sums spent by the clergy. In short, I hold that a very considerable amount of the wealth of the country, derived from the land or from commerce, is continually brought in aid of Church endowments for the promoting of religion; and that, instead of great fortunes being made in the Church and taken out of it for worldly purposes, as is supposed by many, the contrary is the fact, and great fortunes which have been made out of the Church are continually spent by the clergy, either directly upon Church purposes, or in a way which is more or less governed by the Church spirit—the desire to promote the cause of religion and of virtuous living.

The number of benefices returned to the inquiries of the Ecclesiastical Commissioners was 10,540. The number of incumbents, as has been already stated, was much less, because many clergymen held more than one benefice. The actual number of preferments, above mere

---

* I find that, in 1841, the Rev. W. Palmer estimated the number of parochial clergy in England at no more than 12,000. "On the whole," he says, "there is reason to believe that the number of *parochial* clergy does not exceed 12,000." The number which he then thought necessary was 16,000.

curacies, exceeds considerably the 10,540 parochial benefices, as there are chapelries, district churches, &c., which
are, in fact, subdivisions of benefices.   The *net* revenue
of the benefices was returned at the total amount of
3,004,721*l.* ; of these

297	were under £50 a-year.			337	above £600 and under £700			
1629	above	£50	and under	£100	218	„	700	„	800
1602	„	100	„	150	126	„	800	„	900
1355	„	150	„	200	90	„	900	„	1000
1978	„	200	„	300	134	„	1000	„	1500
1326	„	300	„	400	32	,.	1500	„	2000
830	„	400	„	500	18	„	2000 and upwards.		
506	„	500	„	600					

This enumeration makes only 10,478; and in other
places the number of benefices will be found variously
stated at 10,708, and 10,693.   These discrepancies are
always found in public returns, arising no doubt from
differences of interpretation of the word benefice, or incumbency, or whatever term may be used.   But the
average income of the 5430 curates was returned at but
a fraction above 80*l.* a year; and, though many of them
may have to live upon even less than this, yet every one
acquainted with society must be aware that a large proportion of them spend a great deal more—that is, they
spend their own private fortunes, or the allowances made
to them by their families, upon the work of the Church.
The whole Church revenues, including the Bishops' landed
estates and the estates of other dignitaries, may be taken
at 3,500,000*l.* per annum in England—a very large sum,
no doubt, when looked at in the mass, and increased, as
it must be admitted it is, by the revenues of college fellowships reserved to the clergy, by the great school foundations, by the endowed masterships and lectureships in
numerous places, by chaplaincies to hospitals, prisons, and
various public institutions.   But when all these revenues

are put together, let us consider what 16,000 educated
gentlemen, many of them connected with the aristocracy,
and most of them with the gentry of the kingdom, are
likely to spend. Suppose their expenditure to average
300 guineas a year—and I am of opinion that the average
is more than that—the aggregate sum would exceed
5,000,000*l.* a year, which certainly Church revenues of
all descriptions do not amount to.

But if the fixed revenues of the Church were 7,000,000*l.*
a year, instead of half that sum, I cannot see why they
who take even the most democratic views of the division
of property should object. For, of all the property in the
country, it is that alone which may be said, with at least
an approach to correctness, to be set apart as the reward
of learning and virtuous living—it is that alone which the
country has some security for being spent with at least
the intention to do good. Of course it is not meant to be
asserted that the best clergyman generally gets the most
ample reward, or to be denied that there are many instances of the revenues of clergymen being ill spent.
But it may be fairly maintained, as a general truth, that
the revenues of the clergy are more devoted to the promotion of good and the relief of wretchedness than the
revenues of laymen. The Rev. Sidney Smith, when he
was desirous to chide Lord John Russell for a scheme he
had in view of more equally distributing the revenues of
the Church, asked in his peculiar style—

" What harm does a prebend do in a politico-econo-
mical point of view? The alienation of the property for
three lives, or 21 years, and the almost certainty that the
tenant has of renewing, give him a sufficient interest in
the soil for all purposes of cultivation. The Church, it
has been urged, do not plant—they do not extend their
woods ; but almost all cathedrals possess woods, and

regularly plant a succession so as to keep them up.   A single evening of dice and hazard does not doom their woods to sudden destruction; a life tenant does not cut down all the timber to make the most of his estate; the woods of ecclesiastical bodies are managed upon a fixed and settled plan, and, considering the sudden prodigalities of laymen, I should not be afraid of a comparison.   A long series of elected clergymen is rather more likely to produce valuable members of the community than a long series of begotten squires.   Take, for instance, the Cathedral of Bristol, the whole estates of which are about equal to keeping a pack of fox-hounds.   If this had been in the hands of a country gentleman, instead of precentor, succentor, dean and canons, and sexton, you would have had huntsman, whipper-in, dog-feeders, and stoppers of earth; the old squire full of foolish opinions and fermented liquids, and a young gentleman of gloves, waistcoats, and pantaloons: and how many generations might it be before the fortuitous concourse of noodles would produce such a man as Professor Lee, one of the Prebendaries of Bristol, and by far the most eminent oriental scholar in Europe! The same argument might be applied to every cathedral in England.   How many hundred coveys of squires would it take to supply as much knowledge as is condensed in the heads of Dr. Coplestone or Mr. Tate of St. Paul's!   And what a strange thing it is that such a man as Lord John Russell, the Whig leader, should be so squirrel-minded as to wish for a movement without object or end!   Saving there can be none, for it is merely taking from one ecclesiastic to give it to another; public clamour, to which the best men must sometimes yield, does not require it; and, so far from doing any good, it would be a source of infinite mischief to the establishment."

At the time the above was written, squires were held to be the *nimium fortunati* of the country, and the proper marks for satirical attack. Times have now changed, and the contrast may be extended. We may ask whether the wealth of the country is not as well disposed of in the hands of ecclesiastics, as in those of rich cotton-spinners or railway contractors. Behold a man, coarse in his manners and cruel to his workpeople, impudent, ostentatious, and overbearing, who by some one stroke of cleverness in his trade has sprung into great business, and realized an immense fortune—or another, who, by more cunning than that of his employers, has got a contract which he can execute at half the stipulated price—or a third, who has boldly speculated and won a fortune in a transaction which might have turned the other way, and ruined all connected with him—is it rational to suppose that the wealth administered by such persons is more rightfully their own, or distributed more for the public good, than that which is in the hands of ecclesiastics?

It is very often said that the reason of the objection to the large fortunes obtained by some ecclesiastics is, that they are not given to the most worthy, but invariably to persons of aristocratic connexion or influence. Canon Sidney Smith met this by a denial of the fact. He says the Bishop of London was a curate, the Bishop of Winchester was a curate—" almost every rose-and-shovel man has been a curate in his time. All curates *hope* to draw great prizes." He describes a baker driving his son through the streets of London. They stop opposite the house of the Duke of Northumberland ; but the father feels that not the slightest atom of chance has his son of getting in among the Percies, of enjoying a share of *their* luxury and splendour, or of chasing the deer with hound

and horn upon the Cheviot Hills.   But he drives on to
St. Paul's, and all his thoughts are changed when he
contemplates that beautiful fabric.   It is the possession
of the Church, and to a share in *its* revenues, and a seat of
honour within its walls, the humblest may aspire who
will become learned, diligent, and devout.   So the baker
sends his boy to school, and then to college, and at last
sees him earn " purple, profit, and power," in the Church.
I omit the sarcasm and the levity which Sidney Smith
puts into this illustration, because they tend to the
weakening of the serious truth which the illustration is
meant to enforce.   Coleridge argued that a Church was
the only pure democracy.   A state, he said, is *in idea*
the opposite of a Church.   " A state regards classes, and
not individuals ; and it estimates classes, not by internal
merit, but by external accidents, as property, birth, &c.
But a Church does the reverse of this, and disregards all
external accidents, and looks at men as individual persons, allowing no gradation of ranks but such as greater
or less wisdom, learning, and holiness ought to confer.
A Church is, therefore, *in idea*, the only pure democracy.
The Church so considered, and the state exclusively of
the Church, constitute together the idea of a state in its
largest sense."   Upon the subject of the " high prizes "
in the Church, as it was at one time the fashion to call
them, he discourses as follows :—" The argument against
high prizes in the Church might be put strongly thus :—
admit that in the beginning it might have been fairly said
that some eminent rewards ought to be set apart for the
purpose of stimulating and rewarding transcendent merit ;
what have you to say now, after centuries of experience,
to the contrary ?   *Have* the prizes been given to the
highest genius, virtue, or learning ?   Is it not rather the
truth, as Jortin said, that twelve votes in a contested

election will do more to make a man a bishop than an admired commentary on the twelve minor prophets? To all which, and the like, I say again, that " you ought not to reason from the abuse which may be rectified, against the inherent uses of the thing. *Appoint* the most deserving—and the prize *will* answer its purpose. As to the bishops' incomes—in the first place, the net receipts —that which the bishops may spend—have been exaggerated beyond measure ; but waiving that, and allowing the highest estimate to be correct, I should like to have the disposition of the episcopal revenue in any one year by the late or the present Bishop of Durham, or the present Bishops of London or Winchester, compared with that of the most benevolent nobleman in England of any party in politics. I firmly believe that the former give away in charity of one kind or another, public, official, or private, three times as much in proportion as the latter. You may have a hunks or two now and then, but so you would much more certainly if you were to reduce the incomes to two thousand per annum. As a body, in my opinion, the clergy of England do in truth act as if their property were impressed with a trust to the utmost extent that can be demanded by those who affect to believe, ignorantly or not, that lying legend of a tripartite or quadripartite division of the tithe by law."

It is a very serious and a very difficult question whether or no the beneficial influence of the clergy upon society is increased or diminished in consequence of the position which the wealth of the Church, and the peculiar mode of its distribution, enable them to take. The shrewd Sidney Smith is decidedly of opinion that poverty in the clergy would be ruinous to the Church. " At present," he says, " men are tempted into the Church by the prizes of the Church, and bring into that Church a great deal

of capital which enables them to live in decency, supporting themselves, not with the money of the public, but
with their own money, which, but for this temptation,
would have been carried into some retail trade.   The
offices of the Church would then fall down to men little
less coarse and ignorant than agricultural labourers—the
clergyman of the parish would soon be seen in the squire's
kitchen,—and all this would take place in a country where
poverty is infamous." I think there is some ground for
such apprehension as is here rather strongly, if not
coarsely, expressed; but there is, on the other hand,
reason to doubt that, even in England, mere poverty
could so degrade men of learning, if their lives were as
holy as their calling.   Sidney Smith does not deny that
his is a Mammonish view of the subject, but he says that
those who make that objection forget " the immense
effect which Mammon produces upon religion itself."
" Shall the Gospel," he asks, " be preached by men paid
by the State ?   Shall these men be taken from the lower
orders and be meanly paid ?   Shall they be men of
learning and education ?   And shall there be some mag-
nificent endowments to allure such men into the Church ?
Which of these methods is best for diffusing the rational
doctrines of Christianity ? not in the age of the Apostles,
not in the abstract, timeless, nameless, placeless land of the
philosophers, but in the present time, in the porter-brewing,
cotton-spinning, tallow-melting kingdom of Great Britain,
bursting with opulence, and flying from poverty as the
greatest of human evils.   Many different answers may
be given to these questions, but they are questions which,
not ending in Mammon, have a powerful bearing on real
religion, and deserve the deepest consideration from its
disciples and friends.   Let the comforts of the clergy go for
nothing.   Consider their state only as religion is affected by

it. If, upon this principle, I am forced to allot to some an
opulence which some would pronounce to be unapostolical,
I cannot help it : I must take this people with all their
follies, and prejudices, and circumstances, and carve out
an establishment best suited for them, however unfit for
early Christianity in barren and conquered Judea."
Should any one say of this argumentation that, however
clear and clever it may be, it is founded rather on
worldly policy than on Christian principle, and contemplates dealing with society as it is, rather than endeavouring to make it what according to Christian views it
ought to be, I have no answer to make to such objections. But there are many to whom such reasoning
seems more conclusive than another kind which would
pay less respect to the world as it is.

Probably there is a great majority of those who go
with average decency through the world, who think with
Sidney Smith (though they could not say it as he does,
and would not if they could) that the clergyman of
every neighbourhood is a proper person to be at the head
of its intellectuality and civilisation ; and that one of his
main uses is to give by example, as well as precept, a
proper tone to society—meaning thereby not so much the
society of the faithful seeking a kingdom which is not of
this world, as the society which seeks to make the most of
this world, without violating established rules of propriety,
or openly offending against the laws of morality. In this
view of the clerical office it is clear that either present
income, or the position which arises from the chance of
attaining to it, is desirable, if not necessary. " If," says
Sidney Smith, " you place a man in a village in the
country, *require* that he should be of good manners and
well educated ; that his habits and appearance should
be *above* that of the farmers to whom he preaches, if he

has nothing else to expect (as would be the case in a
Church of equal division); and if upon his village income
he is to support a wife and educate a family, without any
power of making himself known, in a remote and solitary
situation, such a person ought to receive 500*l.* per annum,
and be furnished with a house.   There are about 10,700
parishes in England and Wales, whose average income is
285*l.* per annum.   Now, to provide these incumbents
with decent houses, to keep them in repair, and to raise
the income of the incumbent to 500*l.* per annum, would
require (if all the incomes of the bishops, deans, and
chapters, of separate dignitaries, of sinecure rectories,
were confiscated, and if the excess of all the livings in
England above 500*l.* per annum were added to them) a
sum of two millions and a half in addition to the present
income of the whole Church; and no power on earth
could persuade the present Parliament of Great Britain
to grant a single shilling for that purpose.   Now, is it
possible to pay such a Church upon any other principle
than that of unequal division?   But if men of capital
were driven out of the Church, and plans were adopted
which would pauperize the English clergy, where would
the harm be?   Could not all the duties of religion be
performed as well by poor laymen as by men of good
substance?   My great and serious apprehension is that
such would not be the case.   There would be the greatest
risk that your clergy would be fanatical and ignorant,
that their habits would be low and mean, and that they
would be despised."   Such is the deliberate teaching of
a Whig clergyman; one of those who thought that in
politics all "illiberality" was unwise, and all Toryism a
proper subject for scornful banter.   He subsequently
draws a ludicrous and contempt-inspiring picture of an
" average, ordinary, uninteresting minister," appearing

in society in the way in which such persons, having but a small income, must appear, and he demands triumphantly whether any man of *common sense* can say that all these outward circumstances of the ministers of religion have no bearing on religion itself? No doubt these are points which, in a financial view of the Church question, ought to be taken into consideration. In another view of the Church question, namely, whether the ministers of religion are not very often more occupied with the affairs of the world than could be wished, and less devoted to matters of higher concernment than might be desired, perhaps the necessity or expediency of 500*l.* a-year, or some kind of equivalent, might not be thought so important.

The practical question, however, is not between an absolute uniformity of stipend and the excessive inequalities which formerly existed in a greater, and do still exist in a lesser degree; but it is whether, and how far, a readjustment and redistribution of the revenues of the Church have been made necessary by the existing state of society? It may be permitted to those who are of a reforming turn of mind to say, that, though they recognise the usefulness of unequal division of Church property, they do not see why the division should be *so* unequal as it has been. Something has been done upon the principle of " moderate reform " in this matter. The recommendations of a body called the " Church Commission " have been sanctioned by Parliament, and powers have been given to the Commission to proceed with very important arrangements affecting the distribution of Church revenues. The acts of this Commission do not appear, however, to have given general satisfaction either to the clergy or the laity. The spirit of episcopacy, and the spirit of lawyers, are said to have too much predomi-

nated, while the views of the less dignified order of clergy
have met with but slight regard.   But whatever the
success of the Ecclesiastical Commission may have been
in executing the business intrusted to it, it was endowed
with very considerable powers over the funds of the
Church, with a view to their better distribution.

In the Report of the Royal Commission, upon which
the Parliamentary Ecclesiastical Commission and its extensive powers were founded, the episcopal and archiepiscopal incomes (1835) were set down as follows:—

Archbishop of Canterbury . . .	£19,182	a year
„ York	12,629	„
Bishop of Saint Asaph	6,300	„
„ Bangor	4,464	„
„ Bath and Wells . . .	5,946	„
„ Bristol	2,351	„
„ Carlisle	2,213	„
„ Chester	3,261	„
„ Chichester	4,229	„
„ Saint David's . . .	1,897	„
„ Durham	19,066	„
„ Ely	11,105	„
„ Exeter	2,713	„
„ Gloucester	2,282	„
„ Hereford	2,516	„
„ Lichfield and Coventry . .	3,923	„
„ Lincoln	4,542	„
„ Llandaff	924	„
„ London	13,929	„
„ Norwich	5,395	„
„ Oxford	2,648	„
„ Peterborough . . .	3,103	„
„ Rochester	1,459	„
„ Salisbury	3,939	„
„ Winchester	11,151	„
„ Worcester	6,569	„

The prospective incomes of the several sees were not
the same as the actual incomes stated in the Report.

The following was the ultimate plan, showing the estimated prospective income as the sees were before alteration, and the alteration to be effected under the sanction of Parliament.

ARCHBISHOPS AND BISHOPS.

PROPOSED ARRANGEMENT OF EPISCOPAL INCOMES.

	Estimated Income.	Proposed future Income.	Excess.
	£.	£.	£.
1. Canterbury	18,090	15,000	3,090
York	10,270	10,000	270
London	13,890	10,000	3,890
Durham	19,480	8,000	11,480
Winchester	10,370	7,000	3,370
Ely	9,400	5,500	3,900
Worcester	6,500	5,000	1,500
Bath and Wells	5,550	5,000	550
St. Asaph	5,600⎱	5,200	4,110
Bangor	3,810⎰		
	102,860	70,700	32,160
2. Bristol	2,090⎱	5,000	*Deficiency.*
Gloucester	2,130⎰		780
3. Carlisle	3,050	4,500	1,450
Chester	2,900	4,500	1,600
Chichester	3,610	4,500	890
St. David's	2,800	4,500	1,700
Exeter	2,790	4,500	1,710
Hereford	2,650	4,500	1,850
Lichfield	4,350	4,500	150
Lincoln	3,810	4,500	690
Llandaff	1,170	4,500	3,330
Oxford	1,600	4,500	2,900
Peterborough	3,380	4,500	1,120
Rochester	1,450	4,500	3,050
	33,560	54,000	20,440
4. Manchester.	. .	4,500	4,500
Ripon	. .	4,500	4,500
5. Norwich	4,700	4,700⎱	*Unaltered.*
Salisbury	5,000	5,000⎰	

SUMMARY.

	From	To	Excess.	Deficiency.
	£.	£.	£.	£.
1. Nine sees to be reduced. .	102,860	70,700	32,160	. .
2. One see to be raised . .	4,220	5,000	. .	780
3. Twelve sees to be raised to 4,500*l.* each	33,560	54,000	. .	20,440
4. Two new sees at the same .	. .	9,000	. .	9,000
5. Two unaltered	9,700	9,700	. .	. .
	150,340	148,400	32,160	30,220
	148,400		30,220	
	1,940		1,940	

The Commission recommended various alterations of the boundaries of the dioceses, the union of the sees of Gloucester and Bristol, and of those of St. Asaph and Bangor, and the creation of two new sees, one of Ripon, the other of Manchester. In the same Report the Commissioners stated their opinion that where the annual income of a bishop amounted to 4500*l.*, it was not necessary to make any addition, nor would they recommend any diminution unless the income exceeded 5500*l.* They considered, however, that the two archbishoprics, and the bishoprics of London, Durham, and Winchester, ought to have a larger provision than the rest. In a subsequent Report they fixed these incomes as follows :—

Archbishop of Canterbury. . .	£15,000 a-year.
,, York . . .	10,000 ,,
Bishop of London	10,000* ,,
,, Durham	8,000 ,,
,, Winchester . . .	7,000 ,,

---

* Very strong statements have been made in the House of Commons, impugning the correctness of the official returns of episcopal incomes. See specially the debate of the 8th of July, 1850. I believe these statements arise from a hasty confusion of the well-known advance in the annual value of episcopal estates with advance of episcopal income. The property of the Church is so leased, that, in most cases, the increase of value, or the greatest portion of it, goes to the lessee, and not to the

These are large incomes to be possessed by individuals in virtue of their ecclesiastical office ; but let it be borne in mind that they *were* much larger, and that these diminished incomes were recommended by themselves, and not prospectively and for their successors, but immediately and for themselves.* I am not aware of any instance in which laymen have given up vested interests, or any considerable part of them, for the sake of the general good of the order or profession to which they belonged. There are, however, such honourable instances as those of the late Marquis Camden and the late Viscount Sidmouth, the former of whom relinquished a sinecure of 30,000*l.* a year, and the latter a pension of 3000*l.* a year, because they could afford to do without such additions to their private fortunes.

The extensive powers of the Ecclesiastical Commission over the property of the Church were conferred by the 6 & 7 Will. IV. c. 77, and by the 3 & 4 Vic. c. 113. The part of the former Act which united the sees of Bangor and St. Asaph at the demise of the bishop of either diocese has been repealed, and these two sees still exist. Bristol has been united to Gloucester, and the bishops of Ripon and Manchester have been appointed, with incomes provided by the Ecclesiastical Commission out of the

---

Church. It is not the Bishop of London, but the Bishop of London's lessees, or the Ecclesiastical Commission, who reap the advantage of the increased value of the Church-land on the north-west of London.

* This is the conclusion to which any friend of the Church would have come from reading the 6 & 7 Wm. IV. c. 77 ; but it seems from the Bill of 1850 (referred to in the sequel) that the manifest intention of the Act of W. IV. had been carried into effect in but a limited degree ; and that in fact the Bishops' incomes had not, up to the year 1850, been fixed according to the scale of that Act; nor was it even then contemplated so to fix them, except as regarded bishoprics appointed to after the 1st of January, 1848.

Church property placed at their disposal. The nearer approach to an equalization of the incomes of the bishops has also been accomplished through the powers of the Commission, and those preferments, inferior in rank but larger in endowment, which bishops with small episcopal incomes were wont to hold *in commendam*, are now possessed by those who hold no superior rank.

The distribution of the clergy is, however, quite as unequal as that of clerical income. In a pamphlet on ' Church Extension,' by the Rev. W. Palmer, who has a high reputation as an author on ecclesiastical subjects, he says that, judging from a rough estimate, it would seem that about 3000 parishes contain less than 300 inhabitants each, affording perhaps about 200 on an average, or a total population of not more than 600,000. Thus 3000 clergy are engaged in the care of 600,000 souls, while the remaining clergy (he estimates them at only 9000) are intrusted with the care of 15,400,000, showing a total " deficiency" of 6400 clergy for the care of 6,400,000 people. Mr. Palmer calculates that when the proportion of clergy to people is less than one to 1000* there is a " deficiency." In his tract (published in 1848) he says,—

" It appears from a Report of the Ecclesiastical Commissioners, that thirty-four parishes in London and its suburbs, with a population exceeding 10,000 each, contained, according to the census of 1831, a population of 1,137,000, with only 139 parochial clergymen. According to our basis this alone shows a deficiency of clergy for 994,000 people. But there were, by the same census, forty other parishes in London and its suburbs with popu-

---

* The Report of the Ecclesiastical Commission suggests one church for every 3000 persons in London.

lations varying from 3000 to 10,000 : making a total of
235,266, and served by only eighty-two clergymen. This
shows a further deficiency of clergy for about 153,000
souls ; which, added to the former deficiency, presents a
total of 1,151,000 people deprived of spiritual instruction
in 1831. If we add 20 per cent. to represent the increase of the last ten years (which would not, I believe,
exceed the truth), we have now in the above parishes of
London and its suburbs a population of 1,646,400 under
the spiritual care of 221 clergy ; leaving in the metropolis
alone the enormous number of 1,425,000 people unpro-
vided with spiritual aid, and requiring for their care
upwards of 1400 clergy, in addition to the present ecclesiastical force of the metropolis. If, in short, the clergy
of London were multiplied *seven-fold* at this moment,
they would all have full and ample occupation."

Undoubtedly they would, provided the people were
willing to receive their ministrations ; but it is worth
considering whether the Church should not begin by
such earnestness of action on behalf of the best interests
of the people as to create a strong popular desire for
additional guidance and superintendence on the part of
the clergy. In the metropolis the work is going on, and
by one means or another a considerable increase of clergy
and of churches is taking place. The difficulty is to
provide clergy for the poor ; and this difficulty is likely
to continue until men are found willing to devote themselves to poverty, labour, and all manner of privations,
merely for the sake of fulfilling the duty of preaching
the Gospel to the poor. Mr. Palmer thinks that with
the money which the Church has, and with more which
might be raised annually in the parishes of the kingdom
under the authority of a Royal Letter, sufficient funds
might be obtained to pay a very large number of addi-

tional clergy at the usual rate.   Something might no
doubt be done in this way, but not, I think, to the extent
he estimates.

Mr. Palmer advocates the extension of the episcopate
no less strongly than that of the priesthood.   Having
regard to the practice of the primitive Christian Church,
and the modern Romanist system, he thinks that our
English Church manifestly requires more bishops.   The
suggestion of 300, however, is somewhat startling.

"Looking to the invariable rule of the ancient Church
to place a bishop in every great city, for the purpose of
giving energy, unity, and consistency to the large body
of clergy collected there, it seems strange indeed to think
that places like Liverpool, Birmingham, Leeds, Manchester, Nottingham, Sheffield, Derby, Newcastle, Bath,
Plymouth, and many other towns of great population and
importance, should have been so long left without resident bishops.   Romanism has, with its usual quick-
sightedness, availed itself of our deficiencies, and fixed
the residence of its pretended bishops in large cities,
where none of our bishops are stationed.   Birmingham,
Bath, Wolverhampton, Liverpool, Newcastle, Derby,
and other important stations, are thus cicumstanced ; and
in some of these places Romish ecclesiastics are gradually assuming a position which can only arise from the
want of bishops in those localities.

"Since the above was written the case of the English
Church has become stronger by comparison with the proceedings of the Romish communion in this country.   In
England and Wales, where the largest computations of
the Romanists do not give them more than 1,000,000 of
people, and in which they really do not possess above
600,000 or 800,000 adherents at the outside, their hierarchy has been increasing, during the last ten years,

from four bishops to ten, and from ten (the present number) to fourteen; such being apparently the number of their hierarchy under the new arrangements now in progress. There are about 600 priests, so that each bishop will superintend about forty clergy. Were the Church of England equally well provided with bishops in proportion to the numbers of her clergy, she would have about 300 bishops."

By way of raising a fund for the endowment of additional bishoprics, Mr. Palmer proposes a further reduction of the incomes of the existing bishops, which would afford an aggregate of 46,000*l.* for the new sees; and also that the incomes of the deaneries should be added to the same fund. In this manner he suggests ways and means to the extent of 76,000*l.* a year, and proposes the following establishment of seventy-five suffragan bishoprics, under the present bishops as their metropolitans :—

" The ecclesiastical arrangement of England and Wales might be as follows :—

" I. JURISDICTION OF CANTERBURY.

(ARCHBISHOP OF CANTERBURY, PRIMATE.)

Metropolitan Sees.	Suffragan Sees.
Canterbury	Dover, Maidstone.
London	Westminster, Southwark, St. Alban's.
Winchester	Guildford, Romsey, Newport, Jersey.
Rochester	Colchester, Chelmsford.
Chichester	Lewes.
Salisbury	Malmsbury, Warminster, Dorchester, Wimborne.
Exeter	Barnstaple, Plymouth, Tavistock, St. Germain's, Truro.
Wells	Bath, Taunton, Bridgewater.
Gloucester	Bristol, Cirencester.
Worcester	Birmingham, Coventry, Evesham.
Hereford	Ludlow, Radnor.
Lichfield	Wolverhampton, Newcastle, Derby, Chesterfield, Shrewsbury.

Metropolitan Sees.	Suffragan Sees.
Oxford . . .	Windsor, Faringdon, Aylesbury.
Peterborough . .	Northampton, Leicester.
Ely . . .	Huntingdon, Bedford, Bury.
Norwich . .	Ipswich, Dunwich, Yarmouth, Thetford.
Lincoln . . .	Louth, Stamford, Gainsborough, Nottingham, Southwell.
St. Asaph . .	Montgomery.
St. David's . .	Brecon, Carmarthen, Cardigan.
Llandaff . .	Monmouth.
Bangor . . .	Merioneth.

" II. JURISDICTION OF YORK.

(ARCHBISHOP OF YORK, PRIMATE.)

York . . .	Sheffield, Beverley, Whitby, Northallerton, Sodor and Man.
Durham . .	Newcastle and Hexham, Berwick and Lindisfarn.
Carlisle . . .	Kendal.
Chester . . .	Macclesfield, Liverpool.
Ripon . . .	Leeds, Halifax, Huddersfield.
Manchester . .	Rochdale, Preston, Lancaster."

This is indeed a bold scheme of episcopal extension, yet not perhaps going beyond what is expedient, if at any time the public should become convinced that the Church ought to be in reality and practice what it is theoretically —the superintendent of religion, morals, and education throughout the land. This feeling, however, on the part of the public can scarcely be hoped for until the Church is observed to be at unity within itself,* having definite

---

* Dr. Arnold makes a distinction between unity of spirit and unity of opinion, which I fear is but a fond imagination. In the preface to his third volume of sermons he says, " I have endeavoured to assert the authority of law, which fanaticism and jacobinism are alike combining to destroy. I have wished to inculcate Christian unity—the unity of the spirit ; and therefore have condemned that craving for unity of *opinion* and of *form* by which the true unity is rendered impossible. I have upheld one standard and one authority in all moral points, namely, the law of God ; and one standard and one authority in all points of form

objects and definite principles, upon which all possessing authority within its pale are agreed, and having a system of discipline which will exhibit to all whom it expects to guide, that order and obedience — that imperturbable gentleness and unswerving firmness, which will serve as an example and an attraction to the world without.

It has already been incidentally mentioned as a sign of the times, proclaimed in the House of Commons, that about 1500 new churches have been added to the means of devotional accommodation in England and Wales within the last eighteen or twenty years. In the year 1848 the Queen's letter to the Archbishop of Canterbury officially announced that the Society for Promoting the Enlargement and Building of Churches, which was instituted in 1818, had, by means of donations, annual subscriptions, bequests, remittances from local associations, and collections under Royal Letters, contributed 439,698*l.* towards the increase of Church accommodation; and that more than a million and a half had been contributed for the same object by the parishes which the Society had assisted. The number of parishes thus assisted was 2735, and 760,000 additional sittings had been obtained, of which 566,000 were free and unappropriated. This, however, by no means embraces the whole of what has been done for Church extension, many churches having been built by local subscription or individual munificence, without calling upon the Society in question for any assistance.

The number of benefices in England and the different returns respecting them having been mentioned, it may be

---

and order, namely, the law of man; the first of these infallible and eternal; the second fallible and changeable; but both having an absolute claim in their respective departments to the implicit obedience of individuals."

well to state by what patronage these benefices are distributed :—

The Crown appoints to	952
The Archbishops and Bishops	1,248
Deans and Chapters and ecclesiastical corporations aggregate	787
Dignitaries and other ecclesiastical corporations sole	1,851
Universities, colleges, and corporations not ecclesiastical	721
Municipal corporations	53
Private proprietors	5,096
	10,708

Of the livings appointed to by the Crown, about seven-eighths are in the patronage of the Lord Chancellor, and one-eighth in the patronage of the Prime Minister. The above table was made out before the Church Commission had obtained its absorbing and dispensing powers, so that changes may have taken place, but not in the patronage either of the Crown or of private persons.

It is, says Dr. Arnold, quite manifest that the whole amount of Church property in England, including under that name both tithes, so far as they are in clerical hands, and Church lands of every description, is so much saved out of the scramble of individual selfishness, and set apart for ever for public purposes. Now there are few things from which society in England has suffered greater evil than from the want of property so reserved : it is apparent in every town and in every village ; in the absence of public walks, public gardens, public exercise-grounds, public museums, &c., in the former, and in most instances of even so much as a common green in the latter. Let a man go where he will, he is beset on every side with the exclusiveness of private property. The public has kept nothing. This has arisen very much out of the false and degrading notions of civil society which have prevailed within the last century. Society has been regarded as a mere collection of individuals, looking each after his own interest, and the business of government has been limited to that of a mere police, whose sole use is to hinder these individuals from robbing or knocking each other down. This view of society, alike unphilosophical and unchristian, has largely counteracted the good which the world in this advanced stage of its existence has derived from its increased experience; and its pernicious effects have been abundantly shown in the actual state of the poor throughout England. For their physical distresses, their ignorance, and their vices are the true fruits of the system of "letting alone," in other words of leaving men to practise for their own advancement all arts save actual violence; of allowing every natural and every artificial superiority to enjoy and push its advantages to the utmost, and of suffering the weaker to pay the full penalty of their inferiority. I hold it to be an enormous benefit that the property of the Church is so much secured for ever to public uses—a something saved out of the scramble, which no covetousness can appropriate, and no folly waste. Again, it is not only so saved, but so happily divided, that every portion of the kingdom shares in the benefit. The sight of a church-tower, wherever it is met with, is an assurance that everything has not been bought up for private convenience or enjoyment;—that there is some provision made for public purposes, and for the welfare of the poorest and most destitute human being who lives within the hearing of its bells.*

In May, 1850, returns were made to the House of Commons of the number of resident and non-resident

---

* Principles of Church Reform. 1833.

incumbents in England and Wales in 1838 and in 1848, and also of the number of "licensed" curates, and the total number of curates in those years respectively. This return contains much more than the gentlemen who moved for them appear to have asked, and, so far as official documents of the kind may be relied upon, afford a considerable amount of statistical information upon Church matters.

By the return for 1838 it appears that the total number of benefices was then . . .	10,742
Of which those having glebe-houses amounted to	7,364
The number of non-resident incumbents was .	4,307
Of these there were doing the duty of their parishes	1.184
The resident incumbents amounted to . .	5,859
The vacant, the sequestrated, and those from which there was no return, amounted to . .	576
The number of curates in the benefices of non-resident incumbents was	3,078
(Of whom 2627 were "licensed curates.")	

Of these 39 had less than 30*l.* a-year; 64 had between 30*l.* and 40*l.*; 192 had from 40*l.* to 50*l.*; 493 from 50*l.* to 60*l.*; 231 from 60*l.* to 70*l.*; 379 from 70*l.* to 80*l.*; 395 from 80*l.* to 90*l.*; 111 from 90*l* to 100*l.*; 493 from 100*l.* to 110*l.*; 33 from 110*l.* to 120*l.*; 256 from 120*l.* to 130*l.*; 30 from 130*l.* to 140*l.*; 11 from 140*l.* to 150*l.*; 190 from 150*l.* to 160*l.*; and 32 above 160*l.* The rest had weekly or unascertained stipends.

The curates of resident incumbents amounted to 1725, of whom 1233 were "licensed curates:" of these 128 had less than 50*l.* a-year; 804 had from 50*l.* to 100*l.*; 408 from 100*l.* to 110*l.*; 147 from 110*l.* to 150*l.*; 61 from 150*l.* to 200*l.*; and 18 above 200*l.* Thus the total number of parochial curates appears to have been 4803. The number of incumbents does not

appear, many of them being classed as "resident"
on one benefice, and "non-resident" on another; but
it is stated that of the non-resident incumbents no less
than 1878 had an exemption on account of residing on
other benefices.

In 1848 the total number of benefices was . .	11,611
Of which those having glebe-houses amounted to	7,917
The number of benefices on which there was no resident incumbent was . . .	3,094
The number in which the duty was done by the incumbent, though non-resident, was .	1,119
The resident incumbents amounted to . .	7,779
The vacant, the sequestrated, and those from which there was no return, amounted to .	738
(The "sequestrated" were 45 in 1838, and 36 in 1848.)	
The number of curates on the benefices of non-resident incumbents was	1,908
(Of whom 1,688 were " licensed curates.")	

There were 36 curates under 40*l*. a-year; 58 between
40*l*. and 50*l*.; 233 between 50*l*. and 60*l*.; 118 between
60*l*. and 70*l*.; 179 between 70*l*. and 80*l*.; 301 between
80*l*. and 90*l*.; 60 between 90*l*. and 100*l*.; 393 between
100*l*. and 110*l*.; 24 between 110*l*. and 120*l*.; 184 between 120*l*. and 130*l*.; 62 between 130*l*. and 140*l*.; 153
between 140*l*. and 160*l*.; 23 above 160*l*.; 34 having
the whole income of the benefice.

The total number of curates of resident incumbents in 1848 was	2,998
(Of whom 2,378 were " licensed curates.")	

104 had less than 40*l*. a-year; 357 between 40*l*. and
60*l*.; 318 between 60*l*. and 80*l*.; 553 between 80*l*. and
100*l*.; 940 between 100*l*. and 110*l*.; 51 between 110*l*.

and 120*l.* ; 228 between 120*l.* and 130*l.* ; 63 between
130*l.* and 150*l.* ; 109 between 150*l.* and 160*l.* ; 31 between 160*l.* and 300*l.* ; others at weekly rates.

The changes indicated by these returns are all favourable to the progress of the Church in practical improvement. The cases of residence of the incumbent have
increased from 5859 in 1838 to 7779 in 1848, and the
curates of resident incumbents from 1725 in 1838 to
2998 in 1848. The number of curates of both resident
and non-resident incumbents is increased only from 4803
in 1838 to 4907 in 1848; but this is accounted for by
the greater number of incumbents resident and doing the
duty of their parishes themselves. The number of curates
acting for incumbents in their absence from their parishes
was in 1838 no less than 3078; but in 1848 was diminished to 1908. It will be observed, however, that those
at the higher classes of salary were more numerous in
1848 than in 1838.

The returns for 1848 include the see of Sodor and
Man, which was omitted in the returns of 1838, and the
see of Manchester, which was created in the interval.

The number of exemptions in 1848 on account of residing on other benefices was 1373, being 505 less than
in 1838.

The public prints of the 16th of July, 1850, report
that in the debate of the evening before, in the House of
Commons, Mr. Hume said he understood it was determined by the Bill of 1837 that the bishops were to have
fixed salaries, and that the surplus was to be paid over to
the Ecclesiastical Commission. The bishops, however,
had always pocketed the surplus. Lord John Russell said
the honourable gentleman was mistaken in supposing that
the salaries of the bishops were definitely fixed by Act of
Parliament. Mr. Hume observed that there was at least

a resolution of the House to that effect. Lord John Russell answered that he did not remember any such resolution, but he was well aware the Act of Parliament said no such thing. What was proposed in the Bill then before the House—the "Ecclesiastical Commission Bill"—was to fix the sums.

The Act alluded to by Mr. Hume was, no doubt, that of 1836, the 6 and 7 W. IV. c. 77. The preamble of that Act sets forth in detail the recommendations of the Ecclesiastical Commissioners in their several Reports, and amongst other things the recommendation that fixed annual sums shall be paid *to the Commissioners* out of the revenues of the larger sees, for the augmentation of the smaller ones, so as to leave *an average annual income* to the Archbishop of Canterbury of 15,000*l.*, to the Archbishop of York 10,000*l.*, to the Bishop of London 10,000*l.*, and so on, as already detailed. And then by the 10th section of the Act it was enacted that " the said Commissioners shall from time to time prepare and lay before his Majesty in council such schemes as shall appear to the said Commissioners to be best adapted for carrying into effect the hereinbefore-recited recommendations, and shall in such schemes recommend and propose such measures as may upon further inquiry, which the said Commissioners are hereby authorised to make, appear to them to be necessary *for carrying such recommendations into full and perfect effect:* provided always, that nothing herein contained shall be construed to prevent the said Commissioners from proposing in any such scheme such modifications and variations as to matters of detail and regulation as shall not be substantially repugnant to any or either of the said recommendations." This Act was passed on the 13th of August, 1836. On the 15th of July, 1850, we find the Prime Minister declaring in his

place in the House of Commons that the salaries (incomes) of the bishops had not been definitely fixed by any
Act of Parliament !

In legal strictness the ministerial statement was correct.
The Act of W. IV. did not absolutely confirm anything
as to the incomes of the bishops, but it stated very plainly
the intention of the legislature with regard to them, and
it determined the way in which that intention might be
carried out.   As the Act, however, only said that the
Ecclesiastical Commission was to do certain things, without fixing any specific period within which they were to
be done, it appears that the Commissioners did not deem
it necessary to undertake in its full extent the very difficult and delicate task imposed upon them by the 10th
section of the 6 and 7 W. IV. c. 77.

The " Ecclesiastical Commission Bill " of 1850 constitutes a new Commission, in addition to the Ecclesiastical
Commission, to be called the " Church Estates Commission."   It is to consist of two commissioners, appointed by
the Crown, who must be lay members of the Church of
England, and one other member of the Church of England to be appointed by the Archbishop of Canterbury.
The first commissioner appointed by the Crown is to have
1200l. a-year, and the Archbishop of Canterbury's commissioner 1000l. a-year, both to be paid out of the funds
in the hands of the Ecclesiastical Commissioners.   The
first Crown commissioner is to be capable of sitting in the
House of Commons, and it is to be presumed he will be
chosen from the members of that House,* and become
the official or political agent for managing ecclesiastical
matters in that assembly, which now undertakes the criticism, if not the direction, of all affairs in this kingdom,

---

* He has not been.   The new Crown Commissioner is a peer.

from the cleansing of cesspools to the regulation of the hierarchy. Upon the appointment of a first Church Estates Commissioner under the Act, all estates and interests held in trust by the late secretary and treasurer of the Ecclesiastical Commissioners for them, shall vest in the new Estates Commissioner and his successors. The three Church Estates Commissioners, to whom the Ecclesiastical Commissioners may add other two, are to form a committee for the management of all property of the Ecclesiastical Commission; and nothing is to be done at any meeting of the Ecclesiastical Commissioners, unless two of the Estates Commissioners be present. On the other hand, the Ecclesiastical Commissioners may make general rules for the direction of the Estates Committee. The Bill of 1850 recognises two existing funds in the hands of the Ecclesiastical Commission, namely, a fund for episcopal purposes, and a "common fund;" and it is provided that they shall be put together and form one common fund, and the united funds shall be applicable to the purposes of the formerly existing common fund. The section, with regard to episcopal incomes, runs thus :—

"And whereas her Majesty has issued a Commission to certain persons therein named, to inquire, amongst other things, whether any and what improvement can be made in the existing law and practice relating to the incomes of archbishops and bishops, so as to secure to them, respectively, fixed instead of fluctuating annual incomes; and it is expedient that, until the said commissioners shall have made their report, and parliament shall have determined upon some permanent mode of effecting the object last aforesaid, temporary arrangements should be made for that purpose: be it enacted, that, notwithstanding the provisions of the said first-recited Act (6 & 7 Will. IV. c 77), and any order or orders of her

Majesty in council founded thereon, relating to or providing for the payment to or by the Ecclesiastical Commissioners for England of fixed annual sums, it shall be lawful, by the authority and in the manner by and in which the arrangements for carrying into effect the recommendations in the said Act recited may now be made, so to regulate from time to time the amounts, times, modes, and conditions of payments to be made to or by the said Ecclesiastical Commissioners, as the case may be, *by or to any archbishop or bishop who shall have succeeded to a see, upon any avoidance thereof happening after the first day of January*, 1848, or any other archbishop or bishop *who may signify his willingness to accept such annual income* as hereinafter mentioned, in lieu of his present income, as to secure to every such archbishop and bishop the annual income named for the archbishop or bishop of his see in the same or any other Act now in force, or in any order of her Majesty in council duly made and published, and no more ; and any arrangements which may be made for effecting the purpose last aforesaid shall remain in force until parliament shall otherwise direct."

This section sufficiently indicates the difficulty that had been found in carrying into effect the Act of 1836 (6 & 7 Will. IV.), and the unsettled state in which the affair of episcopal incomes still remained.   Even this last recited enactment only empowers, without enforcing, and it is a limitation rather than an extension of the Act of 1836 ; for while that Act appeared to contemplate the fixing of all then existing episcopal incomes, and of others which were then only intended to be called into existence, the new Act has regard only to the appointments since the beginning of 1848, or to other incomes which may be voluntarily submitted for regulation.

CHAPTER XXIV.

CHURCH CONSTITUTION AND DISCIPLINE.

SOME account, although it be but a very cursory one, of the different ranks of clergy in the Church of England, and of the origin of parochial divisions, is necessary to a right understanding of the actual condition of England. The highest rank is that of archbishop. In England there are two—the Archbishop of Canterbury and the Archbishop of York, of whom the first takes precedence. Their sees are as the names import; but, as archbishops, they preside over provinces. The province of York extends over the sees of York, Carlisle, Chester, Durham, Ripon, and Manchester: the province of Canterbury extends over all the other sees in England. An archbishop or bishop is elected by the chapter of his cathedral church, by virtue of a licence from the Crown,* called a *congé d'élire;* and it appears, from the defeat of recent proceedings which were taken in order to prevent the Crown from placing Dr. Hampden in the see of Hereford, that, though the forms of the confirmation of the election seem to recognise a right to object, yet the objector cannot be heard against the appointment which the Crown has authorized to be made.† Anciently, or rather in the

---

* Blackstone, i. 377.

† In Hilary Term, 1848, an application was made to the Court of Queen's Bench for a mandamus to compel the Archbishop of Canterbury and his vicar-general to hear the objectors who were called on to appear at the confirmation of the election of Dr. Hampden; but were not

middle ages, the Pope made the prelate, and the Crown granted the revenues. His Holiness, however, took offence at the mode of investiture, which was *per annulum et baculum*—by ring and crozier. This was considered to be an encroachment on the Church's authority. A compromise was made, and it was agreed that the gift of the temporalities should be *per sceptrum*, and that the sovereign should receive homage from the bishops for their *temporalities* only. Henry VIII. took back by statute (25 Hen. VIII. c. 20) the ancient right of nomination. It was enacted that at every future avoidance of a bishopric the king may send the dean and chapter his usual licence to proceed to election, which is always to be accompanied with a letter missive from the king, containing the name of the person he would have them elect; and if the dean and chapter delay their election above twelve days, the nomination shall devolve to the king, who may by letters patent appoint such person as he pleases. This election or nomination, if it be of a bishop, must be signified by the king's letters patent to the archbishop of the province; if it be of an archbishop, to the other archbishop and two bishops, or to four bishops,

---

allowed to appear, and were pronounced contumacious for not appearing, though they were present and desirous of being heard. The motion was heard by Lord Denman, L. C. J., and Justices Pattison, Coleridge, and Erle. The Court was equally divided, and no rule passed. Lord Denman and Justice Erle were against the rule; Justice Pattison and Justice Coleridge were in favour of it. Justice Pattison, whose opinion is of the highest authority, said that he apprehended the true meaning of the clause relating to the penalty of *præmunire* in the Act of Henry VIII. was that, *unless good and lawful reasons existed* for delaying the confirmation, the penalty would be incurred. Whenever a penalty was attached to the non-performance of a judicial or ministerial act, he apprehended it could only be incurred where no lawful cause or excuse existed to justify the non-performance of the act.

requiring them to confirm, invest, and consecrate the
person so elected, which they are bound to perform immediately, without any application to the See of Rome :
after which the bishop elect shall sue to the king for his
temporalities; shall make oath to the king, and none
other; and shall take restitution of his secular possessions out of the king's hands only. And if such dean and
 hapter do not elect in the manner which the Act ap-
points, or if such archbishop or bishop do refuse to confirm, invest, and consecrate such bishop elect, they shall
all incur the penalties of a *præmunire.* The statute of
præmunire (16 Rich. II. c. 5) enacts that whoever pro-
cures at Rome or elsewhere any translations, processes,
excommunications, bulles, instruments, or other things
which touch the king, against him, his crown, and realm,
and all persons aiding and assisting therein, shall be put
out of the king's protection, their lands and goods forfeited to the king's use, and they shall be attached by
their bodies to answer to the king and his council; a
process of *præmunire facias* shall be made out against
them, as in other cases of provisors.* This is what Pope
Martin V. called " execrabile illud statutum." The Act
of Henry VIII., which makes it applicable to the refusal
of chapters or bishops to comply with the desire of the
Crown as to the election or consecration of bishops of the
Church of England, was, as Mr. Christian's note to
Blackstone informs us, " afterwards repealed by 1 Edw.
VI. c. 2, which enacted that all bishoprics should be
donative as formerly. It states in the preamble that these
elections are in very deed no elections, but only, by writ
of *congé d'élire,* have colours, shadows, or pretences of
election. This is certainly good sense; for the permis-

---

* 4 Blackstone, 112.

sion to elect where there is no power to reject can hardly
be reconciled with the freedom of election.   But this statute (that of Edw. VI.) was afterwards repealed by
1 Mary, s. ii. c. 20." So that the statute of Henry VIII.
and the penalties of *præmunire,* entirely directed against
the conflicting authority of Rome, are now found to be
the bulwark of the Queen's prerogative as to the nomination of archbishops and bishops, when the authority of
Rome has sunk into utter insignificance.   This should be
kept in mind by those persons who take an objection to
the law which at present excludes Jews from Parliament,
that it was not made with *that* object, but with another.
If the statute of *præmunire* were only applied to the
objects which it was intended to be applied to when it
was made, what would now be the condition of her Majesty's prerogative in respect to the appointment of
bishops?   Mr. Christian quotes *Harg. Coke Litt.,* 134,
to show that " the bishoprics of *the new foundation* were
always donative."   He also observes that all Irish
bishoprics are so by the 2 Eliz. c. 4, *Irish statutes.*   He
thinks it necessary also to mention that " it is a prevailing
vulgar error that any bishop, before he accepts the
bishopric which is offered him, affects a maiden coyness,
and answers *nolo episcopari.*   The origin of these words
and this notion I have not been able to discover ; the
bishops certainly give no such refusal at present, and I
am inclined to think they never did at any time in this
country."

An archbishop is the chief of the clergy in a whole
province, and has the inspection of the bishops of that
province as well as of the inferior clergy, and " may de-
prive them on notorious cause." *   In the 11 W. III. the

---

* 1 Blackstone, 380.

Bishop of St. David's was deprived for simony and other offences, in a court held at Lambeth before the archbishop, who called to his assistance six other bishops. The Bishop of St. David's appealed to the Delegates, who affirmed the sentence of the archbishop; and after several fruitless applications to the Court of King's Bench and the House of Lords, he was at last obliged to submit to the judgment.* The archbishop has his own diocese, wherein he exercises episcopal jurisdiction, as in his province he exercises archiepiscopal. As archbishop, he, upon receipt of the king's writ, calls the bishops and clergy of his province to meet in convocation; but without the king's writ he cannot assemble them.† To him all appeals are made from inferior jurisdictions within his province ; and, as an appeal lies from the bishops in person to him in person, so it also lies from the Consistory Courts of each diocese to his Archiepiscopal Court. The *Consistory* Court of every diocesan bishop is held in their several cathedrals for the trial of all ecclesiastical causes arising within their respective dioceses. The bishop's chancellor, or his commissary, is the judge, and from his sentence an appeal lies to the archbishop of each province respectively. The Court of Arches is a court of appeal belonging to the Archbishop of Canterbury, the judge of which is called the Dean of the Arches, from the court having been anciently held in St. Mary-*le-bow* (Sancta Maria *de arcubus*), and the office is united with that of the archbishop's principal official. This judge (as does also the official principal of the Archbishop of York) determines appeals from the sentences of inferior ecclesiastical courts within the province. It was in this court, presided

---

* Lord Raym. 541 ; 1 Burn, Ec. L. 212.
† 4 Inst. 322.

over by Sir H. Jenner Fust, that, on the 2nd of August,
1849, the judgment was given in the "Gorham" case
which has since led to very important results. The
learned judge decided that the law of the Church was
opposed to the declared views of Mr. Gorham, and that
the Bishop of Exeter was justified in refusing to institute
him to the benefice to which the Crown had presented
him. "From the judge of the Court of Arches," says
Blackstone, "an appeal lies to the king in Chancery
(that is, to a Court of Delegates appointed under the
king's great seal) by statute 25 Hen. VIII. c. 19, as
supreme head of the English Church, in the place of the
Bishop of Rome, who formerly exercised this jurisdiction.
This great court of appeal in all ecclesiastical causes,"
he adds, the Court of *Judices Delegati*, "is frequently
filled with lords spiritual and temporal, and always with
judges of the courts at Westminster and doctors of the
civil law." The former appeals to the Pope arose out of
an usurpation; and the statute of the 25 Hen. VIII. was
but declaratory of the ancient law of the realm. But in
case the king himself be party in any of these suits, the
appeal does not then lie to him in Chancery, which would
be absurd, but, by the statute 24 Hen. VIII. c. 12, to
the bishops, abbots, and priors of the upper house of the
Convocation of the province in which the cause of the suit
arises.* A few years ago, however, by statute 2 & 3
W. IV. c. 92, the jurisdiction of the High Court of
Delegates in ecclesiastical suits was transferred to the
Privy Council of the king; and the 3 & 4 W. IV. c. 41,

---

* In the judgments of the several courts of common law appealed
to in the Gorham case, after the decision of the Judicial Committee of
Privy Council, doubts were thrown upon Blackstone's correctness in
thus stating the law of appeal to Convocation. See particularly the
judgment of the Court of Exchequer, delivered 8th of July, 1850.

transferred all the judicial functions of the Privy Council
to a select portion of it, called the Judicial Committee,
consisting of judges and other persons learned in the law.
It was to this Court of the Judicial Committee of Privy
Council that Mr. Gorham appealed, in 1849, from the decision of the Court of the Archbishop of Canterbury.   That
Most Reverend Prelate, being a Privy Councillor, was called
in as an assessor, and gave an opinion opposite to that of
the Judge of his own court.   The Judicial Committee of
Privy Council decided that, notwithstanding the declared
opinions of Mr. Gorham on the subject of baptismal rege-
neration, he ought to be instituted to the benefice to which
he had been presented.

A great sensation having been excited in the Church of
England by the consideration that, as the law stood, a
tribunal, which was neither ecclesiastical in itself nor in
its appointment, had the authority to determine in the last
resort what was or was not the doctrine and teaching of
the Church upon points of the most solemn importance,
a bill was brought into the House of Lords by the Bishop
of London, of which the first clause and the last were as
follows :—

" I. Whereas it is expedient to amend the law with
reference to the administration of justice in her Majesty's
Privy Council, so far as relates to questions of religious
doctrine arising in appeals from the Ecclesiastical Courts
of England : be it therefore enacted, by the Queen's Most
Excellent Majesty, by and with, &c., that in all cases of
appeals which may hereafter be made to her Majesty in
Council from any Ecclesiastical Court of England, if and
so often as it shall be necessary to determine any question
of the doctrine or tenets of the Church of this realm,
arising either in a criminal or civil suit, it shall be lawful
for the Judicial Committee of her Majesty's Privy Coun-

cil, and they are hereby required, to refer such question of doctrine to the archbishops and bishops of the provinces of Canterbury and York in the manner hereinafter provided; and the opinion of the said archbishops and bishops upon such question, when duly certified to the said Judicial Committee, shall be binding and conclusive for the purposes of the appeal in which such reference shall be made, and shall be adopted and acted upon by the said Judicial Committee, so far as may be necessary for the decision of the matter under appeal, and shall be specially reported by the said Judicial Committee to her Majesty in Council, together with their advice to her Majesty upon such appeal.

" VIII. Provided always, that in case any archbishop or bishop shall be a party to the suit in which any such question as aforesaid shall arise, or shall be a patron of any benefice or office the title to which shall be in question in such suit, or which in any event of such suit may be liable to become or be declared vacant, then and in every such case such archbishop or bishop shall not be at liberty to attend any such court as aforesaid, or to take any part in the deliberations or business thereof."

This bill was resisted by her Majesty's Government, and rejected by a majority of the House of Lords on the 3rd of June, 1850. The Lord President of the Council, the Marquis of Lansdowne, opposed it on the ground that it went in diminution of the royal prerogative, and would tend to disturbance rather than to peace. The following was reported as the conclusion of the address of the Lord President to the House :—

" To adopt the principle proposed would be, in his opinion, the surest way of preventing the efficacious union of good, and wise, and holy men for the purpose of advancing those truly great interests in which our religion, our prosperity, our happiness here and hereafter, were involved. Make points of doctrine a question of the decision of a bare majority of the bishops, and the ferment in the public mind, so far from being appeased, would simply resolve itself into the form of agitated speculation as to the time when other bishops should come with different opinions to form a majority deciding the other way. In such a state of things, when a bishop should be appointed, the question with the public would be, not whether he was a good man, a wise man, a pious man, but what were his views with reference to the last decree of the bishops? There would be endless consideration and reconsideration of doctrines, which, if raised, should be decided once for all—decided by an impartial tribunal —that was to say, by a tribunal with no preconceived opinions, learned in the law, accustomed to weigh evidence, and thus best prepared, when called upon by their Sovereign, to inform her what ought to be the doctrine, what was the fact, and what the law. Having said thus much, he had no objection to state that, though not prepared to legislate on the subject, he considered it desirable, while preserving the judicature established by his noble and learned friend opposite and the prerogatives of the Crown as hitherto exercised, that, for the purpose of showing the public that these questions could not be determined without the great authorities of the Church being fully heard, it should not be left to the Crown, or to the President of the Council, as in the recent case, merely to invite the attendance of right reverend prelates, but that any bishop, being a Privy Councillor, should *de jure* be a member of the tribunal in such cases; and he considered farther, that any member of the Council, not being a member also of the Church of England, ought not to sit in such cases. He thought that these regulations might very advantageously be a subject for future consideration."

Thus it appears that even the Ministers of the Crown, who were not prepared to legislate for the amendment of the law, were yet conscious of its anomalous condition, and of the unreasonableness of questions of religious doctrine being decided by a tribunal in which the Church was not necessarily represented.

The next in rank after archbishops and bishops are deans and chapters. They are in theory the council of the bishop, " to assist him with their advice in affairs of religion, and also in the temporal concerns of his see. When the rest of the clergy were settled in the several parishes of each diocese, these were reserved for the celebration of divine service in the bishop's own cathedral ; and the chief of them, who presided over the rest, obtained the name of Decanus, or Dean, being probably at first appointed to superintend *ten* canons or prebendaries." Deans are nominated by the Crown. The patronage of members of the chapters is various. The Act of 6 and 7 W. IV. c. 77, which created the Ecclesiastical Commission, gave considerable powers (which were very largely increased by the 3 and 4 Vic. c. 113) for the remodelling of cathedral chapters, and the appropriation of portions of their revenues to the general purposes of the Church. Great havoc was made of the endowed canonries, and the endowments of two new bishoprics (besides several episcopal palaces) arose out of their ruins. To make amends, a number of honorary or unendowed canonries were created by section xxiii. of the last-mentioned Act. This section has a remarkable and, as I think, an ill-judged preamble. It says, that, "whereas it is expedient that all bishops should be empowered to confer distinctions of honour upon deserving clergymen, the holders of such canonries shall be styled honorary canons, and shall be entitled to stalls, and to take rank in the cathedral church next after the canons." I am not aware· of any former constitution of the Church in which the desirableness of any worldly honour or title is recognised ; and when these things have come, they have been rather incidental civil advantages than direct and necessary adjuncts of an ecclesiastical position. And it seems to assimilate the profession of the clergy too much to professions merely secular and worldly, when we find the expediency of honorary distinctions for "deserving clergymen" gravely set forth in an Act of Parliament.

An archdeacon has an ecclesiastical jurisdiction immediately subordinate to the bishop, either through the whole of his diocese or in some particular part of it. His authority was originally derived from the bishop, but is now independent and distinct.* He visits the clergy, and has his separate court for hearing all causes of ecclesiastical cognizance.

The rural deans are also deputies of the bishop, placed in various parts of his diocese, the better to inspect the conduct of the parochial clergy, and to inquire into and report dilapidations. Blackstone enumerates among their duties the examining of candidates for confirmation, and says they are armed in minuter matters with an inferior degree of jurisdiction and coercive authority.

I now come to the most important of all the orders in that goodly fabric the Church of England, I mean the parochial clergy—the parsons or vicars of the parish churches. A parson, says Blackstone, *persona ecclesiæ*, is one that hath full possession of all the rights of a parochial church. He is called parson, *persona*, because by

---

* 1 Burn, Ecc. L. 68-69.

his person the Church, which is an invisible body, is represented; and he is in himself a body corporate, in order to protect and defend the rights of the Church (which he personates) by a perpetual succession. He is sometimes called the rector or governor of the Church; but the appellation of *parson* (however it may be depreciated by familiar, clownish, and indiscriminate use) is the most legal, most beneficial, and most honourable title that a parish priest can enjoy; because such an one, and he only, is said *vicem seu personam ecclesiæ gerere.*

The history of parochial establishments in England seems to me so interesting, and the actual fact of the existence of an endowed parochial clergy all over the kingdom so important, that I shall here extract a brief account of the whole matter from a little work prepared evidently with much care, and published in 1830.* It is correct in substance, and the most intelligible and popular in style of any I can at present lay my hands on. At the same time I may refer to 1 Blackstone, pp. 384-393, for a more particular account of the legal rights of parochial incumbents, the limitations of those rights, and the mode in which they are acquired or avoided :—

" We are informed that, towards the close of the sixth century, Austin the monk, accompanied by several associates, was despatched to propagate the gospel among the Saxon inhabitants of Britain. Ethelbert, who at the time of their arrival was King of Kent, is said to have received these missionaries with considerable favour; he gave them an edifice at Canterbury to be used as a place of Christian worship, and conferred upon them a spacious residence in

---

* ' The Revenues of the Church of England not a Burden.' J. Murray, 1830.

which they might dwell in common. Austin, under the
title of Bishop, was appointed the superintendent of these
ecclesiastics, who, acting under his orders, laboured to
propagate the new faith in different parts of Ethelbert's
kingdom.

" Thus, in fact, was laid the foundation of an ecclesiastical establishment in this country. At that period the
church which King Ethelbert had given to the monks on
their arrival in the island was the only consecrated place
of Christian worship in the kingdom of Kent; it was the
οἶκος or seat of the bishop, and the whole of what forms
the modern county went under the denomination of
πάροικια, *parœcia*, parish, or district, appendant to the
cathedral church.* At that time the population of Kent
was scattered throughout detached hamlets, which had
been cleared of wood and brought under tillage; these

---

* " These churches are called cathedrall, because the bishops dwell
or lie neere unto the same, as bound to keepe continuall residence within
their jurisdictions for the better oversight and governance of the same;
the word being derived *a cathedra*, that is to say, a chaire or seat,
where he resteth, and for the most part abideth. At first there was but
one church in everie jurisdiction, whereunto no man entered to praie but
with some oblation or other, toward the meintenance of the pastor. For
it was reputed an infamie to passe by anie of them without visitation;
so it was a no lesse reproach to. appeare emptie before the Lord. And
for this occasion also they were builded verie huge and greate: for
otherwise they were not capable of such multitudes as came dailie unto
them to heare the worde and receive the Sacraments.

" But as the number of Christians increased, so first monasteries, and
then finallie parish churches, were builded in every jurisdiction : from
whence I take our deanerie churches to have their originall, now called
mother church, and their incumbents archpreests ; the rest being added
since the conquest, either by the lords of everie towne, or zealous men
loath to travell farre, and willing to have some ease by building them
neere hand. As the number of churches increased, so the repair of the
faithfull unto the cathedralls did diminish."—Harrison's ' Des. of Eng.'
p. 135.

villages, or little colonies of cultivators, were occasionally, or perhaps periodically, visited by itinerant missionaries, despatched from their chief residence at Canterbury. At first, divine worship must have been performed in some private and unconsecrated dwelling situate in the village : here the inhabitants of the surrounding districts assembled, and here the travelling missionary expounded to the peasantry the doctrines of the true faith. That this mode of imparting religious instruction prevailed in the wildest and least populous parts of the country at a later period is a fact which we learn from the ' Venerable ' Bede. Describing the labours of Cuthbert, Bishop of Lindisfarne, he says, that, ' leaving the monastery, sometimes on horseback but more frequently on foot, he went to the surrounding villages, and preached the way of truth among their erring inhabitants; which Basil, in his time, was also accustomed to do.   For at that time it was the custom of the people of England that, whenever an ecclesiastic arrived in a village, all the inhabitants should, at his bidding, assemble together to hear the word of God.' *

"In each village the converts to the new faith gradually multiplied, until they became too numerous to meet in a private dwelling for the celebration of divine worship : hence it was found expedient that ' an oratory,' †

---

* Bede, lib. iv. c. 27.

† At that period these oratories were constructed of wood, and raised, perhaps, in some instances, by the joint labour of the inhabitants. Of these ancient ecclesiastical fabrics a specimen may even now be seen at Grinstead, in the county of Essex. The nave, or body, of that church is composed of the trunks of large oaks, split and roughly hewed on both sides; they are set upright and close to each other, being let into a sill at the bottom and a plate at the top, where they are fastened with wooden pins. This was the whole of the original fabric, which yet remains, though much corroded and worn by length of time. The

as it was then termed, or house of prayer, should be set
apart for the accommodation of the increasing community
of Christians. But no particular ecclesiastic was yet
appointed to reside in the villages where these 'oratories'
had been constructed ; no regular provision having been
set apart for his support. Each hamlet was, as heretofore, visited by an itinerant teacher, sent from the seat
of the bishopric.

"It was natural to expect that the labours of these
able and zealous teachers would finally succeed in making
a deep and lasting impression upon the inhabitants of the
island. In the course of time the great landlord of each
district, yielding to their exhortations, became a convert
to the new religion. His own conversion to the Christian
faith rendered him desirous to secure for his immediate
domestics, as well as the villeins and slaves who cultivated
his estate, a more frequent and regular administration of
religious ordinances than could have been obtained from
the casual visits of an itinerant missionary. To obviate
the manifest inconveniences of this irregular system of
religious instruction, he built, at his own cost and charges,
a church in which the inhabitants of the district might
assemble for public worship, and a house, with an attached
glebe, which the minister might inhabit. Having thus
created a parochial benefice, he voluntarily, freely, and
expressly endowed it with a certain portion of the gross
produce of his estate as an independent and inalienable
provision for each succeeding incumbent constantly resi-

---

modern additions are composed of stone. "There was a time," says
Bede, " when there was not a stone church in all the land, but the custom
was to build them all of wood ; and therefore, when Bishop Ninyas
built a church of stone, it was such a rarity and unusual thing among
the Britons, that they called the place *Candida Casa*, or *Whit-Church*."
Hist., lib. iii. c. 4.

dent upon his cure, and devoting his attention to the religious and moral improvement of the parishioners.

" In this manner it was that not only the county of Kent but the whole of this island became originally divided into parishes; not all at once by a general regulation or legislative enactment, but gradually, according to the disposition and circumstances of the various owners of estates. It was the work, not of one particular era, but of a long series of centuries: a parish was instituted whenever the landowner felt disposed to build a church and found a benefice for the religious instruction of his tenants.

" This furnishes a satisfactory reason for the singular forms and unequal extent of English parishes. Whenever a benefice was instituted by the owner of the soil, the limits of his private estate became the boundaries of the newly-created parish. Hence our manorial and parochial boundaries are in general found to be still coincident; and all exceptions to this rule are capable of being accounted for by a reference to the revolutions which have taken place in the state of landed property at various periods subsequently to the endowment of parish churches.

" The view which has been here given of the origin of parishes is strongly corroborated by an anomaly familiar to all those who have devoted any attention to topographical researches. In every part of the kingdom parcels of land, insulated and surrounded by other parishes, are to be met with situate at a considerable distance from the parish to which they belong. These anomalies appear to be quite inexplicable upon any other hypothesis than that which has been here put forward to account for the institution of benefices and the origin of tithes. In every reasonable mind they must succeed as effectually as the testimony of existing documents in establishing the conviction that the endowments of English parish churches were originally derived from the free and spontaneous grants of the owners of estates. These owners endowed the benefices which they founded with the tenth of the produce, not only of their principal estates, but also of such detached parcels of land as happened to lie at a distance from the churches which they had built.

" The extent to which the institution of parishes had proceeded in the southern division of this island at the date of the Domesday survey is a matter involved in considerable obscurity. The whole number of churches mentioned in that celebrated record amounts to about 1700. But as the precept issued for its execution did not expressly require a return of churches, it leaves room to suspect that, in many instances, these structures were omitted. Hence it has been inferred that the churches actually inserted in the Norman survey fall considerably short of the number of such structures actually existing in this country at the close of the eleventh century.

" But whatever may have been the number of parish churches built before the conquest, little doubt can be entertained that the greater portion of our parochial benefices are of more recent institution, and owe their endowments to the politic munificence of the early Norman barons or their immediate successors.

" Secure in the possession of the manors which their leader had conferred upon them, and naturalized in their adopted country, the followers of the Conqueror turned their attention to the cultivation of their estates and the civilization of their vassals. They vied with each other in the beauty and magnificence of the ecclesiastical edifices which, at their own expense, they constructed for the accommodation of their tenants and retainers. Hence parish churches and parsonage houses sprang up on every considerable estate, built and endowed by their owners. Another circumstance operated very powerfully in adding to the number of parish churches endowed during this period. The original grantees of the Crown, in many instances, split their extensive manors into minor fragments, which they conferred upon subinfeudatories. These sub-grantees claimed and exercised, as of common right, the privilege of building churches on the fees which they thus acquired; and to avail themselves of this privilege they were impelled by two motives :—When the subinfeudatory built a church upon his own estate, his tenants and domestics were relieved from the inconvenience of resorting for religious purposes to the mother church, lying generally at some distance from them. As long as no church existed in the underfee, the tithes of its produce were demandable by the incumbent of the mother church, who was appointed by the superior lord; but as soon as a church was built and consecrated upon the subfee, it became an independent parish, and the tithes vested in an incumbent nominated by the owner of the property, from the produce of which they accrued. The grantees of mesne manors were thus impelled to build churches on their estates, not only for the convenience and accommodation of their tenants, but frequently for the more interested purpose of securing to themselves the right of nominating the individual entitled to receive the tithes.

" That the barons and other landed proprietors of that age, not only enjoyed the privilege of converting their estates into independent parishes, but also practically exercised the right of granting away, to whomsoever they pleased, either a portion or the whole of the tithes accruing from their land, is capable of being substantiated by abundant and indisputable evidence. Of this evidence the following document will serve as a specimen :—

" 'Sciant tam præsentes quam futuri quod ego *Henricus de Malmeins* concedo et confirmo monachis ecclesiæ *Sancti Andreæ Apostoli Rovecestriæ* decimam meam totam de dominico meo et eam vehendam quocunque voluerint et transferendam : cum ante hanc concessionem solummodo granum habuerint. Præterea dono eis et concedo decimam meam de vitulis et porcellis. Has concessiones confirmo illis pro amore Dei et salute animæ meæ et uxoris et antecessorum meorum liberè et quietè possidendas assensu hæredis mei et voluntate uxoris et amicorum meorum.' *

" This grant shows that the owners of land enjoyed the right, not only of conferring their tithes in perpetuity, but also of limiting and defining the particular articles on which they should be levied. The demesne mentioned in this instrument must either have been extra-parochial, or, as it frequently happened in other instances, exempted from tithes on the original endowment of the parish in which it was situate. The owner of this demesne commenced his liberality to the monks of *Rochester* by conferring upon them the tithe of his corn alone. In the document just transcribed, he confirms his previous bounty, and adds to it the tithes of calves and pigs.

" The following is another ancient grant which puts it beyond all doubt that the tithes of the district named in it were derived from the voluntary munificence of the owner of the land :—

" 'Sciant præsentes et futuri quod *Radulphus de S. Georgio* et *Agatha* uxor ejus et *Alnus* hæres eorum dederunt et concesserunt monachis de *Boxgrave*, decimam

---

* Selden's ' History of Tithes,' p. 315.

de *Liparinges* in perpetuam eleemosinam, quam prius dederat eis *Basilia* mater ipsius *Radulphi*. Et ipsi monachi debent facere ecclesiasticum servitium in ecclesia sua de *Ichenora*, vel in capella sua de *Briddeham*, hominibus prædicti Radulphi morantibus apud *Liparinges* et in singulis hebdomadis unum servitium, donec prædictus *Radulphus* vel hæredes sui ibi fecerint quoddam oratorium in quo unus de capellanis monachorum faciat prædictum servitium in hebdomadâ.' *

" From this grant we collect that the district or estate called *Liparinges* was destitute of a church for the accommodation of its inhabitants, and free from the payment of tithes. Being desirous to provide for his domestics and tenants the benefit of religious instruction, the owner of the estate confers on the monks of *Boxgrove* the tithes of his land, on condition that 'his men dwelling at *Liparinges*' should be permitted to attend the church of *Ichenor*, or the chapel of *Briddeham* belonging to the said monks, until such time as either he or his heirs should erect an ' oratory' at *Liparinges*, which should be thenceforward served by a chaplain appointed and maintained by the monks of *Boxgrove*.

" The same motive which induced the owner of the estate called *Liparinges* to settle the tithes of its produce on the monks of *Boxgrove*, operating upon the minds of other landlords, impelled them to build churches and endow them with tithes. The chartulary of the priory of *St. John the Evangelist* in *Brecon* contained a transcript of the deed by which the church of the parish of *Hay* in that county was endowed with tithes. Soon after the conquest the manor of *Hay* came into the possession of *Bernard de Newmarch*. Having as yet no church, it was

---

* Selden's ' History of Tithes,' p. 333.

extra-parochial, and all the land which it contained was
let out to the occupiers tithe-free. About the close of
the eleventh century we find that this great baron, ' various considerations him thereunto moving,' built within
the limits of his manor of *Hay* an edifice in which his
domestics and tenants might assemble for religious worship. He erected also a parsonage-house, to which he
attached fifteen acres of glebe-land, which are precisely
and very particularly described in the grant ; and having
thus founded a parochial benefice, he expressly endowed
it with the tithes accruing from all the land contained
within the limits of the parish.

" The document itself runs thus :—

" ' Bernardus Dei gratia Episcopus de Sancto David,
omnibus Sanctæ Dei Ecclesiæ fidelibus salutem, Deique
benedictionem et suam. Sciant tam presentes quam
futuri, quod quando dedicavimus Ecclesiam Beatæ Mariæ
de Haia, Willielmus Revel, concessu Bernardi de Novo
Mercato qui interfuit dedicationi, dedit et concessit in
perpetuam eleemosinam et dotem ipsius ecclesiæ 15 acras
terre et duas mansuras terre, videlicet, Levenathi pre-
positi et Alverici bubulci et totam illam terram quæ est
ab illis mansuris sursum in nemore usque ad divisas de
Ewyas* et in bosco et in plano ; dedit etiam eidem
ecclesie totam decimam totius terre sue de Haia in
omnibus rebus et de terra Ivoris et de Meleniauc † et de
omnibus illis qui de feudo Haie tenebant. Et ne in
posterum inde fiat dubitatio, has determinate dedit et

---

* The parish of Hay joins part of the possessions of the ancient family
of Laci, called formerly Ewyas Laci, now a parish only.

† Terra de Meleniauc ; Melinog is a very small and mesne manor on
the confines of the parishes of Hay and Llanigon, running in a narrow
slang nearly north and south, and crossing the Wye, where there are
some fields still called " caeau Melinog," the fields of Melinog.

concessit decimas, videlicet, de blado et fœno et de
pullanis et vitulis, de agnis et porcellis, de lana et caseo
et virgulto et de redditu Wallensium et Pasnagio et
placitis. Quicunque vero aliquid inde subtraxerint vel
diminuerint, excommunicentur, et a consortio Dei omni-
umque sanctorum ejus sequestrentur, donec ad emenda-
tionem veniant.' *

"To the benefice thus instituted he presented an
ordained clerk, and reserved to himself, his heirs and
assigns, the right of nominating the incumbent on every
subsequent avoidance.

"With respect to nearly all our ecclesiastical benefices, such I apprehend to be a correct account of the
origin of the endowments now attached to them: the
lord of a manor, or the owner of an estate acquired by a
grant from the Crown, by descent, or by purchase, erected
a church for the accommodation of the inhabitants of the
district who were then his tenants at will, and endowed
it with the tithes of the whole produce. Hence the
ancient limits of a private estate became the public
boundaries of the subsisting parish; and the emoluments
of the incumbents made no addition to the burdens
already pressing upon the occupiers, as they were, in
fact, deducted from that portion of the surplus produce
which fell to the share of the owner under the denomination of rent.

"Assuming this representation of the origin of ecclesiastical endowments to be correct, it necessarily follows
that the advantages which the inhabitants of a parish
derive, in a religious, moral, social, or political view, from
the discharge of the ecclesiastical functions ordained by
the state, were originally a gratuitous boon conferred

---

* Apud Kennet on Impro.

upon them by the proprietor of the estate who first built a church, and endowed it with tithes. The funds now expended in maintaining these institutions are the proceeds of his bounty. He might, had he thought proper, have devised to his heir the whole surplus produce received from his estate as rent, undiminished by a claim on account of tithes. But such was not his pleasure. On the contrary, he bequeathed his landed property to his eldest son, encumbered and charged with a provision for securing, on a permanent foundation, the religious and moral instruction of its occupiers. It appears, from the language of one of the ancient grants already transcribed, that the heir at law was actually consulted as to the intended alienation: it is indeed reasonable to presume that in this instance the grantor was only tenant for life, and that therefore the consent of his son and heir was necessary in order to render the deed of endowment valid. It is surely both reasonable and lawful that every man should be at liberty to do what he likes with his own, provided ' what he likes ' be not injurious to the rights and interests of others ; and it will be difficult to point out a ' reason ' which should debar the lay owner of an estate from setting aside any portion of its produce for the purpose of instructing its occupiers in the duties of religion and morality, until it can be proved that such an object is repugnant to the interest and welfare of society : and when an individual has actually, and for ever, thus alienated any portion of the produce of his estate, it is extremely difficult to comprehend on what grounds his descendants, much less those who have subsequently purchased his property, or their tenants, can represent themselves as bearing any part of this burden. The founder and endower of a rectory, reserving to himself and his representatives the privilege of presenting to the benefice when vacant, conferred upon the parishioners a right to require the appointment of an individual to the living properly qualified to discharge the ecclesiastical duties of the parish: but the emoluments derived from this endowment do not come from the pockets of the parishioners—they are a portion of the surplus produce of the estate, which, before the endowment of the rectory, belonged to the owner, and were received by him as rent, and which, from the moment of their appropriation to ecclesiastical purposes, ceased to be his property."

Upon this it seems proper to observe that a distinction ought to be taken between an endowment in land, which the parson may either occupy himself or let to another, and an endowment in the form of tithe or rent-charge, which gives no right to occupation, but only to a portion of that which arises from the application of labour to the land. It is much easier to acquiesce in the right of a proprietor to settle or bequeath his land for ever to the use of the Church, than to allow the reasonableness of his leaving a charge for ever upon the produce of land which the Church, or its personal representative, has no right to occupy. Notwithstanding the trouble and responsibilities which proprietorship involves, I cannot help regretting that the right of the parochial clergy should so generally be to a charge upon the lands of others, instead of to the produce or rent of their own land. It is to be considered, however, that, as it is easier to rob a man of the money he carries about with him than of his credit at his banker's, so it might have been easier in violent times to have robbed the Church of its land in every parish, if such had been the form of its parochial endowments, than to alienate its claim upon the land possessed and occupied by others. Perhaps, therefore, there is upon the whole no reason to regret that the original parochial endowments of the Church were in the form of claims upon the land, and not in that of the land itself; although at the present time there is undoubtedly a jealousy of the Church's claim both on the part of occupiers and proprietors, as if it were something in the nature of a tax rather than of a joint ownership; and this feeling would probably not exist if the Church had its own portion cut off and set apart from the rest.

In the middle ages the religious houses or monasteries frequently possessed themselves of the parochial tithes, undertaking the parochial duty, which was discharged by some member of the house. But the deputed monk was found in practice a bad substitute for the parish priest, and the Parliament (which in England seems always to have meddled in Church matters) interfered to remedy the evil. By statute 4 Hen. IV. c. 12, it was " ordained " that the vicar of parishes, the tithes of which have been " appropriated " by religious houses, shall be a " secular person," * that is, not belonging to any order or brotherhood of " regulars "—that he shall not be a member of any religious house—that he shall be a vicar perpetual, not removable at the caprice of the monastery—that he shall be canonically instituted and inducted; and be sufficiently endowed, at the discretion of the ordinary, for these three express purposes, to wit, to do divine service, to inform the people, and to keep hospitality. The endowments of vicarages have in consequence *usually* been by a portion of the glebe or land belonging to the parsonage, and a particular share of the tithes which the appropriators found it most troublesome to collect, and which

---

* The monks who lived *secundum regulas* of their respective houses or societies were denominated "regular" clergy, in contradistinction to the parochial clergy, who performed their ministry in the world, *in seculo*, and who from thence were called secular clergy.

are generally called small tithes, the greater or predial
tithes being still reserved to their own use. But one and
the same rule was not observed in the endowment of all
vicarages. The Act of the 47 Geo. III. c. 99, regulates
the residence of the clergy, and provides penalties for
non-residence. Legal residence is not only in the parish,
but also in the parsonage-house, if there be one : for it
has been resolved that the original statute intended residence, not only for serving the cure and for hospitality,
but also for maintaining the house, that the successor
may also keep hospitality there.

A curate is the lowest degree in the Church, though a
highly honourable and respectable office in itself. The
curate is the officiating temporary minister instead of the
proper incumbent. There are some perpetual curacies,
which are unendowed incumbencies, the tithes having
been appropriated, and no vicarage endowment made.
With regard to curacies in general, it is an office known
to the law, and by statute the curate is provided for
who serves a church during a time its incumbency is
vacant. He is to be paid such stipend as the ordinary
thinks reasonable out of the profits of the vacancy. A
great part of the most arduous duties of the ministers of
the Church—especially among the poor—is discharged
by curates. Taking them for all in all, they are a most
deserving and useful class of men, and worthy the regard
of all Christian patriots. The murmurs of discontent,
however, which are sometimes heard respecting the
severity of their work, and the smallness of their pay, are
not only peevish but unjust. Men who devote themselves
to the Church should not do so for the sake of a provision
to support a family. If that be their aim, they should
devote themselves to something else. Curates have not
the responsibilities which belong to incumbents, and the

more they devote themselves to the details of duty allotted
to them, the less will they feel the need of those " advantages " which are required to make idleness agreeable.
How many of the beneficed are there who look back upon
their curacy days with some sighs of regret and some
pardonable pride! The curates themselves, I believe, are
not the most apt to complain of their lot. The com-
plainers are generally those who think so little of the
clergy, that they rank them with counting-house clerks
and warehousemen, whose worth is estimated by its money
value, and marked by the pay which they receive.

CHAPTER XXV.

PUBLIC SCHOOLS.

THOUGH education was not made a concern of the Government in this country until of late years, yet from a very early period it was the custom of benevolent individuals to found schools and to endow them. From the king with his royal revenues, to the opulent tradesman with his gettings vested in the land, it was the desire of the best of every class in the olden time to make provision for education in grammar—that is to say, Latin and Greek—and in religion. Several hundreds of these endowed schools were scattered over England; but when the good old custom died away, the purposes of the endowments which had been made were too often overlooked or forgotten by the trustees in succession, so that various neglects, abuses, and perversions grew like rank weeds about the greater number of the old foundations. Much, however, has been done—at first in a violent party spirit, but ultimately with a good effect—since 1818 to inquire into these old endowments and to restore them to their former uses. Much work has been given to various attorneys-general, and those deputies of theirs who are called by a diabolical name, and sundry Acts of Parliament have been passed to set right what was wrong. The last of which I have any note is the 3 & 4 Vict. c. 77. It was to the energy—not unmingled with party bitterness—of Lord Brougham, then a rising barrister and an ardent popular politician, that the inquiries into the abuses of these endowments must be attributed.   To a considerable number of these endowed establishments large additions have been made for the accommodation of boarders, who pay moderately or largely, as the case may be, for classical education.   These are called our " public schools," such as Eton, Harrow (the first a king's, and the second a yeoman's foundation), Westminster, Winchester, Rugby, and many more ; but those already mentioned are the most eminent and most generally referred to by those who extol the glory or proclaim the wrong of English public schools.

Few questions are of more social interest, or have been more frequently discussed, than that of the advantage or disadvantage to the youth of England of these schools. They who have belonged to them have for the most part enough of the *esprit du corps*, as well as of the fondness of schoolboy recollections, to make them zealous for the old scene of their triumphs, or even their disgraces.

> " Dear the schoolboy spot
> We ne'er forget, though there we are forgot."

It is one of the blessings of our mental constitution that the memory retains more vividly that which has given pleasure than that which has inflicted pain.   The man forgets the miseries of his first years at school, and the tyranny of the senior boys, while he remembers his first triumphs in longs-and-shorts, or in bowling and batting. The days of buoyant spirits and the nights of unbroken sleep recur to his memory rather than the cuffs and curses he received as a fag, or the weary poring over fine passages in Homer or in Horace, dimly discerning the ordinary meaning of the words, while of their poetic beauty he had not the slightest glimmering of a concep-

tion. Nothing is more common than a strong partisan
feeling respecting the particular school in which a man is
most interested. This feeling extends in some degree
even to mammas and sisters, and luckless is the man who,
in English society, should venture to find fault with the
system of Harrow, or Eton, or any other of the eminent
public schools in particular. Perhaps, however, some
criticism, and some citation of authority, upon schools in
general, may be offered without offence. At all events,
when one considers the effect which such schools and their
systems have upon that class of the people who afterwards
take the most prominent part in society, in the legislature,
and in the government, it will be admitted that no complete conception of England as a nation can be formed
without some knowledge of these schools and their tendency. In my own opinion, very much of what is peculiar
to the upper classes of Englishmen is to be traced to the
public school system. The courage and the coolness—
the habit of calm endurance—the light yet unexcited
manner, even in the midst of the gravest and most harass-
ing circumstances—the self-command and the want of
feeling for others—the admiration of talent and spirit, and
the want of sympathy with modest worth—the strength,
in fine, and the unamiableness which seem to me to prevail in the character of the generality of Englishmen of
the upper class, may be traced back to the early days
when tyranny and sometimes torture have to be borne
without wincing—when gravity is mocked at, and delicacy
of feeling flouted and jeered—when boldness, readiness,
and good spirits carry all before them—and when he who
at first is the victim of tyranny, grows by seniority to
become a tyrant in his turn. Such I believe to be very
generally the course of the moral habits of English public
schools, out of which much good and much evil are

evoked—much that tends to the encouragement of manliness and the repression of dangerous sentimentalism—
much also that tends to selfishness, scorn, and disregard
of what is simple, kind, and good in human nature.

In Boswell's ' Life of Johnson ' he gives an animated
account of an evening at the Mitre Tavern, when the
Doctor and Mr. Murray, Solicitor-General of Scotland,
dined with him.   The conversation happening to turn
upon public schools, the biographer says that Johnson
displayed in a luminous manner the advantages and disadvantages of them, but his arguments preponderated so
much in favour of the benefit which a boy of good parts
might receive at one of them, that Mr. Murray was very
much influenced by what he heard in his determination
to send his own son to Westminster school.   To this
passage Mr. Croker, in his admirable edition of the book,
appends a note, in which he quotes Mr. Canning.   " A
peculiar advantage," he says, " of an education in our
public schools was stated in one of his parliamentary
speeches by the late Mr. Canning—himself a great authority and example on such a subject.   ' Foreigners
often ask by what means an uninterrupted succession of
men qualified more or less eminently for the performance
of united parliamentary and official duties is secured?
First, I answer (with the prejudices perhaps of Eton and
Oxford), that we owe it to our system of public schools
and universities.   From these institutions is derived (in
the language of the prayer of our collegiate churches)
' *a due supply of men fitted to serve their country both in
Church and State.*'   It is in her public schools and universities that the youth of England are, by a discipline which
shallow judgments have sometimes attempted to under-
value, prepared for the duties of public life.   There are
rare and splendid exceptions, to be sure—but in my con-

science I believe that England would not be what she is without her system of public education, and that no other country can become what England is without the advantages of such a system." *   In the last opinion I quite agree; but I doubt that England is perfect, or that to become what England is, in every respect, ought to be desired by the wise and good of other countries.   With all deference to Mr. Canning's great authority, he was scarcely the fittest person to judge of the general utility of public schools.   If all men were to be public men, there would be less doubt of the advantages of the system of Eton and Westminster.   If all boys were like George Canning, all doubt would be removed.   Nature formed him for making the most of all the advantages which such institutions offer.   Clever, brilliant, bold, ambitious, and amusing, the system eminently suited him; and as he happened to be remarkably successful in after life, his school companions were ever ready to show their recollection of the friendships and intimacies of boyhood.   Had

---

* " Would you your son should be a sot or dunce,
 Lascivious, headstrong, or all these at once;
 That in good time the stripling's finish'd taste
 For loose expense and fashionable waste
 Should prove your ruin and his own at last;
 Train him in public with a mob of boys,
 Childish in mischief only, and in noise;
 Else of a mannish growth, and five in ten,
 In infidelity and lewdness, men.
 There shall he learn, ere sixteen winters old,
 That authors are most useful pawn'd or sold;
 That pedantry is all that schools impart,
 But taverns teach the knowledge of the heart;
 There waiter Dick, with bacchanalian lays,
 Shall win his heart and have his drunken praise,
 His counsellor and bosom friend shall prove,
 And some street-pacing harlot his first love."
       Cowper's ' Tirocinium.

he recollected this, he would perhaps have refrained from stigmatising as of "shallow judgment" those who thought less highly than he did of a system by which he, beyond any other person of his time in England, was likely to profit.   Take a man of very opposite temperament—a man not less eminent in his own way of life than Canning himself, and certainly not less good and amiable.   Cowper remarks, that " connexions formed at school are said to be lasting and often beneficial.   There are two or three stories of this kind upon record, which would not be so constantly cited as they are whenever this subject happens to be mentioned if the chronicle that preserves their remembrance had many besides to boast of.   For my own part, I found such friendships, though warm enough in their commencement, surprisingly liable to extinction; and of seven or eight whom I had selected for intimates out of about three hundred, in ten years' time not one was left me.   The truth is, that there may be, and often is, an attachment of one boy to another that looks very like a friendship, and, while they are in circumstances that enable them *mutually to oblige and to assist each other*, promises well, and bids fair to be lasting.   But they are no sooner separated from each other, by entering into the world at large, than other connexions and new employments, in which they no longer share together, efface the remembrance of what passed in earlier days, and they become strangers to each other for ever." *   Cowper adds to this, that the man frequently differs so much from the boy, that his principles, manners, temper, and conduct undergo so great an alteration, that we no longer recognise in him our old playfellow, but find him utterly unworthy and unfit for the place he once held in our

---

* Correspondence, Oct. 5, 1780.

affections.   As to this, I apprehend the change is more
generally in our own powers of observation and judgment
than in the character of the matured boy.   Wordsworth
judges more profoundly : —

> " So was it when my life began ;
> So is it now I am a man ;
> So be it when I shall grow old.
> The child is father of the man ;
> And I could wish my days to be
> Bound each to each by natural piety."

Southey says that the letter from which the above passage is taken was written by Cowper in " a splenetic
mood, induced perhaps by the neglect of some who, if
they were men of letters, were also, in the worst accepta-
tion of the phrase, men of the world.   Some of his early
intimates he had at that time lost by death ; and the circumstances which drove him into retirement separated
him from others, of whom nevertheless he continued to
think with kindness and affection—this, too, when he
must strongly and justly have condemned the course of
their lives."   Now, it seems to me that these circumstances go rather to establish the reasonableness of what
Cowper had said, than to show that he had said it under
the influence of spleen.   Southey speaks of Cowper's
school unhappiness as having been far greater at the
private school he attended in Herts than it was afterwards in Westminster.   " The tyranny under which
Cowper for two years suffered there (in Herts) made, as
it well might, a deep and lasting impression upon him ;
and to this it is that the strong dislike with which, in the
latter part of his life, he regarded all schools, must be
ascribed.   I know not whether wicked propensities are
ever cured at school ; but this I know, that they generally
find full play there, and that a system of preventive dis-

cipline, which should impose *some effectual restraint upon brutal dispositions, at that age when they are subject to control, would be one of the surest means of national reformation.* It is needed alike for those who are being trained in our seminaries of sound and orthodox learning for the higher walks of life and the more important stations of society, and for those who are training themselves in the streets and purlieus of every populous place for transportation or the gallows." This observation is, I think, as wise in its matter as it is vigorous in its expression. In England it appears to me that what is chiefly wanting in education is a more careful government of the habitual disposition and manners of the pupils. To this not enough of attention is given at any large school; and at the great public schools there is no discipline of manners save that arising from mere attrition among the boys themselves. This is not enough to subdue the brutal and the strong, who are found more or less in all ranks, and who spread around them an atmosphere of tyranny and grossness, and everything bad except fear. Among the good effects of public schools is the killing of the vice and weakness of cowardice. " He that is afraid of anything," said Johnson, in one of his exaggerating moods, " is a scoundrel." That was a thoroughly English sentiment, and the expression of it a strikingly original exaggeration. Another great Englishman, Dryden, I think it is, who says,—

" A fool is nauseous, but a coward worse."

It need scarcely be said, however, that high courage is perfectly compatible, even in boys, with courtesy and kindness of demeanour; and there is no risk that, in subduing gross and wicked tempers, we should give encouragement to effeminacy or fear.

Of Cowper at Westminster, Southey remarks that it has been said that the treatment he endured there in all probability produced his insuperable aversion to public schools. But that aversion, adds his biographer, " arose from what he saw and what he reflected on in after-life, *not* from any ill-usage he experienced there. His recollections of Westminster were pleasurable. . . . . So far, indeed, were the years which Cowper passed at Westminster from being years of misery, that they were probably the happiest in his life. They were years in which he was not disquieted with any foresight of the obstacles which afterwards impeded his happiness ; neither had he any cause, real or imaginary, for regret or self-reproach. He was exactly one of those boys who choose for themselves the good that may be gained at a public school, and eschew the evil ; being preserved from it by their good instincts, or by the influence of virtuous principles inculcated in childhood. Being equally fond of his studies and his sports, he was a proficient in both. . . . . The figure which he afterwards made in the fields of literature showed the benefit he had derived both from the discipline of Westminster and its indiscipline—from the instruction which a man of genius willingly imparts to an apt and docile pupil in the regular course of school business, and from that play and exercise of the intellect which, in the little less profitable hours of school idleness, he enjoyed with those schoolfellows who may properly be called his peers, Lloyd, Churchill, and Colman." Another of his more recent biographers (Grimshawe) gives a very different account. " He has been frequently heard to lament," says this author, " the persecution he suffered in his childish years from the cruelty of his schoolfellows in the two scenes of his education. His own forcible expressions represented him at Westminster as not daring to raise his eye above the shoe-buckle of the elder boys, who were too apt to tyrannize over his gentle spirit. The acuteness of his feelings in his childhood rendered those important years (which might have produced, under tender cultivation, a series of lively enjoyments) mournful periods of increasing timidity and depression. In the most cheerful hours of his advanced life he could never advert to this season without shuddering at the recollection of its wretchedness. . . . . He, nevertheless, acquired the reputation of scholarship, with the advantage of being known and esteemed by some of the aspiring characters of his own age, who subsequently became distinguished in the great arena of public life." The same writer observes that the relative merits of private and public education is a question that has long agitated the world. Each has its partisans, its advantages, and defects; and, " like all general principles," its application must greatly depend on the circumstances of rank, future destination, and the peculiarities of character and temper. " For the full development of the powers and faculties of the mind —for the acquisition of the various qualifications that fit men to sustain, with brilliancy and distinction, the duties of active life, whether in the cabinet, the senate, or the forum—for scenes of busy enterprise, where knowledge of the world and the growth of manly spirit seem indispensable; in all such cases we are disposed to believe that the palm must be assigned to public education." This being admitted, the only drawbacks are those which regard religion and morality. If we reflect, says Mr. Grimshawe, that brilliancy is oftentimes a flame that consumes its object; that knowledge of the world is, for the most part, but a knowledge of the evil that is in the world; and that early habits of extravagance and vice, which are ruinous in their results, are not unfrequently

contracted at public schools ; if to these facts we add that
man is a candidate for immortality,—it then becomes a
question of solemn import, whether integrity and principle
do not find a soil more congenial for their growth in the
shade and retirement of private education ? The one is
an advancement for time, the other for eternity. The
former affords facilities for making men great, but often
at the expense of happiness and conscience : the latter
diminishes the temptations to vice ; and, while it affords
a field for useful and honourable exertion, augments the
means of being wise and holy. If all this pleading were
undemurrable, *cadit quæstio*. It is, however, far easier to
believe that disregard of religion and vicious habits may
be learned at public schools, than to be satisfied that at
private schools a progress in holiness and purity of life is
probable.

Upon this most important part of the subject Southey
says, that it cannot be gainsaid that " our boarding-
schools are unfavourable to those devotional feelings the
seeds of which have been sown in early childhood, and
destructive of those devotional habits which have been
learned at home ; that nothing which is not intentionally
profane can be more irreligious than the forms of religion
which are observed there; and that the attendance of
schoolboys in a pack at public worship is worse than per-
functory. This is one of the evils connected with public
education, such as it long has been, still is, and is likely
to continue, however earnestly endeavours may be made
to amend it. It is a great evil, but Cowper did not
reflect upon its natural and obvious causes, when he
accounted for it by saying that the duty of the schoolboy
swallowed up every other. In his days, and in my own,
that duty left time enough for idleness, or recreation, or
the pursuits of private study to those who were studiously

disposed ; the *forcing system* had not been introduced.
But at no time has a schoolboy's life offered any encouragement, any inducement, any opportunity for devotion.
Much might be done to prevent or diminish the mischief
incident to such institutions ; but, of all those mischiefs
which are to be set against the great advantages belonging
to them, this would be the most difficult to reach.   In the
natural course of human life an intercourse is maintained
between all the different grades from infancy to old age,
and each in that intercourse exercises a salutary influence
upon the others : in schools, boys are brought together in
great numbers, and kept together apart from all influences, except that of mere authority.   Theirs is the stage
in which, in the wise order of things, the animal part of
our nature predominates over the intellectual, and in a
still greater degree over the spiritual ; but something
more than scholastic authority is required for counteracting the effect of evil example, to which, in such establishments, they are inevitably exposed."

One hesitates in differing, though it be ever so slightly,
from what has been said by a man so wise and so experienced as Southey was when he wrote his life of Cowper.
The impression on my mind is, however, that he had an
exaggerated notion of the difficulty of a due religious
superintendence over boys at school.   It was not then
known how much it was possible to engage the attention
of boys upon religion and virtue by such earnest affection-
ateness and energetic ability as were brought into play
by Dr. Arnold at Rugby.   Of course there will always
be found some in a school community so dull or so per-
verse, that nothing good can be made of them either by
kindness or coercion ; but generally, I apprehend, if the
teachers felt really and deeply interested in the religious
welfare of the pupils, the " great evil " so feelingly de-

plored by Southey might be in a very considerable degree
corrected. In some degree it already has been, and
nothing perhaps has more improved in the last twenty
years than the more serious departments of school
teaching. Still there is so much association between religious feeling and family feeling—so much resemblance
between the union of authority and love, which subsist in
both—that, with reference to this most important of all the
branches of education, and of training up a child in the
way he should go, the wisdom of Dr. Johnson's opinion is
unquestionable, that "the best system is school in school-
hours, and home instruction in the intervals." This
opinion, however, presupposes the fact that there is a
home worthy of the name—a household conducted with
propriety, and presided over with affection. Cowper says,
in one of his letters to his friend Unwin, "you have seen
too much of the world, and are a man of too much reflection, not to have observed that, in proportion as the sons
of a family approach to years of maturity, they lose a
sense of obligation to their parents, and seem at last
almost divested of that tender affection which the nearest
of all relations seems to demand from them. I have often
observed it myself, and have always thought I could sufficiently account for it without laying all the blame upon
the children. While they continue in their parents'
house they are every day obliged and every day reminded
how much it is their interest as well as duty to be obliging
and affectionate in return. But at eight or nine years of
age the boy goes to school. From that moment he becomes a stranger in his father's house. The course of
parental kindness is interrupted. The smiles of his
mother, those tender admonitions, and the solicitous care
of both his parents, are no longer before his eyes; year
after year he feels himself more and more detached from

them, till at last he is so effectually weaned from the
connexion as to find himself happier anywhere than in
their company."

Forty years ago in the *Edinburgh Review* there appeared an article on the public schools of England from
the pen of the Rev. Sidney Smith. It is remarkably
clear and emphatic, and, I think, in the main, just; but
as to the religious view of the question it is a blank.
The reviewer took ground more level with the platform
from which he addressed the public. The force of his
criticism is directed *against* public schools. He does not
dispute about the sufficiency of the classical instruction
that is given, or the ability of the instructors. He as-
sumes that the only points for consideration are whether
boys are *put in the way* of becoming good and wise men
by these schools, and whether they actually gather there
those attainments which *it pleases mankind for the time
being to consider as valuable, and to decorate by the name
of learning*. In my opinion these are *not* the only points
for consideration. We have better standards of what is
good than what it pleases mankind for the time being to
consider so; and schools ought to follow not the fashion
of the day, but the best way of causing boys to become
wise and good men. Not finding fault with the instruction
given by the masters, or the mode of giving it, the reviewer attacks the system established by immemorial
custom in these schools, of which the result is that "every
boy is alternately tyrant and slave." The power which
the elder part of these communities exercises over the
younger is exceedingly great—very difficult to be controlled—and accompanied not unfrequently with cruelty
and caprice. It is the common law of the place that the
young should be implicitly obedient to the elder boys,
and this obedience resembles more the submission of a

slave to his master, or of a sailor to his captain, than the common and natural deference which would always be shown by one boy to another a few years older than himself. The system thus described still exists, but much ameliorated by the general change in manners, which causes both men and boys to be less violent with voice and fist—in command and in contradiction; and to make themselves amends by an extraordinary obstinacy and pertinacity in theory and opinion. The reviewer asserts generally as matter of fact that the system makes many boys very miserable, and produces bad effects upon the temper and disposition. But as this is a point which not a few will probably meet with a direct negative, I shall give the argument in his own words:—" This system we cannot help considering as an evil, because it inflicts upon boys for two or three years of their lives many painful hardships and much unpleasant servitude. These sufferings might perhaps be of some use in military schools; but to give to a boy the habit of enduring privations to which he will never again be called upon to submit—to inure him to pains which he will never again feel—and to subject him to the privation of comforts with which he will always in future abound, is surely not a very useful and valuable severity in education. It is not the life in miniature which he is to lead hereafter—nor does it bear any relation to it:—he will never again be subjected to so much insolence and caprice; nor ever, in all human probability, called upon to make so many sacrifices. The servile obedience which it teaches might be useful to a menial domestic; or the habits of enterprise which it encourages prove of importance to a military partisan; but we cannot see what bearing it has upon the calm, regular, civil life which the sons of gentlemen destined to opulent idleness, or to any of the three learned professions, are destined to lead. Such a system makes many boys very miserable, and produces those bad effects upon the temper and disposition which unjust suffering always does produce; but what good it does we are much at a loss to conceive. Reasonable obedience is extremely useful in forming the disposition. Submission to tyranny lays the foundation of hatred, suspicion, cunning, and a variety of odious passions. We are convinced that those young people will turn out to be the best men who have been guarded most effectually, in their childhood, from every species of useless vexation, and experienced in the greatest degree the blessings of a wise and rational indulgence. But even if these effects upon future character are not produced, still four or five years in childhood make a very considerable period of human existence; and it is by no means a trifling consideration whether they are passed happily or unhappily. The wretchedness of school-tyranny is trifling enough to a man who only contemplates it in ease of body and tranquillity of mind through the medium of twenty intervening years; but it is quite as real and quite as acute, while it lasts, as any of the sufferings of mature life: and the utility of these sufferings, or the price paid in compensation for them, should be clearly made out to a conscientious parent, before he consents to expose his children to them."

Notwithstanding the utilitarian air of all this—which, so far as it goes, is disagreeable—I think the argument is reasonable, except that part in which the author appears to hold that to the young there can be no benefit in submission and in endurance of privation, unless they be preparing for some course of life in which these habits will be called into play. I agree completely to the wisdom of the distinction between reasonable obedience and sub-

mission to tyranny, but I think the habit of deference to
established authority, and of enduring privation with un-
murmuring fortitude, has a valuable effect upon the character of the growing man, if it be combined with sufficient nobleness of motive. If, from a sense of religious
duty, or of philosophic heroism, the boy can thus conquer
himself, he becomes, for so far, elevated above the commonplace tendencies of his nature ; but if he only bears
with tyranny in bitterness of heart, hoping in time to
repay himself by exacting from others the obedience he
now reluctantly gives, then it seems to me that such discipline is worse than none at all. The assertion that boys
become the best men who have experienced the blessings
of a wise and rational indulgence, has more feeling in it
than the reviewer generally betrays. I am afraid, however, that in general it will not be easy to determine what
a wise and rational indulgence is, and it must continually
vary according to the disposition of the pupil. Taking
boys as they for the most part appear in a school, I apprehend that a prevailing system of strictness, without
harsh severity, will be found more applicable than the
pleasanter system of indulgence, however guarded by the
qualification of " rational."

In support of his argument against the peculiar value
of English public schools, the reviewer brings forward a
formidable array of the names of eminent Englishmen*
who did not receive their education at these schools. He
begins with the poets : Spenser, Pope, Shakspeare (a singular classification), Butler, Rochester, Spratt, Parnell,
Garth, Congreve, Gay, Swift, Thomson, Shenstone, Aken-
side, Goldsmith, Samuel Johnson, Beaumont and Fletcher,
Ben Jonson, Sir Philip Sydney, Savage, Arbuthnot, and

---

* The natives of Scotland and Ireland are included under this general
head.

Burns, were not educated in the system of English schools. Next men of science : Sir Isaac Newton, Maclaurin, Wallis, Flamsteed, Saunderson, Simpson, and Napier, were not educated in public schools. Of historians, the three best, according to the reviewer, that the English language has produced, Clarendon, Hume, and Robertson, were not educated at public schools. Of men eminent in the fine arts, Inigo Jones, Vanburgh, Reynolds, Gainsborough, Garrick, &c., were not brought up at public schools. Among medical writers and discoverers, Harvey, Cheselden, Hunter, Jenner, Meade, Brown, and Cullen were not educated at public schools. Of moral and metaphysical writers, Bacon, Shaftesbury, Hobbes, Berkeley, Butler, Hume, Hartley, Dugald Stewart did not arise from public schools. Of discoverers in chemistry, Dr. Priestly, Dr. Black, and Sir Humphry Davy did not come from public schools. Among warriors, the Duke of Marlborough, Lord Peterborough, General Wolfe, and Lord Clive were trained in private schools. So also among lawyers were Lord Coke, Sir Matthew Hale, Lord Hardwick, and Chief-Justice Holt. Among statesmen not indebted to public schools for their education, the reviewer enumerates Lord Burleigh, Walsingham, the Earl of Strafford, Thurloe, Cromwell, Hampden, Lord Clarendon, Sir Walter Raleigh, Sydney, Russell, Sir W. Temple, Lord Somers, Burke, Sheridan, Pitt. In addition to this list he says we must not forget the names of such eminent scholars and men of letters as Cudworth, Chillingworth, Tillotson, Archbishop King, Selden, Conyers Middleton, Bentley, Sir Thomas More, Cardinal Wolsey, Bishops Sherlock and Wilkins, Jeremy Taylor, Isaac Hooker, Ussher, Stillingfleet, and Spellman, Dr. Samuel Clarke, Bishop Hoadley, and Dr. Lardner. If it be urged, he says, that public schools have only as-

sumed their present character within the last century, and
what are now called public schools partook before this
period of the nature of private schools, there must then
be added to the lists the names of Milton, Dryden, Addison, &c. &c., and it will follow that the English have
done almost all that they have done in the arts and
sciences without the aid of that system of education to
which they are now so much attached.

Lord John Russell, in his 'Essay on the History of the
English Government and Constitution,' has done public
schools the honour of devoting a chapter to their discussion. His Lordship appears to assume that a private
education is one intended to produce a "faultless monster,"
and to give its unhappy object a pre-eminence over the
ill-trained generation of his equals and contemporaries.
"The mistake in these instances," says the noble Lord,
"seems to arise from the want of considering that the object of education is not only to store the mind, but to form
the character."   Now, with all deference to the noble
author, the principal point of discussion in all controversies
upon this subject is, the effect of one sort of training or
another upon the formation of character.   But let us hear
the noble Lord further : " It is of little use that a boy
has a smattering of mineralogy, and is very fluent at
botanical names ; it will be of no avail to him to talk of
argil and polyandria if he cries when he loses at marbles,
and is lifeless as a statue when he is obliged to play a
game at cricket.   Now, a public school does form the
character.   It brings a boy from home, where he is a
darling—where his folly is wit and his obstinacy spirit—
to a place where he takes rank according to his real
powers and talents.   If he is sulky, he is neglected ; if
he is angry, he gets a box on the ear.   His character, in
short, is prepared for the buffetings of grown men—for

the fagging of a lawyer, or the fighting of a soldier. Now, this is of much more importance than the acquisition of mere knowledge. Many men only begin to acquire their knowledge between twenty and thirty ; few men change their character after twenty. Considering the question in this view, it is of little importance to enumerate the names of eminent men in England who have not been brought up at public schools. Many of these rose from middle life, and to them my argument does not apply. The son of a tradesman or farmer meets buffetings enough without being sent to any school ; he is ordered to serve a customer or look after the haymakers, and learns practical life much sooner than any gentleman's son can possibly do." This is, no doubt, a lordly style of writing. The allusion to the array of names of eminent men who have not been brought up at public schools shows that the noble Lord was shooting his arrows against the Edinburgh reviewer.

When Whig meets Whig, then comes the tug of war.

Sidney Smith retorted in a foot-note, when he collected his Essays into separate volumes. " A public school is thought to be the best cure for the insolence of youthful aristocracy. This insolence, however, is not a little increased by the homage of masters, and would soon meet with its natural check in the world. There can be no occasion to bring 500 boys together to teach to a young nobleman that proper demeanour which he would learn so much better from the first English gentleman whom he might think proper to insult." This, indeed, is brief and bitter. Whether the aristocratic pen has the advantage or not, I shall be prudent enough to abstain from attempting to decide.

It appears to me that one great disadvantage of all large schools is, that boys have only the society of boys, and thus lose a thousand opportunities of unconsciously gaining knowledge in familiar conversation with grown-up relatives and friends. It is said that at public schools boys attain a knowledge of the world, but I regard that as a popular error, unless familiarity with certain .vices of a very low description,* which boys quickly teach to one another, is to be called knowledge of the world.   I am afraid that few creatures are more destitute of general information than boys who have been brought up at public schools.   Indeed, it is only during the intervals when they are at home, and mix in the society of home, that they have any opportunity of picking up general and ordinary information.   The Greek and Latin grammars, and portions of the easier classic authors—cricket—boating—the price of tarts, and of wine by the bottle, and perhaps the names of the head and assistant masters of the school; these are the particulars of their vast sum of knowledge.   But were you to ask nine out of every ten of the pupils at a public school who was Prime Minister; whether bread and broadcloth were cheaper than they used to be when their fathers were at school; whether

---

* In a select committee of the House of Lords on the subject of beer-shops and habits of intoxication, Benjamin Rotch, Esq., a Middlesex magistrate, was examined on the 12th July, 1849.

" *Question* 429. You are in the Metropolitan district, outside the Police-court district?—Yes, at Harrow: of course the peculiarities of the school occasion me to see a great deal more of these things than perhaps I other-wise should.

" 430. The school draws some bad characters there?—It does: it has some peculiar features with regard to drinking; but I am happy to say that a spirit of change has come over the school lately—very much to its advantage, and to the credit of those who now manage it."

Having mentioned that country beer-shops were used as brothels, he adds (449), " My attention was particularly called to it in consequence of the various Head Masters of Harrow School at different times calling upon me to endeavour to repress the nuisance, if I could; but on inquiry I find that it is very general."

white and brown sugar came from the same plant; whether tea grew in the west and tobacco in the east, or *vice versâ;* whether Napoleon Bonaparte was at the battle of Trafalgar; or whether the Orkney islands did or did not belong to the Emperor of China; I venture to say they could not tell. But this could hardly be the case had they been accustomed to hear—even without *intending* to learn anything—the conversation of their relatives and other grown-up people at home.

Where a great number of boys are brought together, the practical result is, that the idle are neither won nor driven into attention; and the dull and torpid are left dull and torpid to the end of their course. If boys are naturally clever and spirited, and have within them a desire to excel, the means undoubtedly are before them, and they have the excitement of a large concourse to behold their triumphs. But a system of education, in the strict sense of the word—that is, of drawing out the latent powers— encouraging the timid, stimulating the dull, supporting the weak, and directing the strong—such a system, if not impossible, is very difficu t, and scarcely to be expected, in a school where the number of pupils is large. Upon this point the Edinburgh reviewer is, I think, particularly clear and cogent. What he says is as follows :—

" Upon the system of public schools a boy is left almost entirely to himself, to impress upon his own mind, as well as he can, the distant advantages of knowledge, and to withstand, from his own innate resolution, the examples and seductions of idleness. A firm character survives this brave neglect, and very exalted talents may sometimes remedy it by subsequent diligence ; but schools are not made for a few youths of pre-eminent talents and strong characters ; such prizes can of course be drawn but by a very few parents. The best school is that which is best accommodated to the greatest variety of characters, and which embraces the greatest number of cases. It cannot be the main object of education to render the splendid more splendid, and to lavish care upon those who would almost thrive without any care at all. A public school does this effectually; but it commonly leaves the idle almost as idle, and the dull almost as dull, as it found them. It disdains the tedious cultivation of those middling talents, of which only the great mass of human beings are possessed. When a strong desire of improvement exists, it is encouraged; but no pains are taken to inspire it. A boy is cast in among five or six hundred other boys, and is left to form his own character: if his love of knowledge survives this severe trial, it in general carries him very far; and, upon the same principle, a savage, who grows up to manhood, is in general well made, and free from all bodily defects; not because the severities of such a state are favourable to animal life, but because they are so much the reverse that none but the strongest can survive them. A few boys are incorrigibly idle, and a few incorrigibly eager for knowledge, but the great mass are in a state of doubt and fluctuation; and they come to school for the express purpose, not of being left to themselves, for that could be done anywhere, but that their wavering tastes and propensities should be decided by the intervention of a master. In a forest, or public school for oaks and elms, the trees are left to themselves; the strong plants live, and the weak ones die: the towering oak that remains is admired; the saplings that perish around it are cast into the flames and forgotten. But it is not surely to the vegetable struggle of a forest, or the hasty glance of a forester, that a botanist would commit a favourite plant; he would naturally seek for it a situation of less hazard, and a cultivator whose limited occupations would enable him to give to it a reasonable share of his time and attention. The very meaning of education seems to us to be, that the old should teach the young, and the wise direct the weak; that a man who professes to instruct should get among his pupils, study their characters, gain their affections, and form their inclinations and aversions. In a public school the numbers render this impossible: it is impossible that a sufficient time should be found for this useful and affectionate interference. Boys, therefore, are left to their own crude conceptions and ill-formed propensities; and this neglect is called a spirited and manly education."

Allowing for the amplifications and exaggerations of a professed *littérateur*, this seems to be a reasonable statement. Indeed, it is to me surprising that, under such untoward circumstances, boys succeed so well at public schools, or receive so little injury from them, as they do. Perhaps the best defence that could be made of such institutions is, that, with a sort of discipline that prevents any very violent outrage, they leave young people to follow their nature such as it is, and that the best laid plans can often effect nothing better. Accidents, which no one can calculate upon, are but too apt to mar the most carefully elaborated educational designs.

> " Misfortunes, do the best we can,
>   Will reach both great and small;
> And he is oft the wisest man
>   Who is not wise at all."

Still, though one's best plans may turn out no better than the negative method of letting a boy take his chance, it is not possible to recommend a merely hap-hazard mode of proceeding in a matter so important. Lord John Russell, in the essay already referred to, treats the subject as if there were no medium between a strictly private education and that which obtains at public schools, where the multitude is far too great to admit of any study of the character and mental habits of each individual. Undoubtedly, however, there is such a medium, though it may have escaped the noble Lord's attention. Schools may be found where a boy will have enough of companions to derive such good from school as boy-companionship affords, and yet not so many as to be lost in the crowd, unless possessed of conspicuous ability. As a combination of domestic or home superintendence, with careful school instruction, constitutes in my judgment the best plan of education, so the next best I should consider to be that of a boarding-school, so far limited in number that something like domestic life may be mingled with schooling. It seems to be of very great importance, not only that a boy's spirit and "manliness" should be called forth, but that his affections should be brought into play also, and that he should learn from experience the value of kind consideration. A combination of levity and stoicism is not, I think, the best sort of character, though I am afraid that it is most admired among boys, and among men and women too, especially of the upper classes. There is an opposite extreme, of universal benevolence and theoretical sensibility, much more vulgar and quite as opposed to common sense and sound practical Christianity. The one altogether sets aside affection as not belonging to the habits of "society," and forbears to show kindness lest it should be presumed upon and made the foundation of troublesome claims; the other indulges in fanciful schemes, and becomes affectedly and obtrusively beneficent, not perceiving that genuine goodness must be inspired by the spirit of modesty, and be restrained by reasonableness and sobriety of judgment.

While deprecating the system of public schools the

Rev. Sidney Smith, I am sorry to say, lays it down as a positive rule, that the object of a judicious master is " to fit his pupil for the world ;" and therefore he " may connive at many things which he cannot approve, and suffer some little failures to proceed to a certain extent." I must confess that I have no sympathy with this deference to what is called " the world." The master's object (as the same author admits in another part of his Essay) should be to cause his pupils to become wise and good men, whether wisdom and goodness will fit them for the world or will not. After all the consideration I can give to the subject, I am of opinion that to send a boy to a great public school is not the most likely way to make him good and wise, though it *may* possibly succeed as well as any other.

CHAPTER XXVI.

THE UNIVERSITIES.

Our great Universities of Oxford and Cambridge can never be contemplated by any reasonable Englishman without feelings of profound respect, notwithstanding the faults which may be admitted to exist in the system, and the follies which undoubtedly mark the conduct of large numbers of the students. We cannot forget that these great establishments—the result of private and individual munificence devoted to the noble purposes of systematic study—are now, as they have been for centuries, the central points of the erudition of the land, from whence it is diffused, through the means and opportunities of our ecclesiastical system, to every town, and village, and rural parish, where a church-tower shoots up among the trees; and, through the learned professions, into the very heart and life-blood of the world's business. There is also something in the places themselves—the antique beauty of the buildings—the recollections and associations which cannot be severed from the ground on which they stand—and the certainty that they are still the abode of those who have given long years of study to the science and erudition of both ancient and modern times: all these things unite, to suggest sentiments of respectful admiration, in spite of the conviction that there is much in our University system which might be improved, and much even in the outward aspect of university life which the sober-minded man must condemn. Let any man so minded

walk through Oxford or Cambridge of an afternoon at a
time when the colleges are full, and will he not sigh to see
so little evidence of Christian common sense in the outward manners of the people, and in the apparent ordering
of affairs around him?   Will he not see on the surface a
great deal of pompous formalism and stiff methodical vanity
in the teachers?   Will he not be struck with the cool
recklessness and ostentatious self-confidence of the pupils?
Will he not find in the tradespeople the mercenary mean-
ness which gathers about extravagance and pride—the
vermin engendered of that moral unhealthiness?   It is
true, as Mr. Gladstone lately said in the House of Commons when speaking of those engaged in the business of
education at Oxford and Cambridge, that "nowhere
could be found a body of men more competent for their
duties, more devoted to education, more indefatigable in
application, more adorned with virtues and accomplish-
ments as Christians, as scholars, and as gentlemen." This
is all true; but it is only one aspect of University teaching,
and that the most favourable. For the most part the
teachers have not much in them that is genial or sympathizing. Powers and diligence above the ordinary standard
have placed them in the position and exercise of an
authority which is not limited or interrupted by the common incidents of life; and they are not taught, by the
varieties of circumstances which occur in the outer world,
to know their own weaknesses, or to make allowance for
those of others:

> "And custom lies upon them with a weight
> Heavy as frost, and deep almost as life."

They sympathize with intellectual power and application,
but with little else.

In Wordsworth's biographical poem, published since
his death, much is said, in a somewhat indignant spirit, of

what he found, or felt, wrong in that world in little—an English University.   We must remember, however, that he speaks of impressions before a larger and longer experience had mellowed his mind :—

> " And here was Labour his own bond-slave ; Hope,
>   That never set the pains against the prize ;
>   Idleness, halting with his weary clog;
>   And poor misguided Shame, and witless Fear,
>   And simple Pleasure, foraging for Death ;
>   Honour misplaced, and dignity astray ;
>   Feuds, factions, flatteries, enmity, and guile,
>   Murmuring submission, and bald government
>   (The idol weak as the idolater);
>   And Decency and Custom starving Truth ;
>   And blind Authority, beating with his staff
>   The child that might have led him ; Emptiness
>   Follow'd, as of good omen ; and meek Worth
>   Left to himself, unheard of, and unknown."

Thus indeed it is in public schools and in universities, as well as in the world without them, that the best of our fellow-creatures, in a Christian view of the matter (that is, the humble minded), are left to perish of neglect. This is the spirit of the world ; and even the Scripture would lead us to expect from the world nothing better. But schools and colleges might, at least, try to do something more in accordance with the theory of their religion. They might curb the insolence, and punish the idleness, and forbid the self-indulgence and extravagance, which are so offensive in both schools and universities.   It is indeed my belief, and that of others much better entitled to deliver judgment on such a question, that public schools give colour and direction to the whole system of the universities : I do not mean the theoretical system as it appears in the statutes, but the habits, manners, extravagances, and vices with which the universities are exclusively reproached, as if they all began *there*.   Boys turned into precocious men, and coming to college with the habits of public schools, could not be sent back again in the direction of the nursery, or to those sentiments of deference and that facile obedience which are the best for youth.

The House of Commons, without any legal or constitutional authority that I am aware of, has on several occasions assumed a kind of popular right to animadvert upon university affairs ; and early in the Session of 1850 some returns were presented to the House regarding the number of students not only at each of the three old universities, but of the number at each college or hall respectively within those universities.   It appeared that At Oxford the numbers of new students entered were—

438 in 1845.   406 in 1847.
410 in 1846.   411 in 1848.
440 in 1849.

At Cambridge—

533 in 1844.   560 in 1846.
527 in 1845.   515 in 1847.
499 in 1848.

At Dublin—

366 in 1845.   371 in 1847.
368 in 1846.   333 in 1848.
527 in 1849.

About two months after these returns were presented, one of the Members for Lancashire introduced to the House of Commons the following resolution :—

" That all systems of academical education require from time to time some modification, from the change of external circumstances, the progress of opinion, and the intellectual improvement of the people. That in the ancient English and Irish universities, and in the colleges connected with them, the interests of religious and useful learning have not advanced to an extent commensurate with the great resources and high position of those bodies; that collegiate statutes of the fifteenth century occasionally prohibit the local authorities from introducing any alterations into voluminous codes, of which a large portion are now obsolete ; that better laws are needed to regulate the ceremony of matriculation and the granting of degrees, to diminish the exclusiveness of the university libraries, to provide for a fairer distribution of the rewards of scientific and literary merit, to extend the permission of marriage to tutors of colleges, and to facilitate the registration of electors for the universities ; that additional checks might be considered with reference to the continued extravagance of individual students ; and that the mode of tenure of college property ought to be ameliorated, and particularly in Ireland.   That, as it is her Majesty's right and prerogative to name visitors and commissioners to inquire into the ancient universities and colleges of England and Ireland, an humble address be presented to her Majesty, praying that her Majesty would be graciously pleased to issue her Royal Commission of Inquiry into the state of the universities and colleges of Oxford, Cambridge, and Dublin, with a view to assist in the adaptation of those important institutions to the requirements of modern times."

This was considered, on the part of the friends of the universities, to be a motion equally uncalled for and ungracious, because the universities had been actively engaged in making new arrangements for affording " greater encouragement to the pursuit of various branches of science and learning which were gradually acquiring more importance and a higher estimation in the world."   And, besides, even were it admitted that the universities stood in need of some improvement, it was a very different question whether the House of Commons, endowed with no functions of university superintendence, never called upon to vote money for university purposes, and of whose members the great majority were not university men, had any reasonable claim or title to be judge or agent in such a matter. To the great surprise of the public, the Prime Minister, Lord John Russell, who never had belonged to any of the Universities enumerated in the motion, announced that he had already, on the part of the Crown, determined upon a commission of inquiry, which was to receive whatever evidence might be *voluntarily* offered as to the state of the universities. This announcement having been made, the debate upon the motion was adjourned, and not resumed until three months afterwards. Meanwhile considerable indignation arose at such interference on the part of the minister of the Crown—not from any opinion that, as no improvement was required, so no investigation was called for—but from an opinion that urgency from such a quarter was not at all necessary to induce measures of improvement to be undertaken, and was therefore offensive.

In both the English universities the ministerial measure was strongly resented. Cambridge, which at the last election of its chancellor, had paid the Crown the compliment of electing the Prince Consort to that high office, had now the independence to put forth an address, signed by almost every notable resident member of the university, against the proposed intrusion. Oxford spoke through its vice-chancellor; and the Duke of Wellington, chancellor of Oxford university, spoke against the intrusive commission in the House of Lords. To him Lord Brougham, ex-Chancellor of England, who had taken a leading part in all matters of public education for more than thirty years, addressed a letter, containing the following passages :—

" I have studied with great attention the two protests of Oxford and Cambridge, and I agree in general with the reasoning of both those admirable papers.   My opinion is very decidedly adverse to any inquiry of the kind in contemplation; and I feel so strongly the inexpediency of such a proceeding, that I supported the exemption of the Universities and Colleges from the jurisdiction of the Commissioners appointed first by the 58 Geo. III., c. 91, and afterwards by the 59 Geo. III., c. 81.   When I was a minister of the Crown in 1831, and the Commission was renewed, the exemption of institutions having special visitors was removed, but the Universities and Colleges were still exempted (1 & 2 Will. IV., c. 34).

" There appears to me even stronger reasons against a Commission without power to compel attendance and answers of witnesses and production of documents, than against a Commission armed by Parliament with such powers. The Commission acting by voluntary depositions can have no efficacy ; it can only rely on such information as private interest or personal prejudice—or, peradventure, spleen—may induce persons to give. It cannot avoid doing injustice to parties accused, because those must remain unheard unless they choose to submit themselves and undergo a full examination ; so that parties will be placed in the predicament of either being compelled to give evidence respecting themselves and their concerns, or being condemned unheard, and this under Commissioners professing only to exercise a voluntary jurisdiction. Moreover, parties so situated may, in many cases, be unable to make the statements and disclosures necessary for their defence ; because the Commission can give no protection to them in telling that which it cannot compel them to tell, and which, nevertheless, it may be their duty not to tell. I need hardly add, that it seems somewhat inconsistent with the dignity of the Crown to issue a Commission to which no one person in the world needs pay the least attention.

" I cannot but fear the inevitable tendency of this Commission to obstruct all the good work of improvement now going on safely, because voluntarily, and steadily, because uninterruptedly, in both our Universities. The subject is a delicate one, and I am very far from saying that much useful addition has not recently been made to the course of studies pursued in both. Yet I am apt to believe that great caution is also required in meddling with a long-established course of study."

Nor was the Royal Chancellor of Cambridge silent, though his voice was not in harmony with that of the leading members of the institution over which he had the honour to preside. In truth his Royal Highness was placed in a delicate position, and must have perceived, like Othello's wife, " a divided duty," though, unlike her, he did not decide upon abandoning one branch of it in order that he might more fully and freely follow the other. Considering his connexion with the Crown on the one hand, and with the University on the other, his Royal Highness's letter is a composition of remarkable cleverness. It runs thus :—

" MY DEAR VICE-CHANCELLOR—You have represented to me that it would be of importance to the University to be made acquainted with my opinions and views as to the line of conduct which the University should pursue respecting the proposed Royal Commission of Inquiry, particularly as the Duke of Wellington, as Chancellor of the University of Oxford, has stated his opinion in the House of Lords. I have to express my grateful sense of the confidence which the authorities of the University have at all times shown me, and of the readiness with which they have attended to any suggestions of mine, and can bear testimony, since my connexion with them, to the zeal and industry with which they have laboured in the direction of reform and improvement in the system of education and studies.   You are already aware that I did not know of the intention of her Majesty's Government to advise the issue of a Royal Commission in time, before Lord John Russell's speech in the House of Commons, to be able to communicate with the University, or to express any opinion on the proposed course.   I have since felt that it was not unnatural on the part of the University to look with apprehension at the proposed measure as affording a means to those who may be ill disposed towards these venerable institutions to vent their hostility against them, and also to regard it as a proof of want of confidence in their ability or inclination to carry out useful reforms, which would be doubly painful to them a a moment when they must be conscious of having least deserved such a reproach.   I am glad, however, to find, upon further communication with the Government, that nothing could be further from their intention than to cast such a slur upon the University, and they are anxious to show their desire not to expose the University to needless hostility by the selection of persons who are to compose the Royal Commission.

" Although I had hoped that the University would have been allowed to go on in their course of self-improvement without any extraneous interference, now that I find the Government irrevocably pledged to the issue of the Commission, I would recommend the authorities of the University not to meet it with opposition, but rather to take it as the expression, on the part of the Crown and the Parliament, of a natural desire to be

accurately informed upon the present state of institutions
so closely connected with, and of such vital importance
to, the best interests of the nation; and to take a pride
in showing to those who have indulged in attacks against
them that they have conscientiously and zealously fulfilled the great task intrusted to them.

" Any hostility or opposition on the part of the University could not prevent the issue of the Commission by the
present Government; and while it might add strength to
the accusations of their enemies, would only lead to the
result of the inquiry remaining incomplete, and, as based
upon one-sided evidence, probably injurious to the Universities themselves.

                    " Believe me always truly yours."

No doubt his Royal Highness would learn from her
Majesty's Government that, in the steps they had determined upon taking, it was not their intention to cast any
slur upon the Universities; but their policy might be
very injurious though their intentions were very innocent.
Neither does it very clearly appear how the benevolence
or the harmlessness of the intentions of the Government
can do away with the probable ill consequences of the
Commission of Inquiry, so well pointed out by his Royal
Highness himself, namely, that it would give those who
were ill disposed towards the Universities the means of
venting their hostility, and that it is a plain acknowledgment and proclamation, as it were, of the Government's
want of confidence in the ability or inclination of the
Universities to carry out useful reforms of their own
accord—a want of confidence doubly painful, as it is exhibited at a moment when the Universities must be conscious of having least deserved such a reproach. Indeed,
Lord J. Russell's announcement of his intention to appoint

a Royal Commission of Inquiry, without any authority to inquire, was made on the very day that certain important practical improvements, or changes intended to be improvements, had been resolved upon at Oxford.

According to the old system a man might take his degree at Oxford, though he knew no more of the science of mathematics than of the chemistry of moonshine ; or he might take not only his degree, but the highest honours, at Cambridge, without knowing anything else than mathematical science.   By the new Oxford statutes three examinations are required instead of two, and there is a requirement of algebra and mathematics ; but the requirement is not very onerous.   In addition to the books formerly read in ancient history and in the ancient languages, modern history and modern languages have been brought in ; and really, if all were now learned at Oxford which a diligent man might learn, and all were studied which the men are invited, if not compelled, to study, reasonable complaint could scarcely be made of the education received there.

At Cambridge, also, the change has been considerable. In the year 1848, a syndicate having been appointed to consider whether it was expedient to afford greater encouragement to the pursuit of those studies for the cultivation of which professorships had been founded in the University, and if so by what means that object might be best accomplished, the syndicate reported that, " admitting the superiority of the study of mathematics and classics over all others as the basis of general education, and acknowledging therefore the wisdom of their present system in its main features, they were nevertheless of opinion that much good would result from affording greater encouragement to the pursuit of various other branches of science and learning which are daily acquiring more importance and a higher estimation in the world, and for the teaching of which the University already possesses the necessary means." These being the principles laid down, it was resolved to carry them into practice by making it incumbent on all candidates for an academical degree (not being " candidates for honours ") to attend, during at least one term, the lectures of one or more of the professors of the moral or natural sciences, and to obtain a certificate of having passed an examination satisfactory to one of the professors whom they had chosen to attend. This regulation was to apply to all students commencing their academical residence in and after Michaelmas Term 1849. A new honour tripos, called the *Moral Sciences Tripos*, was established, and another called the *Natural Sciences Tripos;* the places in the first to be determined by an examination in moral philosophy, political economy, modern history, general jurisprudence, and the laws of England ; the places in the second by an examination in anatomy, comparative anatomy, physiology, chemistry, and botany, and geology. The first examination for these honours was fixed to take place in 1851. The syndicate, moreover, acknowledging " the great importance of the study of theology," it was resolved by the Senate that those presenting themselves at the examination in theology should produce a certificate of having attended the lectures delivered during one term at least by two of the three theological professors.

Since the establishment of the examination for honours in classics at Cambridge, it has been the rule that all candidates should have previously obtained an honour in mathematics ; in consequence, however, of the recommendation of a syndicate appointed in 1849, the rule will be, from the first examination of 1851, that candidates for classical honours shall have obtained mathematical honours

at the previous examination, or, having been declared by
the examiners to have deserved to pass (according to the
present standard) for an ordinary degree, so far as the
mathematical part of the examination for such degree is
concerned, shall have afterwards passed in the other subjects of that examination.

It is of course always much easier to point out the defects of any system of training and education, where a
great many persons are concerned, than to devise effective
remedies; but this is not a good reason for entirely
abstaining from notice of such defects.   The remedy
perhaps will come in time, if we are not careless, but
zealously seek for it.   Now it is a serious question whether the examination system now existing, is a sufficient
impulse to study, and a sufficient test of proficiency. The
university adopts no other, and the systems adopted by
each separate college with respect to its own members
do not appear to be sufficiently stringent.   The university
examinations occur at distant intervals, and up to this
time, two have been deemed sufficient for the degree. The
result has been that ordinary men do not work while the
examination is distant, and when it is at hand they are
crammed for it, not that they may know throughout their
lives, the subjects in which the questions will be put, but
merely that they may pass their examination.   That
which is so quickly acquired is, in ninety-nine cases out
of a hundred, no less quickly lost; and if education be
the object of passing through the university, that object
is not attained.   And, indeed, it is too much the case that
the severest students among the young men, and those
who contend for " honours," seem to lose sight of the
object for which " honours " were established, in striving
for the prize.   " I am grieved," says Southey, in one of
his letters to Mr. James White, at Cambridge, " I am

grieved to learn from Neville that you are distressing yourself about what I could find in my heart to call these cursed examinations. There are few things of which I am more thoroughly convinced than that the system of feeding up young men like so many game-cocks for a sort of intellectual *long-main* is every way pernicious." There are, no doubt, many young men who break down under it, or are never good for much afterwards, however deep their mathematical lore may be.* Besides, the man who knows most, and who may, in the course of practical life, be able to make the best use of what he knows, may not be able to stand the nervous excitement of an examination, but be forced to yield the palm to persons of less capacity and more nerve. Wordsworth sings what Southey said :—

> —— " I grieved
> To see display'd among an eager few,
> Who in the field of contest persevered,
> Passions unworthy of youth's generous heart,
> And mounting spirit pitiably repaid,
> When so disturb'd, whatever palms are won." †

To avoid these excessive conflicts, for which such exhausting preparation is made, and in which unworthy passions of rivalship are not seldom stirred up, I should think that much more frequent examinations would be

---

* " It is curious to look over the list of names of those who took honours on their degrees at Cambridge from 1784 to 1823. Of two thousand nine hundred names, how very few afterwards obtained in life the smallest distinction ! Even of the septuagint of senior wranglers very few became afterwards known. . . . . . Fame is the spur by which almost all noble efforts are made. How happens it, then, that so few go on, after they have once obtained university distinctions ? Are they quite exhausted ? Do they rest upon their laurels ? or are the requisite tests of talent and mental culture fallacious ? I should assuredly say the latter in the majority of cases, not in all. Gray, Wordsworth, and many others, attained no college honours."—*Autobiography of Sir Egerton Brydges.*

† The Prelude, book iii.

useful, and still more useful as a check upon those disposed to be idle.   If, instead of two or three university
examinations in the course, there were two or three in
each year, gradually proceeding with the books upon which
the students ought to be engaged, and affording some honorary distinction for the best answering at each, it would
compel every student to be always preparing something,
and it would break into more detail the rivalships of the
hard readers, and give them many chances of answering
for a high place, instead of only one.

Both Oxford and Cambridge have always put the
examinations *above* the ordinary intelligence of the men
to be examined, and this is true as well of those examined
for honours as of those who seek merely to pass for their
degree.   And that will always be the case while the
examiners are chosen from among the latest and brightest
scholars.   They examine according to their own scope,
and it is not to be expected that any statute should limit
this.   The examiners may make the hardest statute easy,
and the easiest impracticable.   Human knowledge is so
defective, that, if intelligent and quick examiners were to
seek to detect ignorance rather than to draw forth what a
man knows, the brightest men we have might make but
poor figures.

I understand it to be the general opinion at Oxford that
the change of the number of university examinations from
two to three will have the wholesome effect of keeping
many idle young men more to their books.   As to the
men called "reading men," it will not affect them at all.
They will probably pass the two earlier examinations as
a matter of course, and give all their power to the last, as
they do now.   This might be obviated, if marks of distinction were given in the earlier as well as in the last
examination.

A gentleman who has seen much of European life, and in later years much of Oxford, gives me the following views of English university education in general. " That," he says, " which at first sight one is apt to exclaim against in such education is that there appears to be no discipline at all, or none that is worth the name of discipline. Cheating scouts, unscrupulous tradesmen, and expensive company, seem to have it all their own way. But in this world things often work differently from what one would expect from the apparent elements. It is true that, notwithstanding all defects and want of discipline, Oxford sends out yearly twenty to thirty very able men, and three or four hundred well-educated men : and it is true that, although very many spend one hundred or two hundred pounds a-year more than they ought, they who ruin themselves are but few and far between. It is true also that hundreds of young men carry on their college education for 150*l.* a-year.

" I do not think that stricter discipline would produce German scholars, or French mathematicians. The habits of the English entirely prevent that ; and perhaps the peculiar quality of the English mind has something to do with it.

" Undoubtedly, with better discipline, there would be less display of folly, and greater outside appearance of study ; but the examinations quite force the men up to the range of knowledge of the day, and I doubt whether more *can be done.*

" I think the greatest moral advantage would be gained if tradesmen at the universities were not protected by the law in the recovery of debts contracted by students ; for, so long as they are protected, the recklessness of youth will, in spite of everything, find gratification. If tradesmen were thwarted in recovering the money which they have

encouraged foolish young men to spend ; if the college
tutors were made to do what the private tutors now do ;
if the parents of young men would be more careful, and
not encourage in their sons the practice of tuft-hunting ;
if they would not so much seek for their sons introduc-
tions to the leading young men of their respective counties who happen to be at Christ Church or elsewhere, with
a view to their advancement in society in after-life—no
doubt much good would be effected.

" The great difficulty is to make rules that will touch
the evil without destroying present good.   The London
University shows this.   At King's College, London, there
are plenty of good rules, but we do not find that its name
has very much weight with the public.   Why ?—Because
it produces merely the ordinary range of scholarship and
science, without the thousand little things and matters of
tact which fit a man to carry on the world's work in the
higher ranges of it.   Oxford and Cambridge, when their
means and opportunities are rightly used, make men
scholars ; and, somehow or other, the abuses of Oxford
and Cambridge make polished men of the world, who are
fit for that to which Dominie Sampsons, however learned,
would be inadequate."

The inference from all this is, that, independently of the
learning and science which the diligent may acquire at
our ancient universities, there are manners and habits
and a certain tone of behaviour acquired even by the idle,
which are suitable to English society, at least in its upper
classes, and give a man advantages, in respect to his future
intercourse with that society, apart from the furnishing of
his mind.*   This may be, and yet I think it is still fair to

---

* " To enter college is taking a degree in life, and graduating as a man.
I am not sure that there would be either schools or universities in a
Utopia of my creation : in the world as it is, both are so highly useful,

raise the question whether this tone of behaviour (for I
do not admit that it is polish) is a good thing or a bad,
even though it may be the tone of society in its upper
ranges.   Addison, I think it was, who laid it down as
the characteristics of English gentlemen that they were
modest, thoughtful, and sincere.   Do the uses or the
abuses of the English universities produce this character in
the men brought up within their walls ?   If they do, then
let them be honoured and applauded accordingly.   If, on
the other hand, they produce a habit of quiet, deliberate
self-indulgence—of courage without enthusiasm—of recklessness without excitement—of friendships without affec-
tionateness, and hatreds frozen by contempt—if these be
the results generally produced upon the character and
behaviour of young men at our English universities who
do not give themselves to study, and if these results be
produced also, to a certain degree, even in those men who
do study, then I doubt that the effect is good, though it
may be popular with the upper classes.

It was the complaint of the democratic press, with
reference to the House of Commons debate upon University matters in July, 1850, that both the champions of
the Universities and their " ministerial opponents " went
on the supposition that these great educational institutions
were merely for a certain well-born and well-connected
class, intermingled with a few humble students, destined
to do the work of drudges.   No one, it was said, spoke
of making the Universities " truly national institutions."
Now, as to the latter point, it seems very clear that no
alteration is necessary ; for the Universities, whether
good or bad, are strikingly national.   They are pictures
in little of the whole nation.   The prodigious perseverance

---

that the man who has not been at a public school, and at college, feels
his deficiency as long as he lives."—Southey, *Memoirs*, vol. iv.

of some—the cool, determined, incorrigible idleness of
many—the smooth hauteur of the rich students—the industrious, and not particularly honest, servility of tradesmen, servants, and all those who hope to get large hand-
fuls of money, either now, or at some future time, out of
the fortunes or allowances of these haughty young men—
the discharge of serious duties without any sentiment of
seriousness attached to them—the civility without cor-
diality, the rudeness without roughness, the scorn of
whatever is weak, the constant mingling of contempt with
pity—all this, be it good or bad, is *very* national.   And
as to the Universities being apparently for the good of
the well-connected and the rich, rather than for any other
sort of people—why, the same thing may be said of all
other establishments in England, unless it be the union
workhouses.   The same thing may be said of the Professions ; it may also be said of all the public offices ; it
may undoubtedly be said of Parliament, and of all the
other clubs about town.   These democratic critics, instead
of blaming the Universities for not being national, should
blame the nation for not being simple, sincere, and just.
Why is it that Manchester dissenters, and the like, howl
and gnash their teeth because the Universities are not
thrown open to them ?   Can they not get good education
elsewhere ?   Undoubtedly they can, but *they* too want to
get into the aristocratic society which, according to their
political theory, they should despise, but which the national
habit drives them in secret to worship with a servility
that is even more irrational than the contempt which they
occasionally persuade themselves that they feel.   Man, says
some philosopher, is naturally born a hunter, and habit,
which is second nature, seems to have made most men in
England tuft-hunters ; a curious characteristic to be combined with disdain, which I believe to be the most general

habit of mind in England, from the tradesman's boy who drives his master's cart upon the public road, to the territorial lord who spends on horses and dogs as much as might support a parish, and hunts wild animals for mile after mile upon his own land.

But though the trading middle class may not have much footing in the Universities, for which one reason is that their habits and interests do not lead them to cultivate scholastic learning or abstract science, it is a great injustice to the Universities to speak of them as if they did nothing for the humbler classes, when among these classes a scholar occasionally arises. On the contrary, it is through one or other of the Universities that almost all such scholars have won their way to eminence and to fortune. This was particularly dwelt upon by Mr. Gladstone in the House of Commons debate of July, 1850; and it will be found that, so far from regarding the Universities as institutions for the benefit merely of the upper ranks of society, he rather deprecated the fact that they were in so great a degree the seminaries of those classes. I allude to the following passage :—

"If we look through the history of the Reformed Church of England we shall find that almost every learned man in that Church had been reared in the Universities, and an immense proportion of them had come from the humbler classes. I make this appeal to the noble lord (J. Russell): How did these men find their way to distinction? Through these local foundations. The case is this: that those persons who had not the advantage of that training in their early years which is given to the children of gentlemen, but had to rough it, having the materials in them, and having been educated at some grammar-school in their neighbourhood, came up to the Universities, and by means of these local foundations got

fellowships which they never could have got if they had
at once been put into competition with the sons of gentlemen who had been trained in refined manners and studies
from their earliest years—a competition which would be
very unfavourable to the democratic character—and I
use that word in its most honourable sense—which has
always distinguished our Universities.* If the Universities have a fault now, it is that they have too much the
character of seminaries of the higher classes. I want to
see them embrace a larger number of the middle classes
of society. We may assist them. The noble lord has
large means in his hands of doing good by judicious communication with the Universities; but by the noble lord's
present course, I feel there can be no result but evil.
Whatever might be said against them, the Universities
have borne a great and conspicuous part in the history of
England, and no man can know the history of England
without knowing something of the history of our Universities."†

Mr. Roundell Palmer, another parliamentary defender
of the Universities, or at all events an opponent of that
Commission of Inquiry which the Universities regard as

---

* This character is attested by Wordsworth:—

———— " Nor was it least
Of many benefits in later years
Derived from academic institutes
And rules, that they held something up to view
Of a republic, where all stood thus far
Upon equal ground—that we were brothers all
In honour, as in one community,
Scholars and gentlemen; where, furthermore,
Distinction open lay to all that came,
And wealth and titles were in less esteem
Than talents, worth, and prosperous industry."
                                   The Prelude, book ix.

† Debate, July 18, 1850, *Times* report.

a hostile step, went very much further in his views of the extension of University education, and called the privilege of the existing colleges and halls a monopoly. Mr. Palmer's notion of "progress" is to go back to something like the University system of the thirteenth century; and notwithstanding the contempt in which persons of the "enlightened" school are apt to hold that period of European history, they cannot but admit that, if Mr. Palmer's University annals be truly stated, the liberality of those antique times far exceeded the present. The passage referred to of Mr. Roundell Palmer's speech was as follows :—

"A very important matter, noticed by the noble lord (Lord J. Russell), when he stated that there were only about 1600 students in the University of Oxford, and in which I cordially agree with the noble lord, was that he wished to see the benefits of those great Universities much more largely extended. But how is that to be done, and how would the Commission effectually deal with the difficulty? There was a time when the Universities (I speak more particularly of Oxford) were open to a degree of which we in the present day have lost all trace and vestige. In the reign of King Edward I., just before the foundation of the first college in Oxford, it was stated that there were as many as 30,000 students in that University, and as many as 300 licensed halls for the residence of students. In Oxford it came to pass that 19 most noble foundations, the colleges, were founded. They were not at all intended to supersede the licensed halls that existed before, but it so happened that during the troubles of the Reformation the number of students in the Universities declined very greatly, and so by degrees the Universities dwindled to the dimensions of colleges, and the endowed halls became assimilated to the colleges. Lord Leicester, then being Chancellor, assumed to himself the right to nominate the heads or governors of all the halls in the University, and, that being conceded to him, the power of establishing new halls passed out of the hands of the University into those of the Chancellor ; and from that time to this, unless the power had been taken away by Archbishop Laud's statute, it remained in the Chancellor and not in the body of the University.   Archbishop Laud's statute required that every student of the University should be matriculated a member of one of the existing colleges or halls within a week of his matriculation.   The consequence is, that it would be impossible, unless we reverted to the old system of opening licensed halls, to augment the number of students beyond the capacity of the accommodation to be found within the twenty-four colleges, which appears to me a very serious evil.   I venture to point out another very important matter which I think could be obtained by resorting to the old system and abolishing the present monopoly.   I mean the regulation of expenses.   We have now a scale of living, manners, habits, and discipline, which, whilst approved by the present members, it would be extremely difficult to interfere with.   We could not well begin *de novo* in existing institutions ; but nothing could be more easy, if new halls were opened, than to place them from the beginning under a strict and economical discipline.   Let all the meals be in common ; no expensive private furniture be allowed—habits all in accordance with the class of students likely to frequent them.   Thus we should at once enlarge the benefits of the Universities, and diminish the expense.   There can be no doubt that there are existing powers in the Universities amply sufficient to authorize what I have proposed, and nothing more is necessary than that it should he demanded by public opinion to induce the authorities of the Universities gradually, and of their own accord, to make changes of that description; and if they have not been made before, it is because they have not been demanded by public opinion."*

We know nothing of the details of life at those periods when Oxford and other seats of learning, according to such chronicles as exist, were crowded with such a number of students as in the present day seems quite incredible. Centuries before the period referred to by Mr. Palmer, the multitudes who resorted, for the sake of peace and religious study, to the ecclesiastical seminaries even of Ireland, were, according to the testimony of the venerable Bede, exceedingly great. We read of 7000 at Armagh; and St. Bernard speaks of the monastery of Benchore, in the sixth century, containing many thousand monks, itself the chief of many monasteries, spread not only over Ireland but over Europe. Nothing, we are told, could exceed the regularity of these monks. The choirs of their churches were constantly full of "religious" chanting hymns to the Creator, as well by night as by day. The times of recess from prayer, refreshment, and natural rest, were devoted to tillage, and other useful employments: for they lived only by the products of nature and the labour of their own hands. But all this fell by corruption or by violence, and now there are but the melancholy ruins of the grandeur of past ages, and lands wretchedly cultivated, where, in the ages called "dark," in the self-complacent vocabulary of modern times, God was continually worshipped, and his creatures lived in peace upon the produce of the ground, which was cultivated with the sedulous attention of gardeners.

---

* Debate, July 18, 1850, *Times* report.

It is strange that a practical lawyer should be an imaginative man; but surely Mr. Palmer must have suffered his mind to be filled with the dreams of poetry, when he even momentarily contemplated the revival of so numerous a society at Oxford as the three hundred licensed halls accommodated. It could only be governed and regulated in times of reverence and of submission to discipline, such as have been in times past, and such as may be again in the recoil of the human spirit from the overwrought activities and perpetual strain of these restless days; but such as we must in vain look for *now*. Steam-engines, railways, cotton-spinning, and free opinion, and controversy about everything by everybody, will not allow of these great communities, devoted to simplicity of life— to prayer, to praise, and to study. Society has forfeited this good, and the hope of its return is only a fitting theme for the poet's song :—

> ——— " Oh what joy
> To see a sanctuary for our country's youth
> Inform'd with such a spirit as might be
> Its own protection; a primeval grove,
> Where, though the shades with cheerfulness were fill'd,
> Nor indigent of songs warbled from crowds
> In under-coverts, yet the countenance
> Of the whole place should bear a stamp of awe;
> A habitation sober and demure
> For ruminating creatures; a domain
> For quiet things to wander in; a haunt
> In which the heron should delight to feed
> By the shy rivers, and the pelican
> Upon the cypress spire in lonely thought
> Might sit and sun himself.—Alas! alas!
> In vain for such solemnity I look'd;
> Mine eyes were cross'd by butterflies, ears vex'd
> By chattering popinjays; the inner heart
> Seem'd trivial, and the impresses without
> Of a too gaudy region." *

---

* The Prelude, book iii.

Such must be the result of such a stream of activities of all kinds, whether in good things or bad, as now prevails. In colleges, as in commerce, we have self-will, rivalship, competition, pushed to excess. Things, which are very good in moderation, are driven to extremes; the grave man becomes an ascetic, the mirthful man a mountebank, and the studious man kills himself with labour, instead of finding rest for his soul in stated periods of repose and pious exercise.*

The universities, such as they are, would, I apprehend, scarcely bear additions of the kind which Mr. Palmer proposes; there is not room for them. Nevertheless such establishments there ought to be, where those who are disposed to study and simplicity of life, might find means towards those ends. We cannot, however, disguise from ourselves that the rush for education in these days is like that of the commercialists to California—it is all for gold. To get on in life, and to make the most of life in the most rapid way, is the uppermost idea in the minds even of boys. Therefore, the seminaries for cheap education are fixed in towns, where what is considered useful knowledge may be most quickly acquired, and most quickly turned to account. I doubt whether, if halls existed in these days at Oxford and Cambridge, where

---

* " Lord Bacon, in a passage quoted by Dr. Chr. Wordsworth containing a happy application of a classical image, professes to be of the opinion that the cause of *learning* is promoted by peace rather than by contention. ' The works which concern the learned,' says that great man, ' are foundations and buildings, endowments with revenues, franchises and privileges, institutions and ordinances for government, *all tending to quietness and privateness of life,* and discharge of cares and troubles, much like the stations which Virgil prescribes for the hiving of bees,—

' Principio sedes apibus statioque petenda,
Quo neque sit ventis aditus; nam pabula venti
Ferre domum prohibent.' "—*Q. Rev.,* No. 104.

such a system of living as that sketched out by Mr. Palmer should prevail, they would be much frequented, except by students seeking to get into the Church ; and if anything new is to be devised on behalf of such students, perhaps better localities might be fixed upon than either Oxford or Cambridge.

Of late years the question has been frequently raised, and I think with good reason, whether our University system is sufficient for the preparation of young men for the clerical office; and whether it is fitting that they should step almost directly from the miscellaneous society, the worldly views, and ordinary amusements of young men at Oxford or Cambridge, to the serious duties and responsibilities of clergymen. That some qualms upon this subject have been felt in the universities themselves, appears from the changes which, within a few years, have been introduced. " A voluntary course," says an earnest writer on this subject,* " has been instituted of somewhat longer duration, and of a less general character, than has hitherto been observed ; but no changes that have been yet made, or can probably be made, can compensate for the absence of such institutions, or theological retreats, as were originally contemplated by the Reformers of the Church. Admirable as both our venerable and time-honoured universities are known and acknowledged to be, and have long been, still they are by no means fitted to form, by a course of training, young men who have for some years been otherwise there employed, and whose friendships and associations may in many cases disqualify them for entering on a more rigid course previous to ordination."

The writer of the above remarks does not wish for a

---

* Rev. John Lockhart Ross, M.A., of Oriel College, Oxford.

complete separation of those intended for the clerical profession from others during the whole course of their education. He supposes the academical course to be concluded, and then he would have a theological course of one year, in diocesan colleges attached to each see and cathedral in England. It is, he says, at the period of life when young men are released from the trammels of the school and the university that they are most likely, in the first feeling of emancipation, to wield their scholastic weapons on some abstruse point of polemics, or to try their inexperienced plumes in some ambitious soarings into the misty regions of theological difficulty or doubt. It is, therefore, more necessary at that period than ever, to have the prudent superintendence and the directing aid of an instructor, to whom the path of theological study is no new or unknown course, but to whom long use and acquaintance with the minds of men and their devious tracks, and also with all the points and bearings of theological controversy and science, have made fully conversant with the duties and responsibility of an instructor of the youthful candidates for orders; that their knowledge may be sound, and that there be more prospect of future unanimity respecting the essential doctrines and usages of the Church.

Further, says Mr. Lockhart Ross, it is highly fitting and desirable that candidates for orders should not merely receive theological instruction from experienced and properly informed guides, but should likewise be obliged to undergo a year of retirement, and study, and probation, in some professional retreat removed from the scene of their former pursuits, and more immediately connected with the duties and scenes of their future holy profession. What is wanted is theological training, quite as much as theological instruction; and it is not too much to say, that much of our present diversity of thinking and acting, and consequent disunion through our different dioceses, is owing to our unsystematic preparation of young men for the service of the Church.

It is also desirable that the youthful candidate for orders should, along with the course of theological instruction, receive instruction relative to subjects of a more practical kind in the ordinary duties of his pastoral office, such as the composition of pulpit discourses, the effective reading of the liturgy, the general working of a parish, and, if practicable, visiting and attending the sick ; for which latter purpose it would be well that a parochial cure or district should be connected with the institution.

Great benefit, moreover, would be derived from the association of a body of young men resident in a collegiate building within the precincts of an abbey or cathedral Church, and required to attend daily on its high and solemn services. And in such quiet and holy retirement from the noise, and hurry, and bustle of the world, there is reason to hope that habits of practical piety might be formed—of quiet, unostentatious, and unobtrusive religion, well calculated to qualify the pastor for his future office, " by elevating his views and aims above the secular motives and inducements by which too many have been tempted to seek admission into the ministry of the Church."

Such observations are, I think, well worthy of attention ; for, considering the duties he undertakes, the candidate for orders should generally be made more practically conscious of them than he is likely to be if he go directly from the ordinary routine of college life, and the ordinary habits of college society, to take the clerical vows, and to enter upon the office of a spiritual guide to others.   Men should have dwelt apart, and should have been devoted to habits very different from those of the ordinary world, before they can, with a clear conscience, make the solemn promises which they must make at the ordination service.

There can, I believe, be no question of the fact, that of late years close and diligent study in the universities has been more general than it formerly was, and that to obtain university distinctions a considerably higher scale of proficiency is required than that which would have sufficed twenty or thirty years ago. But I do not perceive that this increase of knowledge has had the effect of giving to the public more eminent or more useful men than were furnished by the universities at former periods. For instance, in the Oxford prize lists from 1775 to 1800 will be found such names as Joseph Warton, Speaker Abbott (afterwards Lord Colchester), Lord Grenville, Marquis Wellesley, Lisle Bowles, Lord Tenterden (Chief Justice), George Canning, Sir John Richardson (the Judge), Bishop Coplestone, Lord Eldon, Lord Sidmouth, Bishop Burgess, Bishop Philpotts, Bishop Mant, &c. &c. Then take from 1807 to 1832, and we have Sir Robert Peel, Rev. J. Keble, Bishop Coleridge, Professor Senior, Judge Coleridge, J. G. Lockhart, Dean Milman, Bishop Hampden, Doctor Arnold, Bishop Longley, Sir Francis Baring, Lord Harrowby, Mr. Labouchere, Sir George Grey, Sir Charles Wood, Lord Wharncliffe, Bishop Denison, Lord Ashley, Lord Carlisle, Lord Stanley, Bishop Wilberforce, Dr. Moberly, Professor Sewell, Archdeacon Manning, W. E. Gladstone, &c. &c. Now turn to Cambridge, and from the same period we have—(of course, I do not pretend to give *all*)—Lord Manners (Chancellor of Ireland), Professor Farish, Herbert Marsh, Professor Christian, Serjeant Lens, J. Wood, Professor Porson, Wollaston, Judge Littledale, Bishop Brinkley (the astronomer), Malthus, F. Wrangham, Bishop Maltby, Bishop

Middleton, Lord Lyndhurst, Professor Woodhouse, Sir John Beckett, Dr. Wordsworth (Master of Trinity), Bishop Samuel Butler, Chief Justice Tindal, V.-C. Shadwell, sundry Freres, Mr. Le Bas, Archbishop Sumner, the poets Coleridge and Wordsworth. All these in the last quarter of the last century. Then we have Lord Glenelg, Baron James Parke, Bishop Monk, Professor Dobree, Bishop Turton, Chief Baron Pollock, Aristophanes Mitchell, Lord Langdale, Bishop Blomfield, Baron Alderson, *Rev. G. C. Gorham*, Justice Maule, Archbishop Musgrave, Sir John Herschel, Dean Peacock, Professor Amos, Doctor Mill, V.-C. Wigram, Dean Waddington, Rev. Hugh J. Rose, John Shaw Lefevre, Bishop Thirlwall, Principal Melville, Professor Airey, Bishop Boustead, T. B. Macaulay, E. L. Bulwer, Whewell (Master of Trinity), Dr. Christopher Wordsworth, Earl of Burlington, &c. &c. I do not choose to go on with names of those who have more recently obtained university distinction, but leave it to readers who take an interest in such matters of investigation to compare the probable public usefulness and renown of the " honour"-men of the last fifteen years with those of previous times.

To some it may be interesting to compare the *academic* character of the late Government (that of June, 1846) with the present (August, 1850). I believe every one of the late Government were university men, unless the Home Secretary, Sir James Graham—a man second in ability to none of his colleagues—be an exception. He is an *honorary* D.C.L. of Cambridge. The Premier (Sir R. Peel), the Secretary of the Colonies (Mr. W. E. Gladstone), and the Secretary of the Treasury (Mr. E. Cardwell), were all double first-class men of Oxford ; the first in 1808, the second in 1831, and the third in 1835. The Lord Chancellor (Lyndhurst) was second wrangler and second Smith's prizeman at Cambridge in 1794. The Chancellor of the Exchequer (Goulburn) was M.P. for his university. The Chief Commissioner of the Woods and Forests (Viscount Canning) was of the first class in classics at Oxford in 1833 ; the Chancellor of the Duchy of Lancaster (Lord Granville Somerset) was of the second-class classics in 1818 ; the First Lord of the Admiralty (Lord Ellenborough) obtained the Latin Ode prize at Cambridge in 1818 ; the President of the Board of Control (Lord Ripon) obtained the same distinction in 1801. The President of the Board of Trade (Lord Dalhousie) was a fourth-class classic (Oxford, 1833) ; and the Secretary at War (Hon. Sidney Herbert) was of the same rank in 1831. The Under Colonial Secretary (Lord Lyttleton) was classical medallist at Cambridge in 1838, and a senior optime in mathematics. Thus twelve of the Government was not only university men, but men of various degrees of academical distinction. Taking a similar number of official persons (21) of the Administration in August, 1850, I find seven who do not appear to have belonged to any English university. Among these are the Premier (Lord John Russell) and the Lord Chancellor (Lord Truro). The Chancellor of the Exchequer (Sir C. Wood) and the First Lord of the Admiralty (Sir F. Baring) were both double first-class men at Oxford ; the former in 1821, and the latter in 1817. The President of the Council (Lord Lansdowne) and the Secretary for Foreign Affairs (Lord Palmerston) have both been representatives in Parliament of the university of Cambridge. The Home Secretary (Sir George Grey) was a first-class classic at Oxford in 1821 ; and the President of the Board of Trade (Mr. Labouchere) had the same honour in 1820. The Chancellor of the Duchy of Lancaster (Lord Carlisle) was a first-class classic at

Oxford in 1822, and obtained the prize for both Latin and English verse in 1821.   The Financial Secretary of the Treasury (Mr. G. Cornewall Lewis) was of the first class in classics, and of the second in mathematics, at Oxford in 1828; and Mr. Tuffnell, his predecessor, was of the second class in the same year.

The only person of any *theological* note in his academic career, belonging to either Government, was—Sir John Cam Hobhouse!   That gentleman, now President of the Board of Control, obtained at Cambridge, in 1808, the "Theological Essay" prize.

Note.—In Carlisle's ' History of English Grammar Schools,' a book of which but a limited number of copies were printed, I find the following antiquarian information about universities and ecclesiastical schools:—

" That those seats of learning which are now called universities were anciently called *studies* is well known; but about the end of the twelfth or beginning of the thirteenth century the modern name seems generally to have prevailed, either because all kinds of learning were taught in them, and students of all countries were welcome to them, or because they were formed into legal communities, which in the Latin of those times were called *universitates*.

" In the darkest of the middle ages, it has been observed, the families of bishops were the chief seminaries of learning, in which young persons were educated for the service of the Church. These episcopal or cathedral schools still continued in this period. They were also better regulated, and consequently more useful and more frequented. In the most ancient times the bishop was commonly the chief, if not the only teacher of his cathedral school, the faithful discharge of which laborious office was hardly compatible with the other duties of his function. But in this period these schools were put under the direction of men of learning, who devoted their whole time and study to the education of youth, and had certain estates or prebends assigned for their support. These teachers of the cathedral schools were called the *scholastics of the diocese*, and all the youth in it who were designed for the Church were entitled to the benefit of their instructions. By the 18th canon of the third General Council of Lateran, in the year 1179, it was decreed that such *scholastics* should be settled in all cathedrals, with sufficient revenues for their support, and that they should have authority to superintend all the schoolmasters of the diocese, and grant them licences, without which none should presume to teach. The sciences, therefore, that were taught in these cathedral schools were such as were most necessary to qualify their pupils for performing the duties of the sacerdotal office, as grammar, rhetoric, logic, theology, and church music. In the year 1215, in the fourth General Council of Lateran, similar ordinances were expressly enjoined. The great increase of *religious houses* in this period very much increased the number of seminaries of learning, as there was a school, more or less celebrated, in almost every convent. And some idea may be formed of the number added to the schools by this means, when it is considered that there were no fewer than 557 religious houses of different kinds, according to Bishop Tanner, founded in England between the Conquest and the death of King John."

Note 2.—Some apology is due for having only incidentally alluded to the University of London, and for having said nothing of the University of Durham. It is from no want of respect that I have been silent regarding them. I believe they are both very useful educational institutions, though the public at large does not take very much interest in them. I hope they may both flourish, and may produce both good scholars and good men.

CHAPTER XXVII.

THE LAW AND ITS ADMINISTRATION.

THERE is nothing which is more injured by the compli-
cations of society, in an old country, than the simplicity of
justice.   Right becomes involved with right, forms mul-
tiply and become confused one with the other, until at
last all is perplexity and doubt, except to those who have
been carefully brought up to thrid the mazes of the law.
And even with respect to lawyers, it may be doubted that
they see their way through perplexed cases *much* more
clearly than others, but it is their business to seem to do
so ; and, at all events, they know the proper forms of
procedure, of which the unlearned in the law are ignorant. In King Alfred's " golden reign" he " obtained, for
a perpetual usage, that the great council of the kingdom
(*wittena-gemote*) should meet twice in the year, or oftener
if need be, to treat of the government of God's people ;
how they should keep themselves from sin, should live in
quiet, and should receive right."   This " meeting of the
wise men" was, doubtless, in so far like our present
House of Lords that it was both a legislative assembly
and a court of justice ; but how refreshing to read the
simple statement of the principles by which it was animated, and the objects it had in view ! Century after
century, since that remote period, has added rule upon
rule, statute upon statute, interpretation upon interpretation ; and though within the last thirty years a great deal
has been done by Parliament with the intention of sweep-

ing away what had become obsolete, and of making the
ways of the law more clear and less expensive, still the
mass of new circumstances, accumulating in modern times
with unprecedented rapidity, seems to render the clear
view of a man's rights, and the means of asserting them,
year by year more difficult.

We have indeed come to such a pass in respect to these
matters, that, in the opinion of many, there is no such
practical tyranny in this country as the condition of the
law. And this opinion is formed in no spirit of hostility to
the Government or the State, but concurrently with the
belief that the State is sincerely desirous of mitigating this
evil as much as it can. But there are evils of society
which grow with its growth, and even strengthen with its
strength, and which become so interlaced and interwoven
with the very framework and structure of society itself,
that, without its dissolution, such evils must—in some
considerable degree—remain. It is, perhaps, not going
too far to say, that all but the very vindictive or the very
rich are, in this country, exceedingly afraid to engage in
law, even when convinced they have a good cause. The
former class are for the moment reckless, and the latter
indifferent ; and so they order law proceedings to be
taken. Many questions also go into the hands of the
lawyers as a matter of course, because they evidently
must go there. But where a choice of going to law, or
not going to law, is to be deliberately exercised, many
persons in England forego their rights every day, either
from policy or in disgust. Three things in our law are
especially frightful; namely, 1. The unintelligibleness of
the proceedings to the popular understanding ; 2. The
uncertainty of the result, however obvious the moral
justice of the case may be ; 3. The certainty of a great
expense. Scarcely any legal document is intelligible
even to the most accomplished scholar, if his scholarship

extend not to the technicalities of the law. Even acts of
parliament, passed at this very day, for the better adjust-
ment of rights, or the better government of society, are
so stuffed with words, so elaborated in detail, and so technical in phraseology, that nine-tenths of those who look at
them give up at once all hope of making sure of what
they mean. And yet this is said to be necessary, because
popular language is too loose for the exactness required
in legislative acts. The result of a lawsuit is very
generally dependent upon the observance of minute for-
malities, or upon technical rules of evidence, which are
quite independent of the merits of the cause, or seem so
to be. No suitor can certainly tell but that he may be
thrown over upon some matter of which he can have no
notion till he hears of his defeat. I remember having
been present in Westminster Hall when some persons of
condition were prosecuted for conspiracy to defraud a
young gentleman, who lost a considerable sum to them at
cards. The party took carriages in London, drove to
Richmond, dined, and then played. The evidence went
on and looked dark enough, but, when it was closed, the
learned Lord Chief Justice Tenterden said, that all the
serious evidence had reference to what took place in
Richmond—that Richmond was not on the Middlesex but
the Surrey side of the river Thames—that the court was
trying a Middlesex cause—and that, unless evidence of a
conspiracy to defraud within that county could be given,
the prosecution must fail. And it did fail, simply upon
that matter of form. But the worst thing of all in the
ordinary proceedings of our law—though it does operate
as a bar to the indulgence of mere litigiousness—is the expense of obtaining justice. Our judges are all highly paid
by the public : the sum annually paid out of the public
revenue for courts of justice exceeds a million sterling ;

and in the equity courts a large part of the expense is
defrayed from the interest of money belonging to suitors
whose rights are not yet, and perhaps never will be, ascertained; yet still the expense to each of the contending
parties who go to law is a great oppression. Efforts have
been made from time to time to remove or mitigate this
evil of expensiveness, but hitherto without much effect.
Even in the new County Courts, lately organized for the
express purpose of settling causes in a cheap and expe-
ditious manner, where the sum in dispute does not exceed
50l., it appears that fees are demanded from the suitor at
the commencement of the cause which deter many from
seeking justice. As to the higher courts, whatever matter is brought into them is sure to be attended with considerable expense; and it is not even contemplated that
the costs awarded to the successful suitor, at the charge
of his adversary, will repay the actual outlay. The
upshot of the whole is, that, though the integrity, learning,
and assiduity of the judges are universally admitted, yet
legal proceedings are generally a terror to all concerned
except the lawyers. Uncertainty and perplexity in
various forms—delays, postponements, disappointments,
and heavy charges—these are the recognised incidents in
the history of all who go to law, even in this " enlightened
age ! "

The question, how this evil is to be cured, is a very
wide one. I doubt, as I have already hinted, whether an
advanced condition of society admits of any complete
cure ; whether the complexity of circumstances and the
accumulation of various properties and rights do not render a plain and cheap road to justice an impossibility.
Unless we get back to more simplicity in the conditions
and transactions of life, we must have law proceedings
difficult to be understood, and men must be largely paid

for guiding us, or pretending to guide us, through the labyrinth.   Still I do not see why a man who makes a complaint against me in the Court of Chancery may write it out in the most verbose of all possible forms and put it on the file of the court, and thus compel me—when I want to know what his complaint is, in order that I may answer it—to pay largely for an office-copy of my adversary's Bill, as the first step in my proceeding.   A writer, of dry and quiet humour, asserts that our Court of Chancery is "the Protestant Inquisition ; only that, instead of confining its victims in dungeons, it allows them to go about for a time, just as if they were not ruined ; *but they know better.*"   I am aware that Chancery lawyers can give very plausible reasons for all the tortures of Chancery suitors, but I remain unconvinced that the pursuit of justice in the Court of Chancery must *necessarily* be attended with such delays and expenses as have made that branch of the administration of justice, in particular, a terror to the people and a reproach to the good sense of England.   In the courts of common law, when matters of account form the groundwork of the dispute, it is usual, in order to save the court the time which a lengthened investigation would occupy, to refer the disputed accounts, by mutual consent, to the decision of some competent professional person.   As these episodical investigations, called " references to the master," are the most fruitful sources of delay in the Equity courts, it would perhaps be an improvement if these questions of account were settled more usually by an authorized arbitration.

However, as Horace Walpole said of mankind, that it was being very partial to think worse of some men than of others, so it may be said of courts of justice or of judicature, that it is being very partial to think worse of the practice in equity than of that at common law.   It is pro-

voking enough to see how much of the valuable time of
the judges, and the expensive time of barristers, is wasted
upon the discussion of points that have no apparent connexion with the justice of the case under consideration.

Of course, there are from time to time great legal principles luminously discussed, and learnedly decided ; but
much more frequently the visitor of Westminster Hall, in
Term time, will hear discussions which cause regret that
men of ingenuity should be so occupied. Some technicality of pleading has been perhaps omitted, and the argument turns upon the point, whether this is fatal to the
whole proceeding or is not, though no one pretends that
the omission has led to any misunderstanding of the real
merits of the case. Some appeal from the decision of an
inferior court is under discussion ; but the point which
occupies attention is not whether the decision of the court
below was right or wrong, but whether, in the notice of
appeal, every unimportant particular was technically set
forth. Perhaps criminal proceedings are under consideration ; and the question is gravely debated, whether a man
who has been found guilty upon unquestionable evidence
of having stolen a sum of money, can be legally convicted
in the absence of all testimony to show of what coins or
notes the money, or any part of it, consisted. Or, it may
be, that some one has been indicted for stealing a ham
and found guilty ; but the judges must gravely decide
whether the indictment was sufficient, seeing that it did
not set forth whether the ham was of mutton or of pork ;
or if the latter, whether of tame pig or wild pig, in which
last case there would be a doubt whether it could legally
be considered property—for wild boar, while alive and
uncaught, is not.

In short, wherever there are law proceedings, whether
written or oral, there seems to be a hedge of forms and

technicalities set up between the plain sense and justice of
the case, and its settlement according to legal principles
and practice.   Whether or no this is an apparent evil
only, and inseparable from the needful exactness of the
law, I shall not undertake positively to determine.

CHAPTER XXVIII.

BARRISTERS AND PROFESSIONAL ADVOCACY.

AFTER briefly considering the condition of the law in
England and its administration, we naturally come to
that important portion of society who give advice in cases
of legal controversy, and who plead causes before the
tribunals. Barristership, or the profession of legal advocacy, holds a very high rank, if not the highest, among
the pursuits by which men attain to fame and fortune in
the affairs of civil life. The highest eminence in this
profession in England, leads almost certainly to official
connection with the Government, and thence to judicial
station, and the acquisition of hereditary honours and
privileges. During the last thirty years the quantity of
barristers has very greatly increased, and with that
increase it seems to be admitted that there has been a coincident deterioration of the quality of Barristership. A
journal which gives considerable attention to these matters says, that "incomes at the bar for the last ten or a
dozen years have diminished a third—brilliant talent has
altogether disappeared—business has diminished in a still
greater ratio than incomes, while moderately capable
practitioners have increased twenty-fold ; producing a dull
dead level of mediocrity, in which we have no Erskine, no
Curran, no Brougham, no Scarlett, no Denman." The
number of barristers has indeed immensely increased of
late years, though not quite " twenty-fold." A publica-

tion by a member of the Bar informs us, that the Law-list
of 1814 contained—of counsel, conveyancers, and special
pleaders   821

And that for 1848   .   .   3176

The number of barristers upon the books of the inns of
court at the commencement of 1850, amounted to about
3400 ; but probably not more than a third of that number
seek for business within the strict line of their profession.
Still the profession seems to be overcrowded, and that not
by merely capable, or "moderately-capable practitioners,"
but by men of very considerable learning, industry, and
cleverness, though obviously destitute of the high gifts of
genius which have at former times made the Bar illustrious.   In no walk of life, indeed, does that inimitable
something, to which we give the name of genius, now
appear.   It seems to have fled from a too practical and
wealth-seeking age : but never were simple ability, and
the powers which industry and attention may command,
more general.   A very learned person, whose experience
goes a long way back, and whose view of the present state
of the Bar I have had the advantage of lately seeing,
admits that the high feeling of the profession and the
ardour of its sympathy with letters have considerably
diminished.   But taking into account the circumstances
of the modern Bar, he considers that scarcely anything
else was to be expected.   Law now-a-days, in its monstrous growth, monopolises the students' time.   Business
and fees are equally diminished from their old measure,
and the competitors for them have vastly multiplied.   It
is to be feared that, as the numbers have increased, the
tone and character of the Bar have not been elevated.
Thirty or forty years ago gentlemen used to be called to
the Bar without any view to practice or to any pecuniary
advantage.   It was simply the rank or honour of the
degree of barrister which was sought.   That fashion has

passed away; and now it is common for young men of an inferior grade, without much of classical or philosophical preparation, to press into the profession more as a means of earning a livelihood than of acquiring an honourable fame—more in the spirit of tradesmen than of students. This spirit makes some, though it is to be hoped they are few in number, stoop to modes of getting business which were utterly unknown in the more heroic days of the profession.

Of late years many persons have crowded to the Bar in the hope of being, by that means, in a more favourable position for profiting by Government patronage. A writer, whom I shall presently have occasion to quote at more length, says,* that "great as the influence of the profession of the law is in this country, many causes have tended of late to perplex the objects of its ambition and to tempt its aspirants to lower means of success than steady industry, and conduct free from stain. The number of inferior offices which suggest the appliances of patronage, and offer low *stimuli* to its hopes—the increase of numbers, which weakens the power of moral control while it heightens the turmoil of competition—have endangered the elevation of the character of the Bar, in the maintenance of which the interests of order and justice are deeply involved." Upon the Whigs coming into office, after their painfully tedious exclusion from its responsibilities and rewards, a fashion grew up among them of executing a great variety of ministerial duties by Commissions, composed of gentlemen of the Bar who had for six years been members of the profession. This standing rule became at length a standing joke; and even so distinguished a member of the Whig party as the Rev. Canon Sidney Smith, poured forth a volley of

---

* *Quarterly Review*, No. 149.

sarcasm against his friends upon this subject; but that was when some of their Commissions ventured to touch interests in which he and his order were concerned. Speaking of some projected Commission with respect to ecclesiastical leases, the excellent Canon breaks forth in the following animated strain:—" The Whig government, they will be vexed to hear, would find a great deal of patronage forced upon them by this measure.   Their favourite human animal, *the barrister of six years' standing*, would be called into action.   The whole earth is, in fact, in commission; and the human race, saved from the flood, are delivered over to barristers of six years' standing. The *onus probandi* now lies upon any man who says he is *not* a commissioner; the only doubt on seeing a new man among the Whigs is, not whether he is a commissioner or not, but whether it is tithes, poor-laws, boundaries of boroughs, church leases, charities, or any of the thousand human concerns which are now worked by commissioners to the infinite comfort and satisfaction of mankind, who seem in these days to have found out the real secret of life, the one thing wanting to sublunary happiness—the great principle of commission and six years' barristration." Such a fire as this, and from the guns of their own forts, too, damaged the Commission system of the party in office, and made six years barristration, even with the advantage of Whig connection, a less sure passport to a place; but the effect upon the profession was very considerable at the time, and has not wholly died away.

Another practice, which has crowded the profession, and has done it more injury than the accession of the place-seeking members, is that of solicitors bringing their sons or nephews to the Bar.   These young gentlemen, by their connexion, become quite sure of obtaining a certain amount of that ordinary business to which any man of

average capacity is equal.   It is this which makes it next
to impossible for a young man without such connexion to
get into business.   The solicitor has a junior of his own
family competent for the junior business.   And even if
by some lucky chance a man who depends only on his
own talents and industry should get an opportunity now
and then of showing the stuff he is made of, he is not to
reckon, as in the old time, that being known, business
will then be pressed upon him.   The family interest is
still too strong, except in cases of difficulty and importance, and these must be given to seniors and leading men.
In his 'Life of Lord Eldon,' the late Mr. Horace Twiss,
who always wrote with good sense and a nice discrimination, thus comments upon the eminent success in one or
two cases, which immediately led to Mr. Scott's rapid
rise in his profession : " At the present day, from the
great competition of very learned and very able practitioners, a few occasional opportunities do little, however
they be improved.   Among the more influential class of
attorneys and solicitors it has become usual to bring up a
son or other near relation to the Bar, who, if his industry
and ability be such as can at all justify his friends in employing him, absorbs all the business which they and their
connexion can bestow ; and the number of barristers thus
powerfully supported is now so great, that few men, lack-
ing such an advantage, can secure a hold upon business.
But at the time when Mr. Scott began his professional
life, the usage had not grown up of coming into the field
with a 'following' already secured.   Education being
less general, fewer competitors attempted the Bar ; and
even among the educated classes a large proportion of
adventurous men devoted themselves to naval and military
pursuits, which have now been deprived of their attraction
by a peace of more than a quarter of a century.   In those

days, therefore, it might well happen, as with Mr. Scott it actually did, that a couple of good opportunities, ably used, would make the fortune of an assiduous barrister in London." These are circumstances with respect to the present condition of the Bar which cannot be gainsaid. No doubt ability, industry, and steady perseverance, will still lead to the ultimate success of those who can afford to persevere—those whose purse and whose patience can stand the wear and tear of long waiting and long watching: but many there are, it may be feared, who sink in the struggle, because they are without the needful *connexion*; while better befriended mediocrity succeeds, and, with success, obtains new friends and the means of further advancement.

In this age of general inquiry and discussion, the question has sometimes been raised whether the profession of advocacy for pecuniary reward is, indeed, at the present day, the high and honourable profession which the custom and courtesy of society have admitted it to be. Some have contended that *indiscriminate* advocacy for a money payment must be a profession of at least doubtful morality; and yet it is understood that no rule of the profession is more strict than that of the practising barrister's obligation to undertake any cause regularly offered to him, if he be not retained on the other side. Again, it has been strikingly said, in contrasting Statesmanship with Barristership, that the Statesman's business is to find out what is right and serviceable, not what can be best said or done *for one side;* and that, therefore, the training of the mind is manifestly better in the case of statesmanship. Recently the question of barristerial duty to clients has undergone a sharp discussion, owing to the assertion of rather extreme views of that duty—views which I think it rather surprising that men of nice conscientiousness should approve. Some thirty years ago, upon a remarkable occasion, it was laid down by a barrister of great oratorical and political importance, who afterwards occupied for several years the highest position in the law, that "an advocate, by the sacred duty which he owes to his client, knows, in the discharge of that office, but one person in the world, that client, and none other. To save that client by all expedient means—to protect that client at all hazards and all costs to all others, and among others to himself—is the highest and most unquestioned of his duties. He must not regard the alarm, the suffering, the torment, the destruction which he may bring on any others; nay, separating even the duties of a patriot from those of an advocate, and casting them, if need be, to the wind, he must go on, reckless of the consequences, if his fate should unhappily be to involve his country in confusion for his client's protection."* This has generally been considered a piece of impassioned exaggeration, intended as an excuse for a degree of licence that trenched even upon the traditional respect due to the Crown. The true excuse for that unwonted licence lay in the particular circumstances of the case, and was not fairly based upon any general rule of advocacy. Another eminent barrister, and now for a good many years an equity judge, has laid down very different principles of advocacy. He says, "No counsel supposes himself to be the mere advocate or agent of his client to gain a victory, if he can, on a particular occasion. The zeal and the arguments of every counsel, knowing what is due to himself and his honourable profession, are qualified not only by considerations affecting his own character as a man of honour, experience, and learning, but also by considera-

---

* Brougham, at the bar of the House of Lords, 1820.

tions affecting the general interests of justice." *   Lord Chief Justice Hale said, that he never thought his profession should either necessitate a man to use his eloquence by extenuations or aggravations to make anything worse or better than it deserved, or could justify a man in doing so.   He held, that to prostitute his elocution or rhetoric in such a way was most basely mercenary and below the worth of a man, much more a Christian.   The present Lord Chief Justice of the Queen's Bench says, in his 'Life of Lord C. J. Holt,' when a counsel at the Bar, that "He was noted for doing his business not only with learning always sufficient, but with remarkable good sense and handiness ; so that he won verdicts in doubtful cases, and was noted for having the ear of the court.   Yet he would not stoop for victory to any unbecoming art, and always maintained a character for straightforwardness and independence."   Of Lord Eldon, though sprung from a trading stock, it has been said that he never could be brought to understand that it was consistent with the honour of a gentleman to misrepresent, *in the slightest degree*, either law to a judge or facts to a jury.   In a recent controversy, however, the theory of advocacy propounded by Mr. Brougham in 1820 has again been brought forward.   " The moment," says Mr. Commissioner Phillips, that the barrister "accepts his brief, every faculty he possesses becomes his client's property.   It is an implied contract between him and the man who trusts him.   Out of the profession this may be a moot point, but it was asserted and acted upon by two illustrious advocates of our own day, even to the confronting of a king, and, to the regal honour be it spoken, these dauntless men were afterwards promoted to the highest dignities."   The

---

* Lord Langdale, in a case quoted in the *Examiner*, Nov. 24, 1848.

allusion is to the Attorney and Solicitor-General of Queen
Caroline at the bar of the House of Lords in 1820. But
since it is a rule of the profession that a counsel must accept a brief offered to him, if he be not retained on the
other side, and since, when he has accepted a brief, according to the statement just quoted, " every faculty he
possesses becomes his client's property," what are we to
say of a set of educated men, who are ready, for a fee,
to devote every faculty to the interest of any one, however
wicked, in order to save him from the penalty of his
wickedness when arraigned before the tribunals? In the
case of the cold, deliberate murderer, Courvoisier, about
which Mr. Phillips writes, he admits, that after the man
confessed his guilt, he strained every faculty to save the
guilty man's life. By his own admission, Mr. Phillips
did everything he could for him, short of trying to cast
the guilt upon others. This seems going very far. One
can readily grant that he might, even after the confession
of the wretch, have watched the proceedings, and have
taken care that nothing but what was fair legal evidence
should go against his client; but to strain every faculty
to induce a jury to find a cruel murderer " not guilty,"
while conscious all the time that he certainly *was* guilty,
is to act according to a professional morality which it is
to be hoped will always, out of the profession, be something more than a moot point.

I am afraid, however, that notwithstanding the disagreeable moral complexion of the *theory* of Mr. Phillips,
and its opposition to other theories I have quoted, which
I infinitely prefer, the general practice of barristers is to
give themselves wholly to the gaining of the cause they
have in hand, without any very nice scrupulosity as to the
means. It is a humiliating thing to think how much conscience is an affair of habit. Men in the law, who would

rather cut off their right hands than do anything which seemed to them dishonourable, and who, beyond the limits of their profession, have, I am willing to believe, as nice a sense of rectitude and justice as men who live in the world can have, will certainly endeavour to obtain decisions which they are aware could not be given if the truth were as well known to the court and jury as to themselves. It is unquestionable that eminent men, who have "the ear of the court," sometimes use their influence to keep their adversaries from a fair hearing of their arguments, and a full understanding of their case.   It is notorious that many successful men at the Bar habitually take advantage of the weaknesses, ignorance, or prejudices of jurymen, in order to get verdicts, which they well know would not have been given by men of sense, acuteness, and intelligence.   Some years ago there was one notable example of a man, at the head of his profession as an advocate—a man whose knowledge of the world and of society was even greater than his knowledge of law—a man whose nice sensibility and manly sense of honour induced many persons to consult him upon points of propriety and prudence, with which law had no concern; and yet he, of all men at the Bar, was conspicuous for taking advantage of the follies, weaknesses, and prejudices of the jury-box, in order to obtain verdicts; as well as for stopping short, and holding back the full truth of a case, if he found it in a favourable position for gaining the decision at which he aimed.   It is worthy of remark, that that very eminent gentleman was not considered to be successful in his subsequent career as a judge.   It is said that no man is first-rate in more things than one.   The excellence which nature and art had given to that accomplished gentleman did not comprehend a judicial mind, though it made him so admirable an adviser and so effective an advocate.

But how strangely and almost inscrutably flexible and plastic must that high-mindedness and delicate sense of honour be which can be unconsciously folded up and put away when inconvenient for professional success! How admirably has it been said—

> " Our better mind
> Is as a Sunday's garment then put on
> When we have nought to do; *but at our work,*
> *We wear a worse for thrift."* *

The most ingenious defence of Barristership, or rather of forensic advocacy, that I have ever seen, was in an essay upon the lives of the brothers Lord Stowell and Lord Eldon, in the *Quarterly Review* for December, 1844. The pith of it lies in this, that under the peculiar circumstances which surround and fill the mind of the barrister, he is not the *conscious* advocate of wrong. The whole statement, however, of the advocate's position is so forcible and vivid, that I cannot forbear quoting it :—

" The grotesque and passionate forms of many-coloured life with which the advocate becomes familiar—the truths, stranger than fiction, of which he is the depositary, and which, implicitly believing, he sometimes thinks *too improbable to be offered to the belief of others*—the multitude of human affections and fortunes of which he becomes in turn not only the representative but the sharer, passioned for the hour even as those who have the deepest stake in the issue, rendering his professional life almost like a dazzling chimera, a waking dream. For let it not be supposed that because he is compelled by the laws of *retainer* to adopt any cause which may be offered to him in the regular course of his practice—with some extreme exceptions—that therefore he is often the conscious advocate of wrong. To him are presented those aspects of

---

* Rev. W. Crowe: 'Lewsden Hill.'

the case which it wears to the party who seeks his aid, and who therefore scarcely appears to him as stripped of claim to an honest sympathy. Is the rule of law too probably against him, there are reasons which cannot be exhibited to the Court, but which are the counsel's 'in private,' why, in this instance, to relax or evade it will be to attain substantial justice. Does the client, on the other hand, require of his advocate that he should insist on the 'rigour of the game,' he only desires to succeed by a course apparently so odious, because technicality will for once repair some secret injury, and make even the odds of fortune. Is he guilty of some high crime, he has his own palliations — his prosecutor seeks his conviction by means which it is virtue to repel — or some great principle will be asserted by his acquittal. In all cases of directly opposing testimony the counsel is necessarily predisposed to believe the statements which have first occupied his mind, and to listen to those which would displace his impression with incredulity, if not with anger. And how many cases arise in which there is no absolute right or wrong, truth or falsehood — cases dependent on *user*, on consent, on *waiver*, on mental competency — and in which the ultimate question arises less from disputed facts than from the arguments to be deduced from them, and all these perplexed, distorted, or irradiated by the lights cast on them from the passions and the hopes of the client, to be refracted through the mind and coloured by the fancy of the counsel ! In the majority of his causes he becomes, therefore, always a zealous, often a passionate partizan ; lives in the life of every cause (often the most momentous part of his client's life) ; 'burns with one love, with one resentment glows ;' and never ceases to hope, to struggle, or to complain *till the next cause is called on,* and he is involved in a new world of circumstances, passions, and affections. Sometimes it will be his province to track the subtle windings of fraud, pursuing its dark unwearied course beneath the tramplings of busy life—to develop in lucid array a little history, or cluster of histories, tending to one great disclosure—to combine fragments of scattered truths into a vivid picture, or to cast the light from numerous facts on secret guilt, and render it almost as palpable to belief as if disclosed to vision. At another time the honour or the life of man may tremble in his hands—he may be the last prop of sinking hope to the guilty, or the sole refuge clasped by the innocent; or, called on to defend the subject against the power of State prosecution, may give to the very forms and quibbles with which ancient liberty was fenced a dignity, and breathe over them a magic power. Sometimes it will be his privilege to pierce through the darkness of time, guided by mouldering charters and heroic names; or, tracing out the fibres of old relationships, to explore dim monuments and forgotten tombs, retracing with anxious gaze those paths of common life which have been so lightly trodden as to retain faint impress of the passenger. One day he may touch the heart with sympathy for the ' pangs of despised love,' or glow indignantly at the violation of friendship, and ask for wrongs beyond all appreciation as much money as the pleader's imagination has dared to claim as damages; the next he may implore commiseration for human frailty, and preach nothing but charity and forgiveness. The sentiment of antiquity, the dawnings of hope, the sanctity of the human heart in its strength and its weakness, are among the subjects presented in rapid succession to his grasp, with the opportunity sometimes in moments of excitement, when his audience are raised by the solemnity of the occasion above the level of their daily thoughts, to give hints of beauty and grace which may gleam for a moment only, but will never be forgotten by his delighted hearers."

This pleasing and animated picture of the variety of subjects which occupy the mind of an advocate in considerable business, is no doubt a very true picture, so far as it goes.   To complete its fidelity, however, it should be added not only that all these various processes of the intellect and emotions of the feelings, are called forth merely in the way of business, and have very little, if anything, to do with an ardent desire that truth and justice should prevail; but also, that the energy with which the arguments of the advocate are brought forward, and the pathos with which his sympathies are expressed, very often depend upon the amount of the fee received, or the importance of the solicitor by whom the brief has been furnished.   Such is human nature.   Further to complete the truthfulness of the picture, it would be necessary to say that the advocate finds it very often needful, or expedient, to attack as well as to defend, and that on such occasions he is not apt to be very scrupulous, or to confine his vituperation within the limits of his knowledge or his convictions.   Many a man has been wounded to the heart by observations of counsel who neither knew nor cared for the pain they were inflicting, but only thought how they might add a chance to the turning of the decision in their favour.   The same careless cruelty even more frequently appears in the cross-examination of witnesses, and one hears with indignation a man belonging to what is called " a liberal profession" occupying himself in a way which, morally considered, is not a whit more respectable, in my opinion, than the occupation of those who worked the screws and pulleys of the torture-chambers of bygone ages.   It appears to me that in a

court of justice, every man who is allowed to take part in
the proceedings should have justice ever in view, whether
he be a presiding judge or an advocate of one side.   Nor
do I think that this rule, however strictly observed, would
too much circumscribe the office of the advocate, or limit
his usefulness to clients in matters contested before the
tribunals.   To develop the whole truth of a case, and to
press upon a judge or jury those views of the facts and
of the law applicable to them, which in strict justice they
ought to consider, but which might have escaped a less
astute intellect or a less careful vigilance than that of the
advocate, is a worthy office for a man of understanding
and of honour.   Nor should I have any objection to the
peculiar prominence which the advocate would naturally
give to arguments in favour of the side for which he
pleads, provided all were done fairly, and there were no
attempt to gain a cause by maintaining either as fact or
as law what the advocate himself did not believe, or to
filch from prejudiced or ignorant men a verdict by playing
upon their weakness instead of appealing to their judgment.   I have sometimes thought that it would be well
to have judges who had not been advocates, and who had
not been taught by habit to tolerate the artifices of advocacy which are at war with justice.   If that were possible,
I should hope that the authority of the Court would be
interposed more frequently and decisively than it is, to
check the licentiousness of counsel, and to keep their
exertions more within the bounds of justice and humanity,
while encouraging them in every effort to assist in the
development of truth and in the elevation of the tone of
judicial investigation.   It must be admitted, however,
that there is no such school for acquiring a competent
knowledge both of law and of the general affairs of mankind, as that which the eminent barrister's practice sup-

plies, and it is not easy to conceive how such information as it is desirable the judges should possess could otherwise be obtained.

It is obvious that the business of advocacy in important causes affords almost unlimited occasion for the use of every species of ability, and almost boundless opportunity for bringing every resource of knowledge into effective action. If the first requisites be knowledge of law, and energetic acuteness in applying that knowledge to the circumstances of the controversy, it must be admitted that, while they are the surest foundations of success, there are many other things necessary to the full structure of an advocate's qualifications. What is an advocate without eloquence? And yet even eloquence is no less "fatal" at the Bar than elsewhere, unless it be tempered with knowledge and governed by discretion. There cannot be a greater nuisance at the Bar, or a more dangerous aid to clients, than a man who thinks to carry everything before him by a flashy speech—a man who trusts to exaggeration of sentiment and gaudiness of language, rather than to knowledge, good sense, energy, and a well moderated appeal to the feelings. On the other hand, there is even a lower sort of legal advocate, though not quite so unsafe—the mere technical lawyer, who pleads causes in the spirit of a copying-clerk—a kind of forensic tradesman, who quotes cases, and makes much ado about forms, without the capacity of understanding the full bearing of the facts which are before him, or of feeling how they may be made to tell upon the judgment of the Court, or upon the sensibilities of the jury. Clients who would give their cause a fair chance must equally beware of the empty adventurer, who relies on his powers of making a florid and fanciful harangue, and of the dull plodder, who depends upon throwing over his adversary upon some matter of form culled from obsolete rules of special pleading.

The Bar was in former times considered the great school of oratory; but that lofty department of human skill, to the perfection of which the highest gifts of natural genius and the nicest strokes of cultivated art are equally necessary, does not flourish in this intellectual age. Though the highest oratory is addressed to the intellect, yet the appeal is made through the emotions of the heart. I do not mean that it is to the sensibilities that the great orator merely or chiefly addresses himself. That is an inferior style, which may find a wider though a less worthy audience. But there is a class of mental emotions connected with high effort, and the key-note of these emotions the gifted orator knows how to touch. He speaks of duty, honour, patriotism, glory; and his voice, like the sound of a trumpet, rouses the hearts of men, and fills them with lofty aspirations. Thence the orator proceeds to the intellect, and shows what is to be done that these noble desires of the mind may be fulfilled. But life at present is either too full of the details of business, or too completely abandoned to the enjoyment of ease and pleasure, to afford opportunity for this high oratory. At the Bar, at all events, it seems out of place; and though a great deal of time is wasted in wrangling about minute points of legal practice, it seems as though there were none to spare for the loftier description of forensic eloquence.

Even in Ireland, which seemed at one time the natural soil of oratory, the decay of it is manifest. A distinguished member of the Irish Bar tells me that it has become " more practical—more businesslike—than it was. The juniors know more *cases;* but the want of great men, such as Plunket, Bushe, Curran, Joy,

O'Grady, Saurin, Pennefather, Burton, is awfully certain, and dismally visible." Nor is this all; therefore, adds my informant—" therefore, the minister has less respect for the profession, and the public less protection from the arts of patronage and corruption." Thus does it happen always and everywhere, that an ignoble despotism gradually arises upon the ruins of energetic intellect and generous public spirit.

Among the excuses for judicial errors or short-comings, Bishop Sanderson (who was possessed of a " learned spirit of human dealing," as well as of Divine things) places the skill on the one hand, or the deficiency on the other, of those who state the case. " Because," says he, " there is mostly in every man's tale a mixture of some falsehoods with some truths, whereby it may so happen sometimes that he which hath in truth the more equity on his side, by the mingling in some easily discoverable falsehoods in telling his tale, may render his cause the more suspicious to him that heareth it, to think the whole tale naught; and he that hath indeed, and upon the whole matter, the worst cause, may yet, by the weaving in some evident truths or pregnant probabilities in the telling of his tale, gain such credit with him that heareth it, that he will be very inclinable to believe the whole tale to be good. Or, howsoever, they may be both so equally false, or at least both so equally doubtful, as no one that heareth them can well tell whether of both to give credit to." And, again, in a higher strain he speaks in direct terms, of advocacy, of its glory and of its shame. " Add hereunto," he exclaims, " the great advantage or disadvantage that may be given to a cause in the pleading by the artificial insinuations of a powerful orator. That same *flaxanimis Pitho*, and *Suadæ medulla*, as some of the old heathens termed it, that winning and persuasive

faculty that dwelleth in the tongues of some men, whereby
they are able not only to work strongly upon the affections of men, but to arrest their judgments also, and to
incline them whither way they please, is an excellent
endowment of nature, or rather, to speak more properly,
an excellent gift of God, which whosoever hath received,
is by so much the more bound to be truly thankful to
him that gave it, and to do him the best service he can
with it, by how much he is enabled thereby to gain more
glory to God, and to do more good to human society
than most of his brethren are. And the good blessing
of God be upon the heads of all those, be they few or
many, that use their eloquence aright, and employ their
talent in that kind *for the advancement of justice*, the
quelling of oppression, the repressing and discountenancing of insolence, and the encouraging and protecting
of innocence. But what shall I say then of those, be
they many or few, that abuse the gracefulness of their
elocution (good speakers, but to ill purposes) to enchant
the ears of an easy magistrate with the charms of a fluent
tongue; or to cast a mist before the eyes of a weak jury,
as jugglers may sport with country-people, to make white
seem black, or black seem white; so setting a fair varnish
upon a rotten post, and a smooth gloss upon a coarse
cloth; as Protagoras sometimes boasted that he could
make a bad cause good when he listed; by which means
judgment is perverted, the hands of violence and robbery
strengthened, the edge of the sword of justice abated,
great offenders acquitted, gracious and virtuous men
molested and injured. I know not what fitter reward to
wish them for their pernicious eloquence as their best
deserved fee, than to remit them over to what David hath
assigned them in Psalm cxx.—" What reward shall be
given or done unto thee, O thou false tongue? Even

mighty and sharp arrows, with hot burning coals." *
By the artifices of advocacy, and by sundry other means,
some of which he enumerates, and others which, " in
regard of their number and his inexperience, he is not
able to recite," the Preacher says, " it may come to pass
that the light of truth may be so clouded and the beams
thereof intercepted from the eyes of the most circumspect
magistrate, that he cannot at all times clearly discern the
equity of those causes that are brought before him."

Noble, indeed, would the calling of the advocate be, if
he were truly and in good faith what, in a recent judicial
address, counsel at the Bar were politely described to be,
namely, the assistants of the court in truly declaring the
law and rightly administering justice.   Who will not say
" Amen " to the prayer of the good Bishop Sanderson,
that the blessing of God may be upon the heads of those
who use their eloquence aright, and employ their talent
in that kind, for the advancement of justice, the quelling
of oppression, the discountenancing of insolence, and the
encouraging and protecting of innocence ?   But the profession of advocacy is one which notoriously takes little
account of justice ; and I myself know that nothing is
more common than the boast of barristers, that they have
saved clients from the penalties due to their indiscretions,
or the punishment which moral justice would have
awarded to their crimes.   The barrister, acting as an
advocate, hesitates not to say that his concern is only with
one side, and his business is to obtain success for that
side, whether he believes it to be in the right or in the
wrong.   The care of the interests of Justice, according to
his theory, is left with the judge.   The interests which he

---

* Sermons *ad Magistratum*.   Second Sermon.   Preached at Lincoln,
1630.

has to take care of are *those of his client*.   The pride of
Protagoras is the ordinary pride of advocacy in Westminster Hall and elsewhere ; but it must be ever worthy
of that denunciation of the sacred poet to which it is left
by Bishop Sanderson in the foregoing quotation.

CHAPTER XXIX.

SOLICITORS AND ATTORNEYS.

DESCENDING from the controversies which are determined in the high courts of law and equity, to the more ordinary business of life in which legal advice and direction are found necessary, we come to the class of practitioners called Attorneys or Solicitors. The number at present in the London Law-list is about three thousand, nearly double what the number was forty years ago. It is probable that five-sixths of the whole are actually candidates for business. They are of various grades, from the low, rapacious pettifogger, who grasps at three-and-sixpenny fees, and is something between the common cur and bull-dog of the law, up to the finished gentleman, who has in his hands the most important affairs, and is professionally acquainted with the most delicate secret histories of the first families in the land. There are many persons of some substance, and some worldly consideration, who pass through the troubles and pleasures of life without having occasion to seek barristerial services, at all events without requiring the advocacy of a barrister in open court; but every one who possesses, or has possessed, or has hoped to possess property, must have had to do with a lawyer, which is the name popularly applied to attorneys and solicitors. No business, almost, can go on without the aid of this profession. Every public office, every joint-stock company, every corporation, every guild, every vestry, every association, whether charitable or uncharitable, every institution for the getting of money or the spending it, every private individual who has bought or sold a house, or had a quarrel with a refractory serving-man, must have an attorney. When anything concerning property is to be settled or unsettled, it is he who dictates what is to be done, or warns us what we shall not do. Other people may have general notions of what is right, but he points out the way and settles the form. He comprehends what it is that means something, and what means nothing, in agreements, leases, contracts, and so forth. He is translator-general of law language, and receives his fee for interpreting in the vernacular tongue the papers which he has been paid for preparing, with due attention to legal language, in his back office. No man should know as well as he does " the intricate stuff quarrels are made of." It is he who " takes instructions " to begin the battle of law, and pile up the dreadful accumulation of " costs," which will one day descend like an avalanche upon the adversary, or recoil with no less destructive weight upon the mover of the controversy. It is he who proceeds step by step, doing many things of which nothing but the expense is in the smallest degree intelligible to the client, and even that is perhaps only known when it is too late to say " hold your hand." It is he who, after having explained at the beginning how sure you were to have redress, is bound to explain towards the conclusion that redress is very doubtful, if not hopeless, and that the most prudent course will be to pay the costs and rest content. To every man and every community the legal adviser is a person of very considerable importance; and, in fact, no serious step can be taken without him, for it is his business to make everything *safe*, so far as circumstances will allow of safety being secured.

The position of those leading solicitors who have the affairs of great personages in their management is really very curious. They stand in the place which is, or rather which was, occupied by Father Confessors in Roman Catholic countries, and scarcely any important family step can be taken without their advice and assistance. With respect to property—it is in most, if not in all great families, the subject of formal arrangement by legal deeds or settlements expressed in language which no one thoroughly comprehends, and which men of the legal profession alone affect to understand. The persons chiefly interested in those arrangements know the general results of them, or what were intended to be the general results ; but the instruments on which these results depend are not intelligible to them, and if they wish to make any new dispositions of their properties, they cannot stir a single step without the solicitor to guide them. Now when people have property, almost every important act on their own part, or that of any of their family, is concerned either with getting or giving money, or money's worth, and the solicitor necessarily becomes a confidential agent in family arrangements. If a son has been extravagant, or a daughter is going to be married, the worthy head of the house knows not what to do till he has stated the case to his solicitor. And these are among the simplest matters in which his advice is required. Perhaps in no walk of life in England are there to be found men of such exquisite discretion as these professional advisers of great families. Their legal knowledge constitutes the least part of their value. They have the nicest appreciation of the prudent, the becoming, and the practicable ; and their legal lore is in many cases only made use of in

giving due form and validity to arrangements which are
based on circumstances and considerations that at first
sight *seem* to be wholly out of the province of the lawyer.
Having become confidential advisers in questions where
property is concerned, they are often called upon in respect to disagreements, doubts, suspicions, and other
domestic troubles, where a calm, impartial judgment is
required, and perfect secrecy may be depended upon.
Some of them might tell very strange histories of confi-
dences no less strange, for your solicitor is the only man
who is enabled by his professional conscience so to identify
himself with his "principal," that he will make nothing
known that is confided to him professionally, no matter
what interests, beyond those of his client, may be concerned. If some man or woman—it may be of rank or
wealth—having committed some great offence, goes to
confess to the parson of the parish, the reverend gentleman may probably deem it his bounden duty to call in
the police, or to inform the injured party, as the case
may be. Not so the solicitor. He advises, soothes, and
lays down the doctrine of *discretion*, which he considers
applicable to the circumstances. Solicitors are the priests
of the *Numen Prudentia*, and thereby many of them
become very important and very rich. As regards morality, the same inconvenience or evil belongs to the
system in which they are the prime movers, as does to
the system of acting by trustees, or any other representation of the interests of an individual by persons who are
not representatives of his conscience. I am far from
saying that respectable solicitors take no account of what
a man is in honour and conscience bound to do, as well
as in law and in prudence. They generally consider
what is becoming to a man in the station which he
occupies and in the circumstances with which he has to

deal. Following that rule, they cannot set aside the obligations of honour and conscience. But passions, and affections, and generous emotions are the natural auxiliaries of conscientiousness, especially when it is to be exercised among persons connected by blood or affinity, and these the solicitor keeps at a distance. He may give a cold opinion as to what might be considered generous, but his business is to advise what is prudent, and to keep his clients on their guard against emotion. And this is another reason why so much is committed to confidential solicitors, for great or rich personages are glad of an escape from the disturbance of what they call " a scene," meaning thereby any occurrence in which the passions or feelings are strongly moved ; and they take refuge from such agitation under the cold shade of professional advice. It is, moreover, but too true that while the eminent professional adviser will generally, if left to himself, either do, or recommend to be done, that which is reasonable and becoming under the circumstances, yet he is not so independent but that he will yield himself in some degree to be the instrument of his employer's anger, or enmity, or prejudice, if the employer be rich, and insist upon that course being taken. Whatever he does will, of course, be done in a respectable manner, and with due regard to professional rules ; but many things which are harsh and domineering, and even unjust, may be done in this way ; and the proud and unfeeling man of wealth will not find much difficulty in obtaining even the most eminent aid to carry out his views, if he be willing—as he generally is—that a decorous and formal manner shall pervade the proceedings, however severe in their substance and cruel in their intention. Whether in such cases the professional adviser charges anything more in his bill, for the pain his mind may have undergone in giving vigour to insensibility, or activity to malevolence, my researches have not been able to discover.

An attorney-at-law, says Blackstone, answers to the *procurator* or proctor of the civilians and canonists. And he is one who is put in the place, stead, or turn of another, to manage his matters of law. Attorneys are admitted to the execution of their office by the superior Courts of Westminster Hall, and are in all points officers of the respective courts in which they are admitted, and as they have many privileges on that account, so they are peculiarly subject to the censure and animadversion of the judges. No man can practise as an attorney in those courts unless he be admitted and sworn an attorney of that particular court. But the greater number of attorneys are solicitors also, and that title seems to be preferred as one of greater dignity. To practise in the Court of Chancery, it is necessary to be admitted as a "solicitor" therein, but the qualifications are just the same as those of "attorney" in the Courts of Common Law. A solicitor is an attorney who has been admitted to practise in the Court of Chancery.

In ancient times every suitor in the Courts of Law was obliged to appear in person to prosecute or defend his suit, according to the old Gothic constitution, unless by special licence of exemption, under the Royal letters patent. The rule still applies to criminal cases. And an idiot, says Blackstone, " cannot to this day appear by attorney, but in person, for he hath not discretion to enable him to appoint a proper substitute : and upon his being brought before the court in so defenceless a condition, the judges are bound to take care of his interests, and they shall admit the best plea in his behalf that any one present can suggest. But as in the Roman law *cum olim in usu fuisset, alterius nomine agi non posse, sed, quia hoc non minimam incommoditatem habebat, cœperunt homines per procuratores litigare;* so with us, upon the same principle of convenience, it is now permitted in general by divers ancient statutes, whereof the first is statute Westm. 2, c. 10, that attorneys may be made to prosecute or defend any action in the absence of the parties to the suit." It was settled by Act of Parliament, 2 Geo. II. c. 23, that every person admitted an attorney should have served as a clerk to an attorney for five years, and it seems the rule was that no change of clerkship should be allowed, for the Court of King's Bench thought themselves bound to strike an attorney off the roll of attorneys of that Court, who had served part of the time with another master, but with the consent of the first.   A clerk in this capacity is called an "articled clerk," and he who is going through this preliminary clerkship is said to be "serving his articles."   Sometimes large fees are paid to masters with the articled clerks to whom they are to teach the art and mystery of attorney-ship.   When it first became a rule that no one should be admitted an attorney without an examination in Latin, it is said that a young examinant of more wit than dis-cretion, on being asked to translate Juvenal's apothegm, *Nemo repente fuit turpissimus,* answered, "It takes five years to make an attorney"!   The 1 & 2 Geo. IV. c. 48, enables graduates at Oxford, Cambridge, or Dublin to practise as attorneys after having served a clerkship of only three years, and persons bound to attorneys as articled clerks may serve a part of that time, not exceed-ing a year, with a barrister or special pleader.   So early as the statute 4 Hen. IV. c. 18, it was enacted that attorneys should be examined by the judges, and none admitted but such as were *virtuous, learned, and sworn to do their duty*   Notwithstanding this precaution to make sure of virtue, learning, and dutifulness, in attorneys, it seems that they very soon got into ill odour, for an Act of Parliament, 33 Hen. VI. c. 7, states that not long before that time there had not been more than six or eight attorneys in Norfolk and Suffolk, *quo tempore*, it observes, *magna tranquillitas regnabat*, but that the number had increased to twenty-four, to the great vexation and prejudice of these counties. It therefore enacts that for the future there shall only be six attorneys in Norfolk, six in Suffolk, and two in the city of Norwich.

This prejudice against attorneys has descended to the present day, and, some say, not without good reason. I have heard a man of much experience of the world remark that many attorneys are excellent and amiable men, apart from business, but the moment they become *professional* their good feelings appear to be laid aside, and their sole object to be the taking of every advantage which the law will permit.*

---

* " You hesitate between the professions of theology and medicine. Morally and intellectually, both are wholesome studies for one who enters upon them with a sound heart and a proper sense of duty. I should not say the same of the law, for that must, in my judgment, be always more or less injurious to the practitioner."—*Southey to Herbert Hill, Feb.* 5, 1831.

CHAPTER XXX.

THE PEASANTRY.

THERE are but few subjects of human knowledge with which " the intelligent classes " in this inquiring age are less conversant than the actual condition of the English Peasantry.   Something is known of the interior of Africa, and shrewd surmises exist as to the geological structure of the moon ; the hieroglyphics of ancient Egypt are read and interpreted ; and the learned begin to be acquainted with the mysteries of Hindu polity, and the details of Assyrian civilization ; but of English peasant life the notions which exist are in the last degree dim and obscure, save among those who seldom approach what is called " Society." *   Formerly the idea of English rusticity was made up of several things, such as rude health, a great appetite for bread and bacon, a comfortable cottage, rosy children, and freedom from care. The peasant, according to general opinion, was Goldsmith's peasant of the olden time :—

---

* " With regard to the general condition of the agricultural labourer, I believe the public to be less informed, or worse informed, than about that of any other class of society. His most common vices are, it is true, pretty well known ; but the hardships of his life at best, its temptations, the hindrances to its improvement, the scanty remuneration afforded to him for his hardest labour, these are parts of his condition on which the public are not so well informed, or at least of which they seem to act in perfect ignorance."—*Rev. S. G. Osborne to the Assistant Poor-Law Commissioner.*

" For him light labour spread her wholesome store,
    Just gave what life required, but gave no more ;
    His best companions innocence and health,
    And his best riches ignorance of wealth."

Of late years it has become known that this picture is
one which rather accommodates itself to the desires of the
mind than to the true state of the case ; but what that
true state is, few have cared to inquire. The severe
truth of Crabbe led him to present to the world different
views of peasant life from those of the poetic tribe who
had gone before him. He knew, as John Wilson says,
" what direful tragedies are for ever steeping in tears or
in blood the footsteps of the humblest of our race, and he
has opened, as it were, a theatre on which the homely
actors that pass before us assume no disguise—on which
every catastrophe borrows its terrors from truth, and
every scene seems shifted by the very hands of Nature."
Among many of his sketches of peasant life, this is one
which perhaps takes the widest scope. He turns his view
from the sea-shore to the country :—

" But yet in other scenes, more fair in view,
    When Plenty smiles—alas ! she smiles for few—
    And those who taste not, yet behold her store,
    Are as the slaves that dig the golden ore—
    The wealth around them makes them doubly poor.
    Or will you deem them amply paid in health,
    Labour's fair child, that languishes with wealth ?
    Go then ! and see them rising with the sun,
    Through a long course of daily toil to run ;
    See them beneath the dog-star's raging heat,
    When the knees tremble and the temples beat,
    Behold them leaning on their scythes, look o'er
    The labour past, and toils to come explore ;
    See them alternate suns and showers engage,
    And hoard up aches and anguish for their age,
    Through fens and marshy moors their steps pursue,
    When their warm pores imbibe the evening dew ;
    Then own that labour may as fatal be
    To these thy slaves, as thine excess to thee."

But suppose them to have health, still that is not happiness. The rich man who longs for the health that gives hunger has no sense of the pain that hunger gives to those who have enough of good health, but not enough of good food :—

> " Yet grant them health; 'tis not for us to tell,
> Though the head droops not, that the heart is well;
> Or will you praise that homely, healthy fare,
> Plenteous and plain, that happy peasants share?
> Oh! trifle not with woes you cannot feel,
> Nor mock the misery of a stinted meal;
> Homely, not wholesome, plain, not plenteous, such
> As you who praise would never deign to touch.
>   Ye gentle souls who dream of rural ease,
> Whom the smooth stream and smoother sonnet please;
> Go! if the peaceful cot your praises share,
> Go, look within, and ask if peace be there;
> If peace be his—that drooping weary sire,
> Or theirs, that offspring round their feeble fire;
> Or hers, that matron pale, whose trembling hand
> Turns on the wretched hearth th' expiring brand."

This is the shadow of the picture, but scarcely any state of life is *altogether* so sad as this, and assuredly peasant life is not the worst. Even Crabbe can paint it in much more cheerful colours :—

> " Behold the cot! where thrives the industrious swain,
> Source of his pride, his pleasure, and his gain;
> Screen'd from the winter's wind, the sun's last ray
> Smiles on the window, and prolongs the day:
> Projecting thatch the woodbine's branches stop,
> And turn their blossoms to the casement's top:
> All need requires is in that cot contained,
> And much that taste untaught and unrestrained
> Surveys delighted."

Enough, however, of poetry for the present. Let me now turn to the most prosaic of all prose literature, the Blue Books. I have already, with reference to the subject of education, quoted the Reports of the Assistant Poor-Law Commissioners, who were sent into different districts of England to inquire into the employment of women and children in agriculture. Their reports contain a vast quantity of information as to practical peasant life. Here are the examinations of a few poor persons that might be taken for Crabbe turned into prose, or for the notes jotted down by him before commencing his descriptive poems. First comes Mrs. Smart, who, before she was married, had been both a cook and a housemaid, and probably fared, if not sumptuously, at least abundantly, every day. Behold her now, the mistress of a family !

" I went out (gleaning) this autumn for three weeks, and was *very lucky* : I got six bushels of corn. I got up at two o'clock in the morning, and got home at seven at night. My other girls, aged ten, fifteen, and eighteen, went with me. We leased* in the neighbourhood, and sometimes as far as seven miles off.

" I have had thirteen children, and have brought seven up. I have been accustomed to work in the fields at hay-time and harvest. Sometimes I have had my mother, and sometimes my sister, to take care of the children, or I could not have gone out. I have gone to work at seven in the morning till six in the evening ; in harvest sometimes much later, but it depends on circumstances. Women with a family cannot be ready so soon as the men, and must be home earlier, and therefore they do not work so many hours. In making hay I have been strained with the work : I have felt it sometimes for weeks ; so bad sometimes, I could not get out of my chair. In leasing, in bringing home the corn, I have hurt my head, and have been made deaf by it. Often, out of the hay-fields,

---

* Gleaned.

myself and my children have come home with our things
quite wet through; I have gone to bed for an hour for my
things to get a little dry, but have had to put them on
again when quite wet.   My health is very good now.

"We pay 7*l.* a year rent for our cottage and large
garden.   There are three rooms in the cottage, two bed-
rooms in which we have three beds; and we find great
difficulty in sleeping our family.   When we wash our
sheets, we must have them dry again by night.   In the
garden we raise plenty of potatoes.   We have about a
shilling's worth of meat a-week; a pig's melt sometimes,
a pound or three-quarters of a pound of suet.   Seven
gallons of bread a-week; sometimes a little pudding on a
Sunday.   I can cook a little.   I was, before I was married, housemaid, and afterwards cook, in a family."

This poor woman's husband earned 15*s.* a-week when
employed, but his employment was not regular.   Her
own wages, when she "went out," were 10*d.* or 1*s.* a-day.
Hers appears indeed to have been a life of hard work,
without a cheerful spirit.   Yet probably she had her hour
of triumph and of joy when she brought home her six
bushels of corn, the result of her gleaning.

The next is a case of darker misery, yet there is a
sunny gleam upon it too.   Who could suppose so much
good to result from a teetotaller's lecture.   The story of
" Mrs. Britton " is this :—

" I am forty-one years old.   I have lived at Calne all
my life.   I went to school till I was eight years old, when
I went out to look after children.   At ten years old I
went to work at a Factory, where I was till I was twenty-
six.   My husband is an agricultural labourer.   I have
seven children, all boys.   The eldest is fourteen, the
youngest three-quarters of a year old.   My husband is a
good workman, and does most of his work by the lump,

and earns from 9s. to 10s. a-week pretty constantly, but finds his own tools—his wheelbarrow, which cost 20s., pickaxe 3s., and scoop 3s.

" I have worked in the fields, and when I went out I left the children in the care of the eldest boy, and frequently carried the baby with me, as I could not go home to nurse it. I have worked at haymaking and at harvest, and at other times in weeding and keeping the ground clean. I generally work from half-past seven till five or half-past. When at work in the spring I have received 10d. a-day; but 8d. or 9d. is more common. My master always paid 10d. When working, I never had any beer, and I never felt the want of it. I never felt that my health was hurt by the work. Haymaking is hard work; very fatiguing, but it never hurt me. Working in the fields is not such hard work as working in the factory. I am always better when I can get out to work in the fields. I intend to do so next year if I can. Last year I could not go out, owing to the birth of the baby. My eldest boy gets a little to do : he don't earn more than 9d. a week : he has not enough to do. My husband has forty lugs of land, for which he pays 10s. a-year. We grow potatoes and a few cabbages, but not enough for our family ; for that we should like to have forty lugs more. We have to buy potatoes. One of the children is a cripple, and the guardians allow us two gallons of bread a-week for him. We buy two gallons more, according as the money is. Nine people can't do with less than four gallons of bread a-week. We could eat much more bread if we could get it; sometimes we can afford only one gallon a-week. We very rarely buy butcher's fresh meat, certainly not oftener than once a-week, and not more than six pennyworth. I like my husband to have a bit of meat now he has left off drinking. I buy half a pound of butter a-week, one ounce of tea, half a pound of sugar. The rest of our food is potatoes with a little fat. The rent of our cottage is 1s. 6d. a-week; there are two rooms in it. We all sleep in one room under the tiles. Sometimes we receive private assistance, especially in clothing. Formerly my husband was in the habit of drinking, and every thing went bad. He used to beat me. I have often gone to bed, I and my children, without supper, and have had no breakfast the next morning, and frequently no firing. My husband attended a lecture on teetotalism one evening about two years ago, and *I have reason to bless that evening.* My husband has never touched a drop of drink since. He has been in better health; getting stouter, and has behaved like a good husband to me ever since. I have been much more comfortable, and the children happier. He works better than he did. He can mow better, and that is hard work, and he does not mind being laughed at by the other men for not drinking. I send my eldest boy to Sunday-school; them that are younger go to the day-school. My eldest boy never complains of work hurting him. My husband now goes regularly to Church, formerly he could hardly be got there."

To me there appears to be something not only instructive, but very touching, in all this. It seems to bear out the judgment of a Mr. Watts, of Over-Stowey, Somersetshire, in a letter to the Commissioner, stating that what experience he had obtained of the labouring population had given him, on the whole, a favourable opinion of them, in comparison with those immediately above them; and that, considering the scantiness of their diet, and their insufficient clothing, their health and strength of body, their activity of mind, and contented cheerfulness, were to him very surprising. I agree with Mr. Watts, and yet

so far as I have seen of English labourers' cottages, the
seeming want of cheerfulness was even more distressing
than the absence of material comforts. In other countries, the philosophy of living on little, with a cheerful
heart, is, I think, more generally attained than in England; but then in England the people labour exceedingly
hard, and for a little money, which is soon expended.
I long to see them labouring upon something which is
their own, and giving only part of their time to labouring
for hire. As it is, masters might do more than they generally do, both by words of kindness to those they employ,
and by warning them against vices which produce so
much domestic misery. The reward of drink to working
people is common, and it has an air of hospitality that I
should be sorry to lose, if it were not for the tremendous
danger of fostering the habit of tippling and intoxication.
But no one who has any influence over the working classes
of society can use it to more advantage than in discou-
raging drunkenness—the fruitful source of every kind of
degradation and wretchedness. A labourer gave evidence
to the Commissioner respecting drinking habits, and the
benefits of being with a master who encouraged men to
look to other rewards instead of drink. This man, George
Small, of Othery, says—

" I work for Mr. Somers. I have always done all sorts
of farm-work. I have laboured hard, but I find my health
now just as good as when I used to have cider. I don't
find any difference. I can work just as well as those that
drink. Last summer I mowed, with two men, from four
in the morning till eight at night; it was job-work. They
drank; I did not. They drank a gallon and a half
each, but I did my share of the work as well as theirs;
quite as well as they did. We were paid in money,
3*s*. 4*d*. each a-day, during the mowing. They drank

their cider, and I had my potato-ground at home. I have
gone on this way for four years. They call me all kinds
of names, and laugh at me for not going to the cider-
shop; but I laugh at them, and ask if they have paid
their rent, as I have.

" Mr. Somers pays me as much as other labourers get,
only instead of cider he lets me have half an acre of
potato-ground. He dresses the ground, and I put in the
seed and dig up the potatoes; my wife and family help.
Mr. Somers draws them. I wish all masters did as Mr.
Somers does; for I think, if the labourers didn't drink so
much, they and their families would get more to eat. I
generally get one pound of bacon a-week; sometimes a
little bit of meat, but seldom. We drink tea and coffee,
and at dinner treacle and water. I keep two pigs now.
Sometimes when I kill a pig I keep a piece for myself.

" It is eight years since I had any relief from the
parish. If I had been in the habit of drinking, my family
would have been in rags. I am sure the liquor would
have been doing me no good; but, without the potato-
ground, we could not have gone on. I think the liquor
is a *matter of form.*

" I went to work when I was nine years old. I had
1*s.* a-week, and three cups of cider a-day. If I had a
boy out at work, I had rather the cider was turned into
cheese. It is a bad thing for the young boys to learn to
drink as they do; it is as bad with girls nearly. My
eldest daughter is eighteen years old; the summer before
last she went out to harvest, and had half a gallon of
cider a-day.* The farmers think people work harder
with so much cider. I don't think they do. Women

---

* " Women do not always drink their cider; they bring it home and
give it their husbands."—*Evidence of Mrs. Cozens.*

are often intoxicated at the end of the day, and young men and women, in drinking all this cider, get together in a very improper way."

Abstinence from drinking, and a disposition towards thrift, together with a pride in property—such as a chest full of linen, or the like, which characterised the peasantry of Scotland sixty years since—might do much for English labourers; but they are not educated to stint and pinch themselves for the sake of laying up a store. Their dependence in the last resort is not on themselves and on their savings, but on the parish. Nevertheless, the Vicar of Hilton, Dorsetshire, deposes that the character of the people is " patient, enduring, thankful, and civil; but, either from extreme poverty, or the habit from earliest youth of seeking their fuel in the woods or fields, they are rather given to pilfering."

But to return to the poor women, many of whom told their simple stories, which were all of them narratives of hard work, yet with a difference, showing the character of the narrator. Here is the story of Mary Hunt, a poor woman of apparently a pious spirit, combined with Amazonian strength :—

" I am in my fiftieth year. I have had twelve children; and, if it please God, I shall very soon have my thirteenth. I was left early without father and mother, with a crippled brother, whom I had to help to support. I began to work in the fields at sixteen. I had to work very hard, and got a good deal of lump work. I have earned as much as 2s. 6d. a-day at digging; but I was always considered a very hard worker. I married at twenty-two, and had to put up with a great deal with a young family, and have often had only salt and potatoes for days together. I was always better when out at work in the fields, and as for hard work, I never was hurt by it.

I have carried half a sack of peas to Chippenham, four miles, when I have been large in the family way. I have known what it is to work hard.

" I think it a much better thing for mothers to be at home with their children; they are much better taken care of, and other things go on better. I have always left my children to themselves, and, God be praised! nothing has ever happened to them, though I have thought it dangerous. I have many a time come home and have thought it a mercy to find nothing has happened to them. It would be much better if mothers could be at home, *but they must work.* Bad accidents often happen. I always hold to it to put out children early, and to bring them up to work; they do better. Families are better altogether when children go out regularly; the children are better than when kept at home, getting into all sorts of mischief."

This good woman's acquaintance with hard work seems to have made her in love with it. Work was in her view the best kind of education. It seems indeed to be the general feeling of the peasant class in England, at least everywhere south of the Trent, that education or schooling is to be held secondary to work; and that in no case is the opportunity of earning a little money, were it but a few pence per week, to be sacrificed for the sake of what may be attained at school.

Hitherto the details of humble peasant-life that have been given, have been connected with large families, so that the disciples of a certain school of political economy would perhaps attribute all the hardships that have been described to imprudent marriages. Let us glance then at a different condition. Here is the story of Mary Haynes, a Wiltshire widow: —

" I have been accustomed to work in the fields for the

last sixteen years, all the year through, except just the
winter months. I am employed in stone-picking, weeding, hay-making, reaping, turnip-hoeing, &c. I have
always been employed by the same master, who is particular in his labourers, and whom he pays well. I have
always received 5s. in summer, and 4s. 6d. in other
months, a week: those are the regular wages. I am a
good reaper, as good as many men; and in harvest, when
I have worked by the job, I have earned 2s., sometimes
2s. 6d. a-day, but only for a short time. The hours in
harvest depend on the work; at other times, from half-
past seven in the morning till five in the evening. I think
reaping the hardest of all the work I have ever done; it
makes me very stiff at first, but that goes off in a few
days. I always work in my stays, which get wet through,
and are still wet when I put them on again in the morning. My other clothes are also often wet when I take
them off, and are not dry when I put them on again in
the morning. I have not a change of clothes; but I have
never had my health affected by the hardness of the work
or damp things. In general, the women don't mix much
with the men whilst working in the fields, except at hay-
making. My master was always particular in choosing
respectable people to do his work. My husband worked
for the same master till he died, not long ago; and had
always 10s. a-week in summer, and 9s. in winter.

" I was married nine years before I had a child, and
never had but one, a boy, now about eight years old.
When my husband was alive we did very well, and lived
very comfortably; for then we had four gallons of bread
a-week, 1 lb. or 1½ lb. of cheese, bacon, salt beef, butter,
tea, sugar, candles, and soap, with beer on Saturday
night. Our master allowed my husband small beer
during work. Since my husband's death the guardians

allow 1*s.* 6*d.* a-week for the child ; and I earn 4*s.* 6*d.*
a-week. I pay—

					s.	*d.*	
For rent	.	.	.	.	1	6	a-week.
1½ gallons bread	.	.	.	.	1	6	„
½ lb. candles, ½ lb. soap	.	.	.	0	4½	„
¼ lb. butter	.	.	.	.	0	2¾	„
Tea	.	.	.	.	.	0	1½	„
½ lb. sugar	.	.	.	.	0	2	„
Rent of allotment	.	.	.	0	5¼	„
					4	4	„

The 1*s.* 8*d.* that is left goes for firing, shoes (which cost a
great deal), &c.   My husband hired fifty-four lugs of
land, and I continued it after his death ; without it I
could not get on.   It produces just potatoes enough for
me and my child ; also, this last year, three bushels of
wheat. I manage the ground entirely myself. My father
had a little property when I was young, and I was sent to
school. I was at school just two years. I was afterwards
maid-of-all-work with the master for whom I have always
since worked, and afterwards in the dairy. I have
always found that being maid-of-all-work was of great
use to me after I was married. The work was hard in
the dairy, but it never hurt me."

One of the Surrey witnesses says that the greatest
poverty and the worst moral habits in this part of the
country are to be found amongst the young men who
have no families. The beer shops and worse places are
much frequented by the young men.

The cases in Wiltshire must not be taken as fair speci-
mens of the general condition of the agricultural working
classes.   There is indeed too much poverty among these
classes all through the south-west of England ; but in
Wilts, and in Dorset too, there seems to be a want of that

English sturdiness which contends with adverse circumstances.   A kind of Irish fate seems to hang over the
lowest grade of the population, and they accept labour
and sorrow, overcrowding and unhealthiness, as their
destined portion.   A clergyman of Stourpaine, in Dorset,
says that, among the peasantry generally, the parents of
children not only do not exercise parental authority, but
do not even possess it.   " Ignorant and vicious themselves, what notion of the parental duties can they have?
What authority can they possess?   Such is the state of
things at present in Stourpaine, and, I am certain, in hundreds of other rural parishes.   For this I can divine no
other remedy than that the owners of lands or houses
should strenuously support parish or Sunday schools, and
exercise that influence which the sense of interest on the
part of their tenants gives them for the promotion of good
morals and religion.   Let the labouring class see that
they depend upon the observance of the decencies of life,
and moral and religious conduct, for employment and the
means of comfortable living—let them thus experience
the respective consequences of virtue and vice.   Till this
take place, ministers will labour and schools will exist,
and be attended to with little permanent good effect.   Let
everything be done that in fairness can be done for the
temporal comfort of the labouring classes, and then let
them be made to feel that their comfort depends on their
own conduct."   The worthy gentleman who recommends
this does not perhaps sufficiently estimate the trouble and
difficulty.   It is an exceedingly dangerous thing to
assume the power of discriminating between the good and
the bad, or to determine absolutely that virtue accom-
panies the outward show of it, or that he is really worst
who makes the worst appearance.

The farmers, and the servants who live in the house

with them, appear to live well enough.   They who suffer
hardships are the labourers, both male and female, who
work for wages, and live in cottages which they rent.   A
surgeon of Blandford deposes that "the food of the
labourer's family is bread and potatoes, with a little cheese
and bacon.   He has known many families who do not
taste butchers' meat from one year's end to the other.
He does not think there is deficiency of food, except in
special cases of distress, arising most frequently from
drunken habits, and such a general loss of character as
to interfere with profitable employment, or, in cases of
very large families, where the children are young; but
he thinks the quality of the food is low.   A great cause
of the present state of the labourer's cottage and way of
life is the want of instruction of the women of that class
in domestic economy.   The women have no knowledge of
cooking, or of anything else to increase the comforts of
their lives; the ignorance of the majority in common
culinary management and economy is excessive."

The Assistant-Commissioner who visited the south-west
says that the women of the agricultural class are in a
state of ignorance which affects the daily welfare and
comforts of their families.   They are ignorant of the
commonest things, needlework, cooking, and other matters
of domestic economy.   When any knowledge of such
things is possessed by the wife of a labourer, it is generally to be traced to the circumstance of her having before
marriage lived as a servant in a farmhouse or elsewhere.
" A girl brought up in a cottage until she marries is
generally ignorant of nearly everything she ought to be
acquainted with for the comfortable and economical
management of a cottage.   The effects of such ignorance
are seen in many ways, but in no one more striking than
in its hindering girls from getting out to service, as they

are not capable of doing anything that is required in a family of a better description. The further effect of this is, that not being able to find a place, a young woman goes into the fields to labour, with which ends all chance of her improving her position ; she marries, and brings up her daughters in the same ignorance, and their lives are a repetition of her own."

The working of a field-labourer's wife in the fields, frequently robs him of all home comforts. There is not the same order in his cottage, nor the same attention to his comforts, as when his wife remains at home. When the wife returns from her labour she has to look after her children, and her husband may have to wait for his supper. He may come home tired and wet ; he finds his vife has arrived but just before him ; she must give her attention to the children ; there is no fire, no supper, no comfort, and he goes to the beershop. But such is the depressed condition of the agricultural labourers in many districts, that the earnings of the women in field-labour cannot be done without.

Among the many causes of the degradation of the poorer classes, none appears to be of more pernicious effect than the confined and limited space in which families are obliged to dwell. In their sleeping apartments age and sex are mingled together, in such a manner as to be subversive of feelings of propriety and decency. The details of this subject cannot be gone into, but there is no complaint with regard to the condition of the peasantry so general as this. Even in the north, where the peasants are a careful, comfortable, economical, respectable class of people, large families are found with only one sleeping-room, and they very rarely have more than two, however numerous may be the sons and daughters.

The Commissioner for Kent, Surrey, and Sussex, after lamenting the difficulty of obtaining house-room, and the high scale of the rent of cottages, and the dangerous consequences of admitting strangers as lodgers, proceeds with the following observations :—

" Along with this close domestic intimacy, it must be mentioned too, as a circumstance prejudicial to the purity of relations between the sexes, that they have no public and social intercourse. They meet, indeed, at church and chapel, and at the fairs, but distinctions of sex are lost at divine service, and the crowd and confusion at fairs produce a privacy which is not beneficial, and is spoken of in some instances as ruinous. Whatever may be the cause of this—whether or not it be inseparable from poverty, which can afford no convivialities—it must be unfavourable to the general purity of manners that such rare opportunities exist for intercourse under circumstances where the natural instincts of the sexes would at once be gratified and controlled. In this point of view the occasional meeting of men and women at the gayer seasons, and lighter kinds of field-labour, is not, perhaps, without some utility. Their demeanour is open to public view, the intercourse is general, and the mind is preoccupied by labour from very criminal or dangerous indulgences. Entire seclusion fosters sensuality ; and it must not be forgotten that there are other immoral, cruel, and inhuman habits of mind to which it is known to contribute."

From the evidence taken upon oath, in Kent and Surrey, the following history of an agricultural lad is collected. The first occupation of boys on a corn farm is to keep rooks from the seed at spring and Michaelmas ; a boy usually begins this work at eight years of age, and is paid about fourpence a-day. About the same age he

is also fit to help his father a little in the barn at thresh-
ing.   Boys of this age are employed also to pick couch
after the plough at ploughing-time, but this is more commonly done in the summer, on the fallows.   The wages
for this work are generally about fivepence a-day.   The
usual time of work is as long as the boy can see in winter,
and, when daylight is longer, from six to six.   An hour
and a half is allowed for meals.   Boys of the same age
pick up potatoes for their father while he digs, and cut
off turnip-tops, or pull the turnips out of the ground, with
their mothers.   The fathers are paid for digging the
potatoes by the sack, the women for the turnips by the
acre.   In the latter case the woman's earnings on each
acre depend upon the crop.   She is paid from 10s. to 12s.
an acre, and may earn about 10d. a-day, or, with her boy,
about 15d. a-day.   A boy can earn about a penny more
in the day at piece-work than at day-work.   Boys of a
later age lead the horses at harrow and plough.   About
thirteen a boy may earn about 8d. a-day at this labour.
But between eight and thirteen a boy continues to do the
lighter work of couching and potato-picking, only for
higher pay than he receives at eight.   Boys from nine to
twelve are also employed in the sheep-folds, assisting at
the cutting and picking and carrying turnips, at about
6d. a-day.   Boys from nine years old to fifteen are often
hired to weed the corn from spring to harvest.   For this
their labour is in greater request than at any other time.
The farmers often desire more labour of this kind than
they can get.   Boys get for this work from 3s. to 5s. a-
week, according to their age, varying from nine to fifteen
years.   Women are paid more, but after the corn gets
high their dress is found inconvenient.

Here is an account of a sturdy young agriculturist who
at twelve years of age speaks as if he were quite accustomed to hard work:—

" I was twelve last Sunday. I work all the year round when it is dry. I lead the horse at plough sometimes, and always at harrow, and at *shim* in the hop-grounds. For all that I get 8*d.* a yoke : a yoke is from six to two, when the horses are taken out. I have my breakfast before I go. I have my dinner at two o'clock. After dinner I go and clean the horses ; this lasts an hour. I then feed them and go away about seven. I thresh too at the machine, and get 9*d.* a-day. Sometimes it goes all night, and for the day and night I get 18*d.* We then watch for three nights, and turn in for three days, that it (the corn) may get dry and hard. I get 8*d.* a-day for turning, and nothing for the night, for I am then only helping my father. I am now keeping cows off the corn at 6*d.* a-day. I get 8*d.* for weeding in the summer. I hull the hills in the hop-ground, and pole and dig, all with my father ; I do not know how much he gets for it. At all this we work from six to six ; half an hour is allowed for breakfast, and an hour for dinner. At day-work we take the half-hour before we begin. I never tie the hops, women tie them. I pick the hops from the ground, not from the bine as others do, and for this I am paid 1*s.* a-day. I work with the others from seven to six. I am paid 1*s.* 6*d.* for digging and for picking potatoes. I have three meals a-day. I have bread and cheese, and bread and butter, for breakfast ; and sometimes, but not often, bread and meat, or meat and potatoes, for dinner. We are eleven in all, there are five brothers and four sisters. We all sleep in one room except father and mother. There are three beds in one room, and there are four rooms. We pay 3*s.* a-week rent. We are badly off for clothes ; there are not many so bad off as we. I work keeping cows on a Sunday ; the others do not often go to church. I once went to school for a week.

I know that twice ten is twenty, because I have heard other boys say so. I cannot read. My mother goes out to work; one of my sisters goes out to work."

I doubt whether anywhere else in the world a similar relation of severe toil could be heard from a boy of only twelve years old; and let us remember it is in England all this happens—that country of which the intelligence is lauded every day, and especially by statesmen, as having discovered such wondrous mechanical substitutes for human labour. These statesmen would do well to refrain their lips from boasting, until they can show that the labouring classes have to endure less toil and less privation than was their lot before machine labour swelled the fortunes of the manufacturers and merchants.

Here is the deposition of another hard-working lad, whose habitual exercise appears to have given him a very considerable relish for " victuals." He says,—

" My father is dead. My mother lives at Wincheap. I work in the fields when I can get work. The day before yesterday I was digging. I dig from daylight till dark. I have an hour for dinner in the middle of the day. I breakfast before I start, and earn 8*d.* in the day. In the summer when the wheat is up I weed the corn; I get 6*d.* a-day for that. I sometimes lead the horse at plough, and get 8*d.* I get 6*d.* only for couching. It is not so hard as digging, or leading the horse at plough. I could not get any bird-scaring this year; 6*d.* is the price of that a-day. I got 8*d.* at poling, for poling the hops. I picked hops; I do not know how much I got for that. I have had no digging in the hop-grounds since my father died. I cut wheat and beans this year with my mother; I do not know how much my mother got: they cut wheat and such as that by the acre. At beans we reap as soon as we like. It don't do to cut

wheat early if there has been any damp—till eight or
nine : we never begin before eight at any time. If we
could get two or three *cants* we would cut beans at two
in the morning, and on till dark. I have done no thresh-
ing. I have set potatoes for 8*d.* a-day. I have dug
potatoes for 8*d.* a-day. I keep sheep sometimes for 6*d.*
Last summer I got 3*s.* 6*d.* a-week for keeping cows in
the stables, milking, and feeding them. I have got 6*d.*
a-day for topping and pulling up turnips. My mother
has relief from the parish : I do not know how much. I
have always three meals in the day ; I have bread and
meat for dinner, and bread and cheese for breakfast, and
bread and cheese for supper. When I am not at work I
do not often get bread and meat for dinner. It is ever so
long since I went to school. I left off going to school
before my father died, when I was about eight years old.
I cannot read. I do not know the names of the months.
I have good health. I never have any pains. When I
do not work I go out to play. I had rather work than
play ; you get most victuals when you work."

Undoubtedly it is a disgrace to England, with her
enormous wealth, and with the indulgences and even
preposterous luxuries, in which the middle classes, as well
as the upper, habitually indulge, that the children of the
peasantry, even in a county which touches upon the
metropolis, are thus devoted from almost infancy to
extreme toil, and have no opportunity to learn the first
elements of civilization. If legislative men conscientiously discharged their duty—if they were but a tenth
part as solicitous for improving the condition of the mass
of the people, as they are for facilitating transactions in
which the wealthy are engaged, and for promoting the
convenience of such as dwell in towns, we should not find
the rural population left as they are. We should not

find measures passed, amid infinite self-gratulation, of
which the immediate consequence, as admitted by all
parties, is the increase of the hardships of the agricultural population, and the augmentation of the difficulty to
obtain remunerative employment. The boys who work
hard from eight years of age to fifteen, at wages gradually
increasing from 4*d.* to 10*d.* a-day, at length achieve
manhood, and the climax of 18*d.* to 20*d.* a-day, in this,
the dearest country in the world, and the country in which
agricultural labourers work the hardest! They have no
civilized enjoyments, for they have never known anything
but rough labour from their earliest years, and the
coarsest animal satisfactions of food and rest. Is there
never to be an end of this, and shall we always find our
legislators aiming rather at making labour cheap (for
the benefit of their own class), than at making labourers
more comfortable and more civilized, for the benefit of
their country and of the human race?

In Kent and Surrey a peculiarity in the state of rural
society arises from the annual influx of a stranger-popu-
lation at the time of the hop-picking. The curate of
Farnham said that his parish was under considerable
disadvantage owing to the nature of the labour which is
employed at the hopping. At that time there is a vast
influx of strangers of all kinds, who are partly admitted
into the cottages of the inhabitants, and are partly received in buildings for the purpose. Nearly every cottager takes his tenement on the condition of admitting
hop-pickers for his landlord's plantations. The curate has
seen the cottages crowded with strangers and their
families at the picking season, who so much disturb the
order of the households that provisions are bought for the
day instead of a longer period, lest in the confusion of
the establishment they should be lost or made away with.

Such at least is the statement of shopkeepers, who justify the opening of their shops on Sunday upon that ground. The crowded intercourse, both in the cottages and on the hop-grounds, must be productive of mischief, especially to the young. There is very little uproar anywhere, and not until the close of the hop-picking. The labour of the day, and—as it is commonly alleged—a soporific influence from the hop itself, dispose them to quiet. At the close of the labour on the grounds, when the workmen are being paid off, the scene changes, and there is much drinking, fighting, and bad language. During the whole hop-picking, church is but slightly attended either by strangers or natives.

Hop-picking generally begins about the second week in September. All hands are employed at it, men, women, boys, and girls, down to the youngest that can work. In an average year a shilling is given for the picking of ten bushels, and an active boy or girl of twelve years old could pick a dozen bushels. A good picker (women are the best) will complete twenty bushels a day, or more, in an average crop. The work generally continues for three weeks, the hours being from seven in the morning till five or six in the evening.

In Kent there is a great deal of woodland, which, in the winter, gives work to men and boys: the men cut hop-poles and faggots; the boys cut small faggots and shave the rind off. A boy of fifteen years old can make fifty kiln faggots in a day; 2s. the hundred is the price; 4s. a hundred for the large faggots. The hop-poles are paid for according to the size.

Among the grievances of the agricultural peasantry is the want of opportunity to make the best market with their wages. A clergyman of Kent says that " a great and oppressive misfortune to the labourer's family " is

the difficulty of expending his earnings to advantage.
Confined to the limits of his little circle, and perhaps only
late on the Saturday evening receiving his wages, his
dealings are solely with the village shop. In these shops
articles for consumption are sold of but moderate quality
at very high prices. There are numerous instances of
large fortunes made in places where the farmers and
labourers are the only customers—" such fortunes as
could only be accumulated by excessive profits and want
of competition." It is a hard case, says this informant,
to have earned 12s. by the sweat of the brow, and to be
able to procure not more than 9s. would command in a
town where competition exists.

"The cause of the high price of village shops," continues this gentleman, "arises, I apprehend, from want
of competition. A labourer (it is considered) is allowed
credit for a small amount, and then obliged to deal, under
fear of having his debt called for, and of thus being left
destitute for the time. It may be true that the shopkeeper by deaths and other causes loses money, but with
such large profits the effect is slight; and as he knows
everybody, he has good tact, and generally avoids a bad
creditor. Millers commonly pursue the same system.
Blankets are double the price of a wholesale shop in
London; shoes, too, are excessively high. The labourer
in consequence finds himself ill off, and complains that he
cannot live upon his wages, when, in fact, he cannot lay
them out to advantage. Averages and quotations serve
little purpose; 'Deal here, or pay your debt,' is the
practical argument. I believe one great cause of the bad
condition of the poor is to be found in this."

The remedy for this is to relieve the peasant from
being so utterly dependent upon the shop. There is too
much buying and selling and giving of credit—too much

of the various tricks of trade. Instead of being so anxious to get money, the peasant would do well to bargain for as much time to himself as would suffice, were he clever and industrious, to provide many of the things for which now he pays. A well-managed garden—some poultry— a pig—a little traffic of his own—a little skill in shoe-making on his own part, and in tailoring on the part of his wife—domestic industry, in short, and a determination never to lay out a penny when by an effort he may him-self do the thing which he is tempted to pay another for doing—these are the ways in which the exactions of the shopkeeper are to be met. I wish that in every school for the children of the peasantry the rudiments of shoe-making, carpentry, and kitchen-gardening were dili-gently taught; and I should not object to a law prohibit-ing young women, in the peasant condition of life, from marrying, till they could bring trustworthy certificates of being able to make not only a woman's petticoat but a boy's smock-frock and trowsers. With all the English love of comfort, it is lamentable to see how little ingenuity and skill the labouring classes have in effecting that object. They think only of getting so many shillings a week at their work in the field or in the factory, as the case may be, and spending the money as soon as they get it in the supply of their various wants. If they are thrown out of employment they have no resource, and such comforts as they cannot buy it has become their habit to do without. If they ever learn to cultivate in-dependence in a rational manner, they will discover that to make themselves less dependent than they are on money-wages, is the most important step they can take.

In the north—under the same laws as prevail in the south, but with very different habits and manners—the peasantry are a more independent, and, I believe, a

happier race. The learned Commissioner who was sent
into Yorkshire and Northumberland says—" What I
saw of the northern peasantry impressed me very strongly
in their favour : they are very intelligent, sober, and
courteous in their manners ; their courtesy, moreover, is
not cringing, but coupled with a manly independence of
demeanour ; added to this, crime, as I was told, and as,
indeed, from the annals of the northern circuit, I was
previously aware, is all but unknown in agricultural
Northumberland." He admits that breaches of female
chastity are somewhat common in Northumberland, and
much more so than in the neighbouring shire of York.
Commissioners must, unfortunately, account for everything, so our Commissioner accounts for this, partly by
the common employment of young unmarried females in
field-work, and partly by the want of proper cottage-
room. The custom is to give the cottages rent-free, but
the ordinary cottages contain but one room—perhaps
seventeen by fifteen feet—for the construction and ventilation of which nothing can be said ; " but," adds the
Commissioner, " as the Northumbrians are, in spite of
everything, a healthy and vigorous race of men, such inconveniences do not amount to a crying evil ; but when
we find that a whole family—father and mother and
children, of both sexes and of all ages—live together and
have to sleep together in the same room, any degree of
indelicacy and unchastity ceases to surprise, and the only
wonder is that the women should behave so well as they
do. The restraints of religion, which in this province is
Scotch in spirit, and indeed usually in form also, exercise
a more than common influence upon life, and probably
mitigate an evil which would otherwise be of a most
serious character ; but, mitigated or not, I fear that in
this respect the Northumberland character is not exempt
from reproach."

Farm-servants in Northumberland, as in the southern counties of Scotland, are engaged upon a different system from that which prevails in other parts of England. Villages being rare, and each farm being dependent on its own resources, a necessity exists for having a disposable force of boys and women always at command, and this is effected by what is called the system of " bondagers." Each farm—they are generally large farms—is provided with an adequate number of cottages having gardens, and every man who is engaged by the year has one of these cottages. His family commonly find employment, more or less, on the farm ; but one female labourer he is bound to have always in readiness to answer the master's call, and to work at stipulated wages. To this engagement the name of bondage is given, and such female labourers are called bondagers, or women who work the bondage. Of course, where the hind (as such yearly labourer is called) has no daughter or sister competent to fulfil for him this part of his engagement, he has to hire a woman-servant, and this may be a hardship to him ; but such cases are not very common, and upon the whole the advantages of the system are held to be unquestionable. The Commissioner goes into minute detail on this peculiarity of peasant labour in the north, and here is his statement :—

" Each man, instead of working for weekly wages, is hired for a year. He is provided with a cottage and small garden upon the farm for himself and family, several of whom in many cases are engaged for the year as well as himself. The wages of the hind *are paid chiefly in kind;* those of his sons, &c., either in money, or partly in money and partly in kind. The conditions of this engagement vary slightly in different parts of the county ; but a woman to be found by the hind as a bondager is

universally one of them.   I subjoin the conditions as given
me by Mr. Grey, the resident agent of the Greenwich Hospital estates in that quarter; secondly, by Mr. Fenwick, of
Netherton, near Morpeth; and thirdly, by Mr. Hindmarsh, an extensive farmer in the neighbourhood of
Wooler:—

" *Mr. Grey.*	*Mr. Fenwick.*	*Mr. Hindmarsh.*
36 bushels oats.	10 bushels wheat.	36 bushels oats.
24 „ barley.	30 „ oats.	24 „ barley.
12 „ peas.	10 „ barley.	12 „ peas.
3 „ wheat,	10 „ rye.	6 „ wheat.
3 „ rye.	10 „ peas.	1000 yards potatoes.
36 to 40 bushels po-	A cow's keep for a	A cow's keep.
tatoes.	year.	House and garden.
24 lbs. wool.	800 yards potatoes.	Coals led.
A cow's keep for the	Cottage and garden.	5*l.* in cash.
year.	Coals led.	
Cottage and garden.	3*l.* 10*s.* in cash.	
Coals carrying from	2 bushels of barley,	
pit.	in lieu of hens.	
4*l.* in money.		

" The following, which is a specimen of the half-year's
account between Mr. Hindmarsh and one of his labourers,
will put the condition of the hinds of Glendale before your
eyes much more clearly than anything I could say.   I
should remark, that the stipulated wages of the bondager
over the greater part of Northumberland are 10*d.* a-day
for what is called small work, and 1*s.* a-day for harvest.

' *Wm. Hindmarsh, Esq., debtor to John Thompson.*

Jane Thompson (the bondager), 121½ days at 10*d.* . .	£5	1	3
Catherine Thompson (a child), 24 harvest-days at 1*s.* .	1	4	0
„ „ 73½ days at 5*d.* . .	1	10	7½
Eliz. Thompson (a younger child), 7½ days . . .	0	1	9½
Isabella Thompson (a dress-maker at other times), 35¾ days			
at 1*s.*	1	15	9
„ „ 20 harvest-days at 2*s.* 3*d.*	2	5	0
Carried forward . . .	£11	18	5

Brought forward . . .	£11	18	5
Wife, ——, 9 harvest days	1	0	3
His old father, 52 days	3	18	0
John Thompson's half year's cash . . .	2	10	0
	£19	6	8 "

Let us bear in mind that John Thompson besides this
had his cottage and garden, his cow's keep, his 1000 yards
of potatoes, his oats, barley, peas, and wheat; and then
contrast his condition with that of the wretched households
in Wiltshire. In Northumberland the old habits and
rates of payment remain; and it is easy to see how much
more favourable they are to the labourer than those of
the south, where the *real* bondage of excessive poverty
exists. It is, indeed, but too plain that, however squires
may have advanced in refinement and farmers in the use
of luxuries, the farm-labourer has no reason to bless the
"progress" of the last fourscore years; and it would be
well for his class if they could universally step back into
the position occupied by their great-grandfathers.

Let us return, however, to the Commissioner's statement :—

" What follows are the half-year's accounts of several
hinds, resident upon a considerable farm in another part
of Northumberland, being a surplus arising from the
labour of all the members of the family who remained at
home, which they had not found it necessary to call for in
the course of the half-year, but left in their masters' hands
till the settlement at Martinmas :—

George Cranston .	. £8	3	6½	Thos. Robson . .	. £4	3	11
Alex. Tunnah . .	. 15	0	4¼	James Cranstone .	. 6	12	4½
John Redpath . .	. 9	7	11½	Andrew Young .	. 7	2	5½
Saml. Ewart . .	. 5	5	9½	Edw. Davison .	. 5	15	1
Andrew Gray . .	. 7	1¾	4½	Geo. Chernside .	· 5	16	7
Andrew Elliot . .	. 23	2	2	Thos. Middleman .	. 4	9	10½

" Thomas Fullarton in debt to his master 7*l.* 9*s.* 8½*d.* Thomas Fullarton had lost a valuable cow by death, and his master had lent him 10*l.* to replace it.

" This system, which in its effects (except in one respect) appeared to me deserving of all the commendation which the gentry and practical farmers of Northumberland united in bestowing upon it, has not however escaped animadversion. Cobbett, towards the close of his life, attacked it, and others have since echoed his opinions ; they enlarge upon the misery and iniquity of bondage upon the free soil of Britain, and topics of a like description. As, however, this bondage is simply an engagement for a year upon specified terms, it indicates, I think, some confusion of thought to speak of it as slavery. An outcry, however, on this and other grounds, was raised against the system, and many of the hinds were thus induced to resist it. Mr. Jobson, of Chillingham, whose local situation rendered him independent of it, yielded to the wishes of his men and hired them at certain wages, with regular employment for the year ; and, singular enough, before the year was out, they desired, one and all, to be replaced on their original footing. In fact, there can be no doubt, that, owing to the thinness of the population, the great farmers, who have sprung up on the borders, find some such system necessary, in order to carry on their agricultural operations, and the labourers receive an equivalent for submitting to it."

The peasantry of Yorkshire are described as being generally well off. In many villages the labourers have, all of them, gardens ; and the more prosperous have land to keep a cow. They are shrewd and careful compared with the southrons, and their womenkind understand better how to keep the house, and to make the most of a little. The Commissioner, however, much disapproves of a mode

of paying wages which he found to prevail in the East
Riding. The labourers are fed in the farm-houses, and
men at 13s. a-week had a shilling a-day kept from them
on account of this feeding. They are well provided for ;
but the wife and family at home have to " confront life,"
and to pay for house, food, clothing, &c., with a sum of
money very little more than that which is appropriated to
the food of the labourer himself. The farmers, it appears,
like this system, either because they profit by it, or because they have a notion that men work better in proportion as they are heavily fed. The men like it, because
no doubt they get a better dinner than would otherwise
fall to their share ; but upon the women and children it
cannot but have an evil effect. It must also tend to
generate selfishness and to loosen family ties. The Commissioner states, however, that several intelligent gentlemen, quite incapable of upholding such a practice from
sinister motives, stoutly defended it, though they did not
thereby convince him that it was a system worthy of
defence.

In the north-west of Yorkshire there is a district called
the Dales, of which the circumstances are peculiar. There
is no tillage : the whole country is one large grazing and
breeding farm. With the exception of a few men employed in draining, there are no field-labourers. The
house-servants of each farm are sufficient to perform all
that is requisite. This state of things has driven the
people to seek subsistence by indoor occupation—by knitting stockings, jackets, sailors' caps, &c. There is a
manufactory of things of that kind at the small town of
Hawes. The master of the concern delivers woollen
yarn to the villagers as far as ten miles round ; they work
it up at home, and bring back the articles when finished
to the mill. A clever knitter might perhaps earn 3s. in

any given week by incessant toil, but on an average it would require industry and skill to earn half-a-crown in that time. Children, according to their age and proficiency, may earn 6*d.*, 9*d.*, up to 1*s.* 3*d.* per week. The people are poor and live hard; but the small amount of their earnings is, in some degree, compensated by the cheapness of provisions and the low rent of their cottages. On this account they are more on a level with the rest of Yorkshire than the rate of their wages would seem to indicate.

In Yorkshire and Northumberland women are frequently employed to clear and manure the land, pick weeds, hoe turnips, gather in hay, and in winter attend the barn-work. In harvest-time the Northumbrian women " shear " the corn, which is not the custom in Yorkshire. The Commissioner says it was not considered by those whom he consulted that the bondagers were less chaste than the other women of the county, though their occupations render them somewhat masculine. The Northumbrians have a saying, " Never take a household servant from north of Bremish " (the river Till), which implies that the turnip-hoe and the scythe do not train up girls to be neat-handed indoors. Children are not employed to the same extent as women; and in neither case can it be said that the occupations are unwholesome or beyond their strength.

The food of the peasantry of the north of England consists chiefly of oatmeal-porridge, bread made of barley and pea-meal mixed, potatoes, and occasionally bacon. In the southern counties the pea and barley bread would probably not be liked; it is, however, wholesome and nutritious, and there is official authority for declaring it to be by no means disagreeable. The " conditions," as they are called, under which hinds engage in Northumberland are proved, in very numerous instances, to be adequate—under proper economy—to the support of a man, his wife, and any ordinary number of children. It often happens, indeed, that a hind with but few in family has, at the end of the year, a good deal of corn to dispose of, for which his master is always willing to give him the market price.

The education in Northumberland, the Commissioner says, is very good ; the people are intelligent and acute, alive to the advantages of knowledge, and eager to acquire it. It is a rare thing to find a grown-up labourer who cannot read and write, and who is not capable of keeping his own accounts. The men are possessed of thoughtful and earnest minds, they take an interest in grave matters, and are particularly prone to religious speculations.

The Commissioner supplies a very interesting and curious specimen of a Yorkshire peasant's account-keeping, in the form of a minute record of every penny laid out upon his household expenses for a year, or, according to his own orthography, " the vareas expinces belonging to Housekeeping for seven in famale kept by Joseph and Jane Allen. Begun March 1, 1841, ended Feb. 28, 1842." This is too long an account to copy out entire, but, as it unquestionably gives the most exact view that I have ever seen of the distribution of a peasant's earnings, I shall transcribe the account for the first seven weeks :—

" March 1.	2 stone of Flower	.	.	.£0	5	0
	Yest 2d., ¼ lb. soap 3d.	.	.	0	0	5
	Suger 9½d., coffee 4d.	.	.	0	1	1½
„ 3.	½ lb. candels	.	.	.	0	0	3½
„ 5.	Panchean 3d., candels	.	.	0	0	9¼
	Carried forward	.	£	0	7	7½

		Brought forward	.	£	0	7	7½
March 8.		Yest 3d., coffee, ½ lb. sope .	.	0	0	7
		Oatmeal 1 stone	. .	. 0	2	4
„ 15.		Flower 3½ stone	. .	. 0	5	4
		Bacon 2s., yest, suger	.	. 0	3	0
		Tatoes 2s., coffee 6d.	.	. 0	2	6
		Milk 1s., salt 2d., yest	.	. 0	1	3
		Worsted 2s., suger 9½d.	.	. 0	2	9½
		Sope 3d., butter 7d. .	.	. 0	0	10
„ 22.		Tatoes 3s., meat 5s. 3d.	.	. 0	8	3
		Candels 3½d., yest 3d., suger	.	0	1	3½
		Flower 10s. 8d., tea 9d.	.	. 0	11	5
		Milk 5d., soape 9½d., butter 8d.	.	0	1	10½
		Total for 3 weeks	.	. £2	18	5

March 29.		Coffee, candles 7d. .	.	£0	1	1
		Suger 8d., seane (senna) and salts		0	0	3 (an error).
		Flower 3 stone at 2s. 8d.	.	. 0	8	0
		Tatoes . . .	.	. 0	0	8
Aple. 5.		Suger 8¼d., coffee 6d.	.	. 0	1	2½
		Flower 4 stone at 2s. 8d.	.	. 0	10	8
		Candels 6d., milk 7d., yest 2d.	.	. 0	1	3
		Bacon 2s., boy's school 2s. 6d.	.	. 0	4	6
„ 6.		Pade for house rent	.	. 2	0	0
„ 12.		3 stone Flower . .	.	. 0	8	0
		Treackel 6d., Brimstone 2d.	.	. 0	0	8
		Tatoes 2s. 9d., candels 7d. .		. 0	3	4
		Suger 8¼d., sope 6d. .	.	. 0	1	2½
		Eggs 3d., tape 3½d., brush 1s.	.	0	1	6½
		Coffee 6d., suger 8¼d., tea 5d.	.	0	1	7½
		4 stone of Flower at 2s. 8d. .	.	0	10	8
		4 lbs. of bacon at 8d., yest 3d.	.	0	2	11
		Milk 2s., eggs 3d. .	.	. 0	2	3
		Total for four weeks	.	. £4	19	10"

So the account goes on, the items not very much varying, to the end of the twelve months. The total sum for housekeeping appears to have been 47*l*. 8*s*. 6*d*. Shoes, or " showes," are charged several times, and also leather, and the " Talor for cloes making " comes in for 1*l*. 15*s*., but I find no charge for cloth, nor any sum charged for women's clothing. There is an equally strict account of wages received by the labourer himself, at 2*s*. 4*d*. a-day, and by his wife and boy at sundry times, the whole amounting to 50*l*. 12*s*. 6*d*. This is considerably more than labourers in the south can generally obtain, and I apprehend they do not, in fact, give such good value for their wages as the northern labourers do.

The Commissioner who went into Suffolk, Norfolk, and Lincoln, does not succeed in giving so intelligible an account of the state of the peasantry as the other Commissioners give. He complains very much of what is called the gang-system in Norfolk, a species of migratory labour, headed by a person who contracts to do work for a given sum, and is called a gang-master. He then brings his troop, gets the work done, and gets paid for it, giving as little as he can to the workers, and keeping as much as he can for himself. These gangs are composed of the worst sort of people, though they sometimes work very well. It is complained that this system of doing work throws the whole labouring population into the power of the gang-master, who, if he be a low, hard man, illustrates the proverb that no tyranny is so grinding as that of " a poor man who oppresseth the poor." He has neither the will nor the power much to mend their condition ; he may, on the other hand, exact any amount of toil from them on any conditions he pleases.

Lincolnshire appears to be a far happier land for the peasantry than either Norfolk or Suffolk. Part of the evidence quoted is to the following effect :—" Labourers here (Kelstern) seldom miss a day without having meat. The agricultural labourers, generally speaking, who confine themselves by the year, have about 28*l*. in money ; a cottage and garden rent free ; the keep of a pig in the

crews in the winter, and run upon the farm in the
summer; a rood of land to set potatoes on; four quarters
of barley, at 20s. per quarter; two quarters of wheat, at
50s. If they milk a cow, they have 10l. less in money.
The labourers are generally better fixed in Lincolnshire
than in any county in England."

Certainly the terms here described give a notion of
comfort very different from anything that the reports from
Wilts or Devon, Surrey or Sussex, suggest to those who
read them. In these days of inquiry into so many things,
would it not be worth while to endeavour to find out how
it is that in different localities of the kingdom the state of
the bulk of the population is so different? What work
can be more worthy of a patriotic statesman than that of
raising the condition of the peasantry in districts where
they are depressed to the level of other districts within
the kingdom where the labourer receives a more reasonable share of the good things which he is so mainly
instrumental in producing?

CHAPTER XXXI.

SMALL FARMS—ALLOTMENTS.

THERE is no country in Europe in which the labour of the people is so generally *hired* labour as in England. Almost every man who works with his hands, works for wages. The passion of proprietorship, which reigns so widely, and even to a mischievous extent, in France, is scarcely recognisable among the working classes of England. Where it does exist, few think of indulging it until they are above the necessity of continuing to labour for their support. When they acquire fixed property they think it is time they should cease to be labourers, and should become employers of labour. Every one knows that in wide districts of France, Belgium, and Germany, the case is very different. The owners of small portions of land and their families are the hardest workers in the Continental kingdoms. Whether their labour be what a merchant would call " profitable " or not, it is all for themselves. It very often is, if measured by a money standard, of very little value ; but still it is something which increases in some degree their own store. Such labour might not be worth buying by any capitalist ; and if these labourers depended upon an external demand for labour, they would probably find themselves uncalled for and redundant. But upon their own land there is always something to be done. The demand of the ground is almost constant ; and though the return may be small

in proportion to the pains bestowed, it is always something, and few proprietors of the labouring class lose any
of their time in positive idleness.   That the result of this
Continental habit is in every respect for the best, I am
far from contending.   Elevation of thought, and refinement of taste, *generally* spring from leisure, attended by
the various circumstances which await on wealth.   I think
it is better for *the labouring classes*, as a whole, that they
should labour for themselves than for others ; but then
the few of superior ability among them would have less
chance of escaping from that condition, and of attaining
not only independence, but ease and leisure, and a higher
position in society.   The evils of poverty and of depend-
ance upon hire are by no means the only evils that afflict
society ; and though we might, perhaps, almost get rid of
them by means of small proprietorship and hard work,
yet, if we must at the same time forego the advantage of
a superior station maintained with dignity, and superior
means administered with benevolence, there is reason to
doubt whether society would gain by the bargain.   What
we should aim at is the avoiding of extremes or excess
on either side ; and in England, I think, our working
classes fall into the extreme of being too much dependent
on hire, and too little ambitious of property.

In a national point of view, and with reference to the
obtaining of the largest possible amount of food from our
own soil, it is contended by many observant persons that
small proprietorships are the most effectual means to that
end.   Mr. Laing, in his ' Observations on the Social and
Political State of the European People,' maintains that
" the luxuriance of the crops in Flanders shows that the
stock of cattle producing manure must be greater, or the
manure must be better preserved, than in our large farm
husbandry; for no such crops can be seen with us, unless

on some small pet field. The clean state of the crops—
not a weed in a mile of country, for they are all hand-
weeded out of the land, and applied for fodder or
manure; the careful digging of every corner which the
plough cannot reach; the headlands and ditch-slopes
down to the water-edge, and even the circle round single
trees close up to the stem, being all dug, and under crop
of some kind,—show that the stock of people to do all
this minute hand-work must be very much greater than
the land employs with us. The rent-paying farmer, on a
nineteen years' lease, could not afford eighteen-pence or
two shillings a-day of wages for doing such work, because it never could make him any adequate return. But
to the owner of the soil it is worth doing such work by his
own and his family's labour at odd hours, because it is
adding to the perpetual fertility and value of his own
property. He may apparently be working for a less
return than ordinary days' wages, and, it may be, is
making but a bare subsistence, worse than that of a hired
farm-servant, or a labourer on day's wages on a large
farm; but, in reality, his earnings are greater than those
of any hired servant or labourer, however well paid, because they are invested in the improvement of his own
land, and in the continual advance of his own condition
by its increasing fertility, in consequence of his labour
bestowed on it. His piece of land is to him his savings-
bank, in which the value of his labour is hoarded up, to
be repaid to him at a future day, and secured to his
family after him. He begins with a potato-bed on the
edge of a rough barren piece of land, and with the
miserable diet it affords him; but the land being his own,
he gets on, by the application of his labour to it, to crops
of rye, wheat, flax, sour grasses, and to the comforts of a
civilized subsistence. Where land, whether it be a single

farm, a district, or a whole country, has not merely to
produce food, fuel, clothing, lodging, in short, subsistence
in a civilized way, to those employed on it, but also a
rent to great proprietors, and a profit to large farmers,
the tenants of the landowners, it is evident that only the
land of the richest quality can be let for cultivation, and
can afford employment. What cannot afford rent to the
landlord and profit to the tenant, as well as a subsistence
to the labourer, cannot be taken into cultivation at all,
until the better sort of land becomes so scarce, that the
inferior must be resorted to, and, from the scarcity and
consequent dearness of the better, can afford a rent and
profit also."

That which is most painful to the patriot, in contem-
plating our own great land improvements, is the consideration that, of all this great accession of wealth, the working
classes get so little share. Some of them—but, in the
agricultural world, certainly not many—have risen to the
station of employers ; but the great mass have not at all
advanced in condition. With regard to Scotland, Mr.
Laing observes,—" What has been the improvement,
what the benefit to the great mass, of the people of Scotland by this improving? Rents, it will at once be
answered, have been doubled, trebled, quadrupled, since
it began, some sixty years ago ; and as the large farmers,
or tenants of adequate capital and skill, who pay those
increased rents, are also making greater profits, as well
as their landlords higher rents, it is evident that the land
is now sending greater quantities of food to market, that
there is a corresponding improvement, in short, in the
productiveness of the land ; and Swift or Burke has told
us that he is a benefactor of mankind, and has accomplished a great improvement for society, who makes two
ears of corn grow where only one grew before. But

softly. Let us examine this proposition. What is pithily said is not therefore necessarily true. One should be always on his guard against these pithily expressed sayings. Unless in mathematics and religion, there is no squeezing a general truth into the nut-shell of an axiom. Swift or Burke, or whoever said it, forgot that, unless those who raise the two ears of corn can also eat them, or enjoy, at least, a part and portion in them, it is no improvement in *their* condition,—and they are the great mass of the population of a country,—but only a benefit and an improvement to the small body of landowners and great tenants to whom the corn belongs. The labourer in Virginia or Carolina has no benefit from his master's raising two hogsheads of tobacco or rice where only one was produced before. This additional productiveness is no improvement in his lot or condition, whether he be slave or free. He is not better fed, clothed, lodged, or remunerated with higher wages in consequence of it. Is the Scotch labourer in husbandry better fed, lodged, or clothed now, than he was sixty years ago, although the rents and profits of landlords and tenants have doubled, trebled, or quadrupled? This additional gain from the land is an improvement only to those who, as landlords, large farmers, factors, lawyers, bankers, are connected with the manufacture of food from land. But what are those classes compared to the great mass of the population of Scotland? The class of landed proprietors in Scotland does not, it is said, exceed 5000 or 6000 individuals; and probably all who derive any direct benefit by this improvement will not amount to 100,000 persons, in a population of 2,500,000. Of what benefit is it to the remaining 2,400,000, that three or four times as much grain is raised and sent to market, if only half as many of them are employed and subsisted by raising it as lived from the land before this improvement in agriculture?"

Upon these passages the critic will naturally observe that, while in the first of them it is attempted to be made out that cultivation in a small way is by far the more perfect, and that in which there is least waste of land, in the second it appears to be admitted that the large-farm system has trebled rents and profits, and doubled the produce; the complaint is, however, that the labourers are none the better, but only the proprietors and the capitalists who farm the land. It is, indeed, to this hour a very difficult question to decide whether the large or the small farm system leads to the greater degree of productiveness. Careful writers are found to affirm that, where the land is most divided in France, the cultivation is wretched, compared with that of England. They come to that conclusion from a comparison of the official returns of French produce with what is generally known of English produce. There are, however, numerous travellers who, judging from what they have seen, do not hesitate to say that the small farms of France are very favourable to production.* The late Commander-in-Chief in India,

---

* Mr. Joseph Kay, M.A., of Trinity College, Cambridge, and late travelling Fellow of the University, in a book which he has lately published on the social condition and education of the people of England and of Europe, says that "the moral, intellectual, and physical condition of the peasants and operatives of Prussia, Saxony, and other parts of Germany, of Holland, and of the Protestant Cantons of Switzerland, and the social condition of the peasants in the greater part of France, is very much higher and happier, and very much more satisfactory, than that of the peasants and operatives of England." He describes the land as "nearly all divided into small estates, which is held and cultivated by peasants; the process of conveying estates is very simple and cheap, and they are constantly in the market to be sold." He does not explain why these estates are so frequently to be sold, if the cultivators who own them are so generally prosperous. As to the towns—no children, he says, are

Sir Charles James Napier, who, fifteen years ago, wrote
a book about colonization and small farms, did battle on
that occasion with another author (Mr. Richard Cobden,
I believe) on this question of small farms, and contended
that the agricultural condition of the north of France
proved the case in favour of the existing division of land.
"I will," he says, "meet the author of 'England and
America' on his own ground. He says that the division
of land into small farms is *unfavourable to production*.
This is denied by Lichtervelde, the Belgian writer on
agriculture, whose reports and opinions were sought for
by the ruler of the French empire, with a view to national
improvement. I also made inquiries in Normandy, where
I passed the last year, and where the advantage of small
farms is universally asserted. Mr. Armstrong, the Vice-
Consul at Caen, told me that the English government
had sent queries through his office to ascertain whether
the division of land in France did good or harm in that
neighbourhood; and that the answers to these queries
were, that the opinion was general of its great advantage;
that France owed the improved state of agriculture, and
the comparatively happy state of the peasantry, entirely to
this division of land; that the only dissentient voices to
this opinion were those men who had lost great estates—
in short, the *Carlists*, whose opinions are naturally influenced by their personal misfortunes, or rather biassed
by their politics." The gallant author runs on in this
strain with great vehemence, till at last, having, as he
says, Belgian and French authorities, he comes to this

---

left idle in their streets; no children are allowed to grovel in the gutters;
no children are allowed to appear at the school dirty, or in ragged clothes.
Mr. Kay seems to lay great stress on the superior cleanliness of the peasantry of the Continent, a point of superiority which I should have thought
the very last likely to have been claimed.

point—" No one can deny that the man with twenty acres
will observe the operations of nature more closely, and
consequently more accurately, than he who has a thousand,
and is obliged to use other men's eyes ;* that the man of
twenty acres will have the assistance of his family, and
he will work harder for himself than the labourer hired
by the farmer of a thousand acres, whose family do not
work at all." This appears to be a very reasonable theory,
but I have asked several persons of considerable rural
experience in England their opinion upon this subject,
and they have unanimously answered that of all conditions
in this country none is so beggarly and wretched as that
of the farmers of twenty or even forty acres. As matters
have hitherto gone in England, such small independent
concerns do not appear to suit the circumstances of the
country and the habits of the people ; but that may be
because heretofore the comfortableness of an inferior condition in life has not been, in a general sense, an English
object. The general object is to rise out of that condition,

---

* In a curious old book still to be found in some agricultural libraries
the following passage occurs, with many more, containing matters which
are now put forward as the results of modern observation :—

" Deficiency is that men do usually covet great quantities of land, yet
cannot manage a little well. There were amongst the ancient Romans
some appointed to see that men did till their lands as they should do, and,
if they did not, to punish them as enemies to the publique ; perhaps such
a law might not be amiss with us, for without question the publique
suffereth much by private men's negligences ; I therefore wish men to
take *Columel's* counsel, which is, *laudato ingentia rura, exiguam colito.*
For *melior est culta exiguitas, &c.,* as another saith, or, as we say in
English, a little farm well tilled is to be preferred, for then we should
not see so much waste land, but more industry, greater crops, and more
people employed than are at this present, to the great profit of the com-
monwealth. I know a gentleman who yearly letteth more and more of
that land he used to keep in his hands, yet confesseth his barns are fuller,
because he more diligently manageth what remaineth."—*Samuel Hartlib,
his Legacy of Husbandry,* printed 1655.

not to make it such as a man of sense and energy might be content to abide in, and leave to his children after him.

As a further illustration of the difficulty of coming to a settled conclusion upon the question of fact—whether farming upon a small scale is or is not favourable to large production—it may be mentioned that, while Mr. Laing and many others dwell upon the great fertility of Belgium as a thing notorious and undeniable, Mr. M'Culloch, in his 'Geographical Dictionary,' states that in the richest part of Belgium the produce of wheat is less than three quarters to the acre.* This is certainly not what we should in England make any boast about. Five quarters is no uncommon crop on our very good farms, and some projectors, who have great confidence in "science," talk of seven quarters as a rate of produce by no means unattainable.

Sir C. J. Napier gives a very exaggerated account of the extravagance of the great farmers in England, whom he describes as dining at eight o'clock, drinking claret, and sending their daughters to Paris to learn to speak French. This, he says, comes out of the thousand a-year which is the remuneration for a man's skill and time in managing a farm of a thousand acres, and for his capital invested. "But let us," he adds, "divide the thousand acres among the day-labourers who worked the great farm, giving to each twenty acres on a long lease, thereby securing to these poor men constant profitable work—for what is the poor man's fate who is not sure of constant work? Yes such is the hired labourer's destiny, that he

---

* The following, says M'Culloch (*Geographical Dict.*, art. 'Belgium '), is the *average produce* of the principal crops per acre in the Waes country, the most fertile and highly cultivated part of Flanders :—Wheat, 20½ bushels ; rye, 25½ bushels ; oats, 41 bushels ; clover, 13 tons ; potatoes, 10 tons ; flax, 483 lbs. of yarn and 6½ bushels of seed.

may lose work by the invention of machinery, or from the pique of his employer, who may take offence at some hasty expression. The constant fear of this makes the hired labourer a slave, and, it may be, a rogue, and starves him besides. But now we have divided the thousand acres the poor man is no longer a hireling, but a small farmer. The thousand a-year which gave farmer Middleman the gout, would be divided among fifty hard-working sturdy spadesmen, whose support and comforts would never cease. Thus, in addition to the wages they formerly received as day-labourers, each would have twenty pounds a-year (that is to say his share of the thousand pounds) for managing his own portion of the great farm. They would have a gradual increase of comforts ; they would have constant occupation for themselves and their children ; they would one and all scorn the thoughts of parish assistance, which they would consider as the right of the poor and miserable, and, not being either, they would consider any such assistance to be a degradation, revolting to their honest pride. The son would not marry a woman that he could not support, and the daughter would not marry a dissolute man. No one, as M. de Sismondi says, *voluntarily descends from their condition.* The small farmer—the English yeoman—bestows, but does not ask, alms."

I wish there were more practical ground for all this ardent anticipation. I hope, not very sanguinely however, that the time may come when the English peasant's condition will generally be far better than it is ; but at present I doubt whether there be one English farming labourer in a hundred who could thrive upon a farm of twenty acres, however long the lease and moderate the rent. Such farming is not the custom of the country, and would not bear the expenses which general and local taxation, and the habits of English life, cast upon all occupiers. I do not say that the existing system is more desirable than that of small farms, if there were reasonable ground for believing they would lead to such results as Sir C. J. Napier anticipated, but neither the habits of our peasantry, nor the circumstances of the country, admit the expectation that the possession of farms of twenty acres, on the condition of paying rent and taxes, would place our labourers in a better condition than they hold as labourers for hire.

I believe there is scarcely any such thing in England as a large estate let out in small farms, but across the Irish Channel it is very common; and that not only in the parts of Ireland where the state of the people generally is degraded and disgraceful, but in those parts of the north of Ireland where the people are industrious, frugal, and obedient to the laws. In an enormous "Blue Book," which contains a Report of the evidence taken before Her Majesty's Commissioners for inquiring into the occupation of land in Ireland, popularly called "Lord Devon's Commission," there is a great deal of curious information about rural matters in that kingdom. In the county of Tyrone, as we learn from the evidence, the Marquis of Abercorn possesses an estate of 43,040 statute acres, which appears to be managed with great care. The population upon the estate at the time the evidence was taken was 16,168, residing in 2826 houses. This number did not include the town of Strabane (in the vicinity), but was strictly confined to the rural population. The total number of farms on the estate was 1041 :—

Under 16 acres	137
From 16 to 32 acres	395
,, 32 to 65 ,, . . .	417
,, 65 to 130 ,, . . .	78
130 acres and upwards	14

The particulars of nine "townlands" are given which contained together 3600 acres, producing a rent of 1280*l.*, but in this it is to be supposed there is some mountain or bog, for one of the townlands, containing 767 acres, lets for but 25*l.* a-year.

In reply to a question asked him as to the condition of the farming population on Lord Abercorn's estate, his lordship's agent answered that the condition of the larger farmer was comfortable and respectable. The small tenantry, he said, were a struggling, industrious people, with little or no capital. They consequently depend very much upon the produce of the season for the means of paying their rents, and for their own subsistence. Labourers he described as " a mixed class," who gave two days' work in the week for a cottage, to which sometimes a small garden is attached. The hired labourers live with the farmers, are fed by them, and get from five to six guineas a-year. Farmers in comfortable circumstances frequently educate one of their sons as a surgeon, or for the Presbyterian ministry ; the other male members of the family work on the farm until farms are purchased for them, as circumstances permit. The daughters get portions on marriage, from twenty pounds upwards. When the tenant dies and leaves a widow with young children, she generally keeps on the farm and supports them by it. When children are left without parents, some relation or friend manages the farm till the eldest son is of an age to take care of it. The labourers hold their cottages under the farmers, who build, and ought to keep them in repair, but this, in many instances, is sadly neglected.

Lord Abercorn's Donegal estate consists of 16,165 statute acres ; the population upon it being, according to the last census, 5673, who inhabit 995 houses. The number of farms is 383 :—

62 farms under 10 acres.	108 farms from 20 to 40 acres.
55 ,, from 10 to 20 acres.	112 ,, 40 to 80 ,,

46 farms from 80 acres upwards.

The Church property of the Marquis, amounting to 6269
acres, is similarly divided, but the tenants, being, as the
agent says, "under no control," have sublet their holdings, and covered the land with a pauper population.
Certainly M de Sismondi's apophthegm, that no one voluntarily descends from his condition, does not apply to Ireland, for, except under control, it appears to be the deliberate will of a very large majority of the people of that
kingdom to sink as low as human beings can sink without
forfeiting life.   But there are people who seek to maintain
their families and pay rent from an acre or two.   The
small farmer of from twenty to forty acres is frequently in
what is considered a comfortable way of life.   Still they
do not arrive at that degree of wealth and independence
which the small farmers of Belgium are understood to
possess.   Whether this arises from larger produce, or a
better economy, on the part of the foreigners, or from the
circumstance that they are themselves proprietors, and
pay no rent, I have not evidence before me to determine.
As, however, Charles the Second's wise men, who occupied
themselves in endeavouring to explain the reason that a
live fish put into a vessel already full of water did not
cause the vessel to overflow, would have been thought
wiser had they in the first instance tried to ascertain
whether the fact were so, it may perhaps be thought that
the first point to be ascertained is the certainty of the
comfortable condition of the Belgian small farmers.   I
believe there is a considerable resemblance between their
way of life and that of the Scotch farmers of fifty or sixty
years ago, who have been so well described by Mrs.
Hamilton the novelist.   Their ordinary habits are very

coarse, and not particularly clean; but their pride is in
having stores of household stuff, which they keep not for
use, but for show; and, while living in the most economical and thrifty manner, not sparing themselves hours
of hard labour to save the fraction of a sous, they have
always great stores of linen, and even hereditary gowns
and boddices, which they exhibit to visitors. There is
hardly any condition of poverty so extreme that persevering thrift will not improve it into a sort of humble
affluence. Whatever be the truth in national affairs,
there can be little doubt that, as regards the domestic
economy of those who live by labour, *magnum vectigal est
parsimonia*. England is, however, the least promising
place in the world for those who wish to become independent by severe economy. In the first place, it is a
virtue which brings no respect, but on the contrary contempt and scorn, which are hard to bear. In the next
place, the general habits will scarcely permit it. Taxation, both national and local, is at war with thrift. A
late writer upon agriculture reminds the public that four
or five pounds an acre for wheat-crops "cannot sustain
a landlord, a tenant, a rector, police, bridges, gaols,
churches, lunatic asylums, union workhouses, labourers,
and a Chancellor of the Exchequer."* He might have
added highways, drains, artificial water-courses, Sanitary
Commissioners, and many other things which the govern
ment and legislature have determined must be paid for,
whether the mass of the people wish for such expensive
conveniences or do not. The richness of Belgian agriculture mainly depends upon habits which are utterly
opposed to the whole sanitary code of England, and are
made penal by our Public Health Act. We pay for getting

---

* *Quarterly Review*, No. 173, June, 1850.

rid of that which the Belgian hoards as treasure. The smells which in England are condemned as public offences, are to the Belgian sweetly redolent of coming crops. Instead of paying to be clean, he bears in mind how much wealth there is in dirt. Instead of going to large expenses for water to sweep away impurities, he is aware that agricultural economy is consulted by solidifying these impurities till they are spread upon the fields. He does not calculate upon the noxious effects of certain malodorous gases, and his nose is slow to take offence.

Supposing, then, that we give up the small-farm system as incompatible with the existing habits and prevailing expensiveness of England, there is yet to be considered the question of "allotments" for the labourers in country parishes, or gardens sufficiently large to be of important assistance to the support of their families. Even upon this matter there exists considerable difference of opinion, owing to varieties of experience, or of the principles upon which judgments are formed ; but the great preponderance, both of opinion and of evidence, appears to be in favour of these garden allotments. The Report of the Commissioners (published in 1834), upon which the existing Poor Law was founded, cites a large body of evidence in favour of allotments ; but its own recommendations on the subject are cold and curt in comparison with the language of the authorities which it quotes. The general results, the Commissioners say, seem to be—

1. That the extent of land which a labourer can beneficially occupy is small—seldom exceeding, even when his family is large, half an acre. Such an amount appears to be the utmost he can cultivate, and continue to rely on his wages as his regular and main support.

2. That where the system of letting land to labourers has been introduced and carried on by individuals, it has

generally been beneficial, and, on the other hand, that where it has been managed by parish officers it has seldom succeeded.

3. That the occupation of land by the labouring classes may be made, and in fact is made, *beneficial to the lessor as well as to the occupier.*

This, the Commissioners are pleased to observe, appeared to them "*the most important result of their inquiries on the subject.*" The Reports obtained from various parts of England are all favourable to the allotment system, though they are not all equally favourable. The general result is, that such allotments answer the purpose of giving the labourers a feeling of dependence on their own exertions, and a hope of bettering their condition and obtaining more comforts than they have possessed before. The Report from Cambridgeshire states that the farmers object very generally to allotments for labourers, as an interference with their own business, and as making the labourers too independent. The reporter observes that allotments are not to be looked on as a source of rent, and that " those influences which have caused the absorption of small farms into large ones will check the breaking up of the latter into small ones again." As to the increased independence of the labourers, he says that the fact is so, to a certain degree, and he very properly " exults " that so it is.

In Somersetshire the late Bishop of Bath and Wells gave much attention to this mode of improving the condition of the labouring class, and the Report of the Commissioners contains a very satisfactory statement regarding one of these allotment experiments, which is as follows :—

" At Wells, fifty acres are now granted by the Lord Bishop of Bath and Wells to 203 persons, in quantities

varying from one-twelfth to one-half of an acre, at a rent
of 12s. 6d. the quarter of an acre.   Of these persons, not
above ten are unmarried, and many are widows.   The
average of each family being taken at five, upwards of
1000 persons are thus benefited.

"The conditions are, that no lot shall exceed half an
acre ; that the land shall be tithe and tax free ; that the
holders shall pay their rents regularly, and previous to
the crop being dug up, unless the agent shall allow a part
to be removed (not exceeding the half) for the purpose
of paying the rent ; that the land shall be kept properly
manured ; that no damage shall be done to the walls or
fences round the land ; and by way of encouragement,
the sum of 2s. 6d. annually is allowed to each on punc-
tually paying his rent, and who has not broken any of the
above conditions (thus reducing the rent to 10s. the
quarter acre) ; and the Bishop also annually gives premiums to those occupants who produce the largest quantity of potatoes on the same portion of land.   The tenure
is considered as secured during the lifetime of the Bishop,
and during good conduct.

"No stipulation is made against the receipt of parochial relief, but the result has been to the same effect, as
only three of the number actually receive such relief ;
two of whom are infirm persons who would otherwise be
in the workhouse, and the third, also infirm, belongs to
Bristol ; twenty-nine names were pointed out of persons
who formerly had received relief, but had discontinued it
since they had got land.   Many Dissenters have allotments.

"The system was commenced in 1826, with three
pieces, amounting to thirty acres, which were given in lots
to 109 families ; a fourth portion was added in 1831,
and a fifth has been given in 1832, but has not yet been

brought under cultivation, making the whole amount to fifty acres.

" The land, which was previously worked out, is much improved, and the crops very abundant.

" The following is an account, on an average of six years, of the profits of a quarter of an acre (furnished by the agent) :—

	£.	s.	d.
Rent	0	12	6
Digging	0	8	0
Manure	0	10	0
Seed	0	3	0
Planting	0	4	0
Hoeing, &c.	0	8	0
Digging and hauling	0	10	0
Supposing the man to hire and pay for everything	2	15	6
Produce:—			
Twenty sacks of potatoes	4	10	0
Other vegetables	1	0	0
	5	10	0
Less labour, &c., as above	2	15	6
Clear profit, supposing man to hire and pay for everything	2	14	6
If all be done by the man	4	4	6

" The opinion expressed by the agent was, that a man who works for a farmer for twelve hours, from six to six, with the help of his wife and family, can manage half an acre, supposing it half potatoes, keep a pig, and support his family, and that a mechanic can do more.

" The continued increase in the demand for allotments is the best proof of the advantage derived from them.

" There is a general improvement in the character of the occupiers, who are represented as becoming more industrious and diligent, and as never frequenting those

pests the beerhouses.   Frequently they have been known
to work by candlelight.

" Not a single instance has occurred in which any one
thus holding land has been taken before a magistrate for
any complaint."

The success of this experiment not only led the Bishop
to extend it to other neighbourhoods, but induced many
others who had land at their disposal to follow his example.   It is worthy of observation that the success of
the allotment plan depends a good deal both on the
nature of the soil and on local circumstances.   A stiff
clay soil, in the neighbourhood of a town, is favourable,
for it answers well for spade husbandry, and the ashes
which a town affords, form the best manure ; but a light
soil does not so well repay spade labour, and requires
more expensive and skilful treatment.

The mercantile spirit which prevails so strongly among
all classes in England is evidently averse from the
attempts which labourers make in some quarters to obtain
land, and work entirely on their own account.   The
reporter from Cornwall, in a strain almost peevish, remarks that " there may be something very captivating,
with cursory observers, in the praiseworthy efforts of a
poor miner who contrives to erect a cottage for himself on
a dreary common, and to enclose acre after acre, full of
quartz stones, which must be removed at infinite pains
before cultivation can begin ; yet, judging from the usual
results, I am persuaded that such attempts should not be
encouraged ; and with respect to cottagers generally, and
miners in particular, that they should confine themselves
to gardens, and lay up their little savings in some neighbouring savings'-bank."   The writer of this seems to
have forgotten that the savings'-bank will only take
charge of money, and that a poor man may have spare

labour which he cannot turn into money. The great usefulness of land to a poor man lies in this, that it is an inducement and an opportunity to employ time which otherwise would be lost. In a mercantile view of the matter, and taking the labourer's time at an assumed money value, the reclaiming of waste land, and establishing thereon a little farm, would seem to be a bad speculation. But it is a mistake in the calculation to assume a money value for labour that probably would never be called into action at all, if it waited to be hired. As Mr. Laing says of the small farmer in Belgium, his *land* is his savings'-bank, in which he deposits those hours of labour which would otherwise be lost. It is true that farming on a small scale does not generally answer in England, for in that, as in most other descriptions of business, the tide and surge of great capital and great competition swamp the humbler adventurers. But the man who by great and persevering industry turns a corner of the stony waste into a few small fields deserves praise, and if, instead of looking to the sale of the produce, he contents himself with adding to his comforts in consuming it, he will have his reward, though he may make small progress towards affluence.

The Assistant-Commissioners of 1842 speak almost uniformly of the favourable effect of allotments, generally admitting, however, that it is requisite to limit the quantity of land, and pretty uniformly adding (I am sorry to say) that farmers have for the most part a jealousy of these allotments, and a dislike to the circumstance of the labourer having anything to depend upon but his wages. An intelligent witness in the county of Suffolk says, with regard to allotments, that care should be taken in the first place to set them out as near as possible to the labourers' houses—the nearer the better, and in no case

more than half a mile off. Secondly, none of them should
be more than 30 perches—from 16 to 30 perches probably: one rood he has always found enough. For if
the land is at a greater distance it is apt to interfere with
their day-labour, and they cannot get on the manure but
at great labour, or by getting donkeys, which is not approved of. Again, he advises no more than these quantities of land, because more will either take them away
from their labour, or be badly farmed, or become like
that prejudicial Irish system, where a family lives on and
out of an acre of ground. The more allotments that can
be laid together the better; it stirs up emulation, and
they improve each other; besides, they can have a little
chat together, which they like very much. By giving
labourers land sufficient to grow potatoes enough for their
own use, and a comb of wheat, the benefits are so great
that they are more careful of their own conduct, better
behaved, and have a little stake in the country. If owners or agents attend to them, and see they manage them
well and properly, this system gives them the real comforts of life ; but the allotment should be mainly attended
to and cultivated by the wife and children, and not take
up the labourer's time, which belongs to his master.
The allotment-system should be in addition to the labourers' general employment, to give them comforts over
and above their daily wages. If this object can be
attained, the labourer becomes satisfied, well behaved,
and industrious. His allotment, in summer evenings,
keeps the man from the beer-house. Generally speaking,
farmers don't like the allotment system : they think it
interferes with the labour they are entitled to. Many of
the labourers get pigs ; and as they have access to the
corn, turnips, &c., on the farm, it is often supposed the
temptation to help their own pigs may be too strong for

them. The witness says he coincides in part with the
farmers, as touching the pig. The labourers may gather
and make manure enough for the land without a pig.
A pig, adds this witness with due solemnity, is no doubt
a good thing; but, if possible, let these people be kept
out of the way of temptation, and make their masters
satisfied on that point.

The Sub-Commissioner who reports upon the northern
counties has a very different feeling with regard to porcine
connections. Upon the general question of allotments,
he observes that there is a prejudice against them in the
minds of many farmers, which, when the allotments are
too large, is not wholly unreasonable. When a man has
to grapple with a piece of land which, added to his daily
work, is more than he can manage, it is probable that his
land will be ill cultivated, and his work ill done; but,
with this limitation, the Commissioner is of opinion that
allotments of land produce advantages which it is difficult
to estimate too highly. Where the allotment is small
enough—say one rood—and has a great rent put upon it,
it seems to produce unmixed good, moral as well as
physical. In the more prosperous districts of Yorkshire
most of the cottages have gardens, and many of them
cow-gates, as they are called. It is also common for the
farmers to allow their labourers so many yards of land to
grow potatoes, on condition of receiving from them the
manure of the pig, which the potatoes feed. " Of such a
pig," adds the Commissioner, " the first product of allotment, garden, or potato head-land, it is the fashion among
political economists to speak disrespectfully. Now, whatever might be the superior profit to the cottager of saving
the money which he spends upon his pigs, and buying
his bacon in the market, this, as it never has been, and
never will be so saved, we may dismiss. In the mean

time his pig, besides its usefulness, is also a real pleasure
to him—it is one of his principal interests in life: he
makes sacrifices to it; he exercises self-control for its
sake; it prevents him living from hand to mouth, stupidly
careless of the future. I am persuaded that a greater
act of cruelty could hardly be perpetrated than the discountenancing this practice, or rather amusement and
enjoyment, among the poor."

One of the Assistant-Commisioners, who reported to
the Poor-Law Commission of 1834, suggests that, the old
domestic industry of the cottage having been taken away
by the competition of machinery, the allotment system
must be resorted to as a just recompense. The allotment
of land to labourers divides itself, he says, into two chief
points: first, as to that quantity of land just sufficient for
the cultivation of a labourer and his family during their
spare hours; and secondly, as to that larger quantity
which requires to be worked by the assistance of others,
or by the entire dedication of the labourer's time. " The
day is not long past since, in every industrious cottage
family, the wheel and the distaff, the shuttle and the
knitting-needles, were in full activity. At present, to
compete with machinery would be a useless waste of time,
money, and labour. We must, however, see if the hours
formerly devoted to manufacture may not be profitably
applied, and habits of industry created. I cannot suggest
any mode of doing so more profitable to the agricultural
labourer and his family than the cultivation of exactly
that quantity of land which will occupy these hours as
well as his own spare time. The quantity is calculated
to be the sixteenth of an acre, or ten roods to each individual capable of work." I admit with slow and hesitating
reluctance the proposition that household manufacturing
industry must be wholly given up on account of the com-

petition of machinery. Granting that the produce of the spinning-wheel and the knitting-needle can rarely be brought into the market in competition with machine-work, still it may be used in the family ; and if the time occupied in spinning and knitting would otherwise be thrown away, I think it might be well to resume domestic manufacture for home use, no matter how small might seem to be the remuneration for such industry, if measured only by its money value. It is incorrect to speak of a waste of time and labour upon such industry, if there be no other more valuable occupation of the time and labour within reach. All classes seem but too willing to estimate things by their money value, and the labourer or his family would rather remain idle than do that which, when done, would be worth only a few pence. It should be remembered, however, that " in all labour there is profit " other than that which coin can measure ; and that by occupation mischief may be avoided, even though money be not made. At all events, it has become a manifest duty, even of statesmen, who have done their utmost to stimulate manufacturing industry by means of great capital and extended machinery, to recollect the effect upon cottage occupation and welfare, and to try to make the cottage amends. If they do not, the evil will one day fall upon their own heads, or upon the heads of their children. The poor will not alway be forgotten, nor their homely industry. Even the spinning-wheel will be avenged.

> " ———— Venerable art,
> *Torn from the poor !* yet shall kind Heaven protect
> Its own, though rulers, with undue respect,
> Trusting to crowded factory and mart,
> And proud discoveries of the intellect,
> Heed not the pillage of man's ancient art."

Another of the Sub-Commissioners of 1834 (Mr. Majendie) reported that of the acquisition of land by labourers the effect was invariably beneficial ; their character and conduct seemed immediately raised by having means of exerting themselves for their own advantage, in addition to the uncertain demand for labour. " It is," he emphatically adds, " contrary to the principles of human nature that labourers should be happy and contented when they are turned off at a short notice to the parish roads or gravel-pit, or degraded by what they term convict-labour, while land immediately before their eyes is passing out of cultivation."   This was under the old Poor Law : but are these things better now ? The poor in England are not now sent upon the parish roads when regular employment fails, but within the workhouses their lot more resembles that of convicts than it did in any out-of-door labour. Indeed it is not an uncommon thing for men and women to seek the condition of convicts as a refuge from the greater miseries of mere pauperism.   And yet, while this is notorious in our rich country, statesmen either are, or appear to be, far more anxious about the profits of the capitalist, and the promoting of mercantile transactions on a large scale, than they are to secure an improved condition for the country labourers, by keeping from them the things which lead to their ruin, and by furnishing them with the means of making themselves comfortable by industry.   Instead of taking away beer-shops, and giving allotments of land, statesmen are willing to leave such matters to " find their own level "—a level of ignorance, wretchedness, and vice, in which are breeding the monsters that may yet destroy society.

" There is," says Mr. Majendie, " no class in society whose feelings and opinions are so much known to each other as the labourers.   It can be no secret to them that the crops which may be raised by their exertions on small plots of land are infinitely greater than those produced by ordinary cultivation. The denial of land to them will constantly produce an increase of ill-feeling on their part. It is to the proprietors that they must look for this boon; and it seems probable that nothing can more effectually tend to restore the good feeling *which formerly prevailed between the different classes of society* than the allotment system, under prudent regulations."

Fifteen years having passed away since this warning was given, and great changes affecting the land and its profits having taken place in the interval, a writer in the *Quarterly Review** very coolly acquaints the landowners that, " having seen the domestic spindle and loom swept into the unsightly factory—almost every independent brook-side producer, in every class, absorbed into some leviathan steam-driven establishment—Her Majesty's mail-coach and Mr. Newman's neat post-chaise attached to the rail—we can hardly hope that agriculture alone will be able to retain its old relations, and to resist the *economical pressure*." That pressure, and pressure of every other kind, the landed proprietors may indeed look for; therefore let them strengthen themselves. Let them give the labourers a common interest with themselves in the support of British agriculture. The time may come when they will want such friends to back them. Let the proprietors take care that they shall be found friends, and not discontented adversaries.

---

* No. 173, June, 1850.

CHAPTER XXXII.

SUPPLY OF LONDON WITH MEAT.

A COMMISSION appointed by the Crown in November, 1849, to inquire into the state of the Smithfield Cattle Market, produced in due time a Blue Book, containing a great deal of information on a rather unpleasant subject. The details of the process by which between 4000 and 5000 beasts per week, and nearly 30,000 sheep, are brought to London, crammed together in the market, driven thence through the streets to slaughter-houses, and there killed by persons who have lost all sensibility to the suffering they inflict—such details are very painful, and almost enough to make one forswear the use of animal food, except for the reflection that, whether one did or did not eat flesh, the same thing would still go on for the supply of the dinner-tables of others.

Mr. Giblett, the eminent London butcher, estimates the annual cost of the stock sold in Smithfield and the meat sold in Newgate Market at the enormous sum of 10,020,400*l.* a-year,* though he estimates the Smithfield sales at 1,000,000*l.* a-year less than Mr. Hicks, the eminent sales-master. The Commissioners (whose Report is not remarkable for the care with which it is drawn up) say that they estimate the sales at the two markets in question at 9,477,177*l.* yearly. But, as they had previ-

---

* Evidence attached to Report, p. 96.

ously estimated the Smithfield sale of live-stock at
6,594,977*l.*, and the sales of dead meat from the country
in Newgate Market at 2,878,200*l.* (in addition to 959,400*l.*
worth of meat prepared for the same market in London),
the gross amount is 10,432,577*l.*, if we include what is
slaughtered in London for Newgate Market. But if we
exclude it on the ground that it had already been included
in the Smithfield sales of live-stock, then the gross
amount—according to the figures of the Commissioners
themselves—would be 9,473,177*l.*, or 4000*l.* less than
they state. They say that the number of foreign cows
brought to the London market in 1849 was 19,921, but
the returns of the Board of Trade to Parliament say that
the whole number of foreign cows brought into Great
Britain in 1849 was 17,921. I cannot say which of these
public documents is the correct one. I only know that
one of them must be wrong.

Smithfield, says the Report, " has since the charter of
Edward III., in 1327, been the sole market for the supply
of the metropolis with live-stock. Experience has shown
the tendency of the metropolitan cattle-trade to support
only one large market, and Smithfield has thus received
the constantly increasing supplies required for the growing
population by which it is surrounded. Stowe, who
wrote in the year 1698, says, ' It has been calculated
that the number of cattle sold in Smithfield and within
the bills of mortality, one year with another, are—

Neat cattle, or oxen, or cows . . .	70,000
Sheep and lambs	540,000
Calves	200,000
Hogs and pigs	252,000 ' "

It is difficult to believe that the quantity sold could
have been so great in Stowe's time, particularly as he did

not write in 1698, as the Commissioners say, but exactly
one hundred years before. The first edition of Stowe's
'Survey of London' was published in 1598, the author
being then upwards of seventy years old. The Commissioners say that Maitland's 'History of London' gives the
actual number of cattle sold in Smithfield on each market-
day in the year 1725, taken from the accounts of the
clerk of the market. Their total amounts were—

Bulls, oxen, and cows . . .	73,691
Sheep and lambs	555,620

He adds, that the metropolitan supply of cattle obtained
through other sources would cause an addition of one-
third to these numbers; and he estimated the number of
calves sold in the metropolis—of which only an inconsiderable portion were sold in Smithfield—at about 194,732,
and of pigs at 186,932.

The Return of the City Chamberlain, appended to the
House of Commons' Report of 1828, gives the number of
animals sold in Smithfield, in the twelve months ending
with April in that year, as follows :—

Cattle	155,714
Sheep and lambs	1,412,030

A similar Return, appended to the House of Commons'
Report of 1849, shows the following numbers sold in
1848 :—

Cattle	236,975
Sheep and lambs	1,417,010

The constantly increasing current of supply has suffered
no interruption, except with regard to sheep, which
reached their maximum in 1844, when in 19 markets, in
the latter part of that year, the number exceeded 30,000,
and in one market reached 39,920. Various reasons

have been given for the cessation of increase in the supply of sheep; but the principal one is that, though the sheep brought to London may not increase, the mutton brought to London has increased very much. London must have everything of the best, and, since railway communication has made transport so much more quick and easy, the sheep are killed in the country, and the "hind quarters" are sent up for metropolitan dinners, while the shoulders, necks, and so forth, are retained to stay provincial appetites!

Mr. Hicks, the salesman, estimates the number and value of the animals sold at Smithfield in 1848 as follows:—

	£.	s.	d.			£.
224,000 horned cattle, at	18	10	0 each	.	.	4,144,000
1,550,000 sheep „	1	18	0 „	.	.	2,945,000
27,300 calves „	3	15	0 „	.	.	102,375
40,000 pigs „	1	10	0 „	.	.	60,000

£7,251,375

Mr. Giblett the butcher's estimate on the same interesting subject runs thus:—

	£.	s.	d.			£.
280,000 beasts, at . .	16	0	0 each	.	.	3,328,000
1,560,000 sheep „ . .	1	15	0 „	.	.	2,730,000
20,800 calves „ . .	4	0	0 „	.	.	83,200
20,800 pigs „ . .	2	0	0 „	.	.	41,600

£6,182,800

It might be thought that in a matter of this kind there was no need for estimate or calculation, and that the clerk of the market could state the fact certainly and accurately from his books; but here occurred a very formidable difficulty of detail. The clerk of the market, when called upon for information, stated that the number of sheep returned as sold was considerably greater than

the actual number sold. The salesmen are in the habit
of paying toll for more than they have in the market for
the purpose of getting room, and gaining an advantage
over their neighbours. He described this as a regular
practice, and he estimated that it caused a fictitious
addition of at least 4000 sheep in the numbers accounted
for at each Monday's sale. From the information obtained through the clerk of the market, and from the
other evidence received, the Commissioners made an
estimate for themselves of the annual sales at Smithfield,
which was as follows:—

		£.	s.	d.			£.
236,975 beasts, at	. .	17	5	0 each	. .		4,087,819
1,291,770 sheep „	. .	1	16	6 „	. .		2,357,479
28,856 calves „	. .	3	17	6 „	. .		111,817
27,350 pigs „	. .	1	15	0 „	. .		37,862

£6,594,977

For many years past the space within the City of
London devoted to the sale of cattle has been inconve-
niently small, and, though from time to time enlarged at a
great expense, still it is found too small for the increasing
business. Great cruelty is habitually resorted to by the
drivers of the animals to force them through narrow
thoroughfares into the confined space where they are
exposed for sale. Another fact, which in this mercantile
age will perhaps be deemed more important, is that the
fatigue and excitement of the animals, owing to this
pressure, deteriorates the quality and diminishes the
value of their flesh. But though this is on all hands
admitted, yet it is found so convenient for wholesale
sellers and buyers to have all the cattle for the immense
metropolis of London sold in one place, that no suggestion
for having other markets in different quarters of London
or its environs has met with any success. Between 1832

and 1850 the cattle-market, at an expense of 43,000*l.*,
was enlarged from 4 A. 2 R. 35P. to 6 A. 0 R. 15 P., its present
extent. Six acres appear a very considerable extent, but
3000 bullocks, and nearly 30,000 sheep, besides drovers,
salesmen, butchers, dogs, horses, and all the noisy, dirty
crowd of a great market, would require more than double
the space, in order that the business might be conducted
with convenience, and with as much decency and humanity
as is possible in a concourse of which the most brutal
part is not, perhaps, that which goes on four legs and is
sold for food.

The dead-meat market is only second in importance to
that for live cattle. It is held daily, beginning at a very
early hour in the morning, and continuing until the
afternoon. It is estimated that the value of the dead
meat brought to London from various parts of England
and Scotland by railway or steamboat, and sold in Newgate Market, is 2,878,200*l.* a-year ; and the stock
slaughtered in London to supply the same market is
estimated at the additional sum of 959,400*l.* The business of this market varies greatly, according to the season
of the year. During the hot months the trade in dead
meat falls off to a great extent, and a simultaneous
increase takes place in the sales of live-stock at Smithfield. Since the introduction of steam-carriage, the increase of supply in this market has been very great.
Formerly it drew its chief supplies from places in Surrey,
Berks, Oxford, Hants, and Wilts, all within a hundred
miles of London ; but now the supplies come also from
Suffolk, Norfolk, Lincoln, York, Northumberland, Durham, Bristol, Liverpool, Berwick, Aberdeen, Edinburgh,
Fife, and even from Holland, Hamburgh, and Bremen.

Another market, that of Leadenhall, is chiefly for
poultry, but still from 700 to 1000 sheep, and 100 head

of horned cattle, are slaughtered in the cellars of this place each week, and their carcases sold in the shops. This consumption was not taken into account in the estimate of the annual value, already given, of the meat sold in London.

In considering the amount of population supplied with animal food by these markets, the Commissioners state the population of London and its environs to have been, in 1841, 1,690,084, and they estimate its probable amount in 1850 at 1,886,413. I do not know what authority they have relied upon for these figures. The Population Returns, derived from the Census of 1841, gave the amount as 1,873,676; and the present population, in an area of eight miles round St. Paul's, is estimated at considerably more than 2,000,000. Supposing that to be the number, and taking the value of the flesh or living animals sold for food in London at 10,000,000*l.* a-year, we have 5*l.* worth of animal food for each man, woman, child, and infant in arms, who dwells in the metropolis or its environs. Rich and poor, young and old, sick and well, consume on the average each day of their lives 3½*d.* worth of meat, besides hundreds of tons of fish; innumerable hampers of fowls, hares, and rabbits; venison from country parks and forests; millions of eggs from France; salt beef and pork from America in barrels innumerable; hundreds of tons of butter and cheese; and many millions of loaves of bread, thousands of tons of potatoes, and cartloads of cabbages, together with turnips, carrots, parsneps, and all other kinds of vegetables. Threepence and a third of another penny may be considered to represent, at the least, three-quarters of a pound of flesh-meat. Now many thousands in London are so poor that they rarely can obtain a meal of meat: women who do not work, and very young children, forming together a very considerable portion of the 2,000,000 of metropolitan population, do not consume on the average more than a few ounces of animal food daily. If then the Returns of the Commissioners be correct, some portion of the population must consume very enormously; and that they do so may be conjectured from the number of druggists' shops all over London and its environs, and the 1800 general practitioners, besides consulting physicians, whose names appear in the London Directory.

CHAPTER XXXIII.

BEER SHOPS—DRINKING HABITS.

A COMMITTEE of the House of Lords sat during a part of the parliamentary sessions of 1849 and 1850, to consider the operations of the Acts for regulating the sale of beer. A great deal of evidence was obtained by this Committee, both as to the consumption of various kinds of drinks and the effect of beer-shops upon the moral habits of the lower orders. I have had frequent occasion to take notice that, apparently, the habit of drinking so as to produce temporary stupefaction, or a temporary excitement amounting to madness, is the greatest curse of the working classes of this country. No other cause so much tends to degradation of character and brutality of manners. A very large proportion of the heinous crimes which are committed arise from drunkenness. All this is very generally admitted, but it is nevertheless held by many advocates of freedom that the restraints of law and government should not be applied to these habits. They contend that, though it is wise to endeavour to teach the people better habits, if they can be taught, it is not wise to impose any restriction even upon the sale of intoxicating drinks, or to prevent people from having their own way in obtaining the pleasant poison with which they temporarily destroy their reason, inflame their passions, and brutalise their manners. I have no agreement or

sympathy with such friends of freedom. It is true that
legislators and governors, after using their best exertions
to discourage vice and to promote virtue, will often find they
have had small apparent success; but to have thus employed themselves is a great good in itself, whether the
immediate result be promising or the contrary. Moreover, though few things are more to be deprecated, or are
more mischievous in the end, than fastidious meddling or
puritanical severity, yet a Government should not forget
that it has a moral duty to perform, and that it should
spare no pains to effect, in a temperate and reasonable
manner, the reformation of every pernicious popular habit,
while it encourages every improvement in sound knowledge and good manners. The evidence now printed, by
order of Parliament, proves, as clearly as anything can be
proved by evidence, that the beer-shops in the country
are frequently made use of for the indulgence of every
depraved passion, and for the concocting and maturing of
all kinds of villanous schemes. It is manifestly absurd
to say that nothing can be done to remedy such an evil,
and it is both a moral and a political mistake to urge that
the remedy of such an evil is of less importance than the
maintenance of the principle of non-interference with the
trade of beer-selling.

The Lords' Committee report that the expectations of
those who proposed the existing system of the sale of beer
have not been realised. Their object appears to have
been the creating of a class of houses of refreshment,
respectable in character—brewing their own beer—diminishing, by the supply of a cheap and wholesome beverage,
the consumption of ardent spirits—and thus contributing
to the happiness and comforts of the labouring classes.
But it appears that, of all the houses licensed under the
beer-shop system, only one-twelfth brew their own beer;

that a very large proportion are, as in the case of public-houses, the actual property of brewers, or bound to them as debtors; that they are notorious for the sale of an inferior quality of beer; that the consumption of ardent spirits has, from whatever cause, far from diminished; and that the comforts and morals of the poor have been seriously impaired.

It was already, say the Committee, sufficiently notorious that drunkenness is *the main cause* of crime, disorder, and distress in England: and it appears that the multiplication of houses for the consumption of intoxicating liquors, which under the Beer Act has risen from 88,930 to 123,396, has been thus in itself an evil of the first magnitude, not only by increasing the temptations to excess, which are thus presented at every step, but by driving houses which were originally respectable to practices, for the purposes of attracting custom, which are degrading to their own character and most injurious to morality and order.

Coincident, they say, with this increase in the facilities for intoxication, has been the increase of crime in a frightful ratio; the commitments for trial in England and Wales, in the years 1848-49, being in the proportion to those of 1830-31 (the first two years after the enactment of the Beer Act) of 156 to 100; and that this is not a mere casual coincidence, the Committee have the strongest reasons to believe, from the general evidence submitted to them, but more especially from that of the chief constables of police and the chaplains of gaols, who have the best opportunities, the one of watching the characters of beer-shops and of those who frequent them, the other of tracing the causes of crime and the career of criminals. The Committee do not mean to assert that there are no houses under the beer-shop licence conducted with pro-

priety, and even advantage to their neighbourhoods. On
the contrary, they have evidence of the existence in London, and some other towns, where houses, kept by parties
of a respectable character, furnish a valuable accommodation to the middle and working classes; but they
allude to the great mass of low-rated houses in town and
country, frequented by persons of the lowest character,
" and giving no security for good conduct by the capital
invested in the business ! "

Mr. Rotch, the Middlesex magistrate, says (Evidence,
447) that the country beer-shops are used as brothels and
receiving-houses.   " Nowadays, almost all the ill-conducted beer-shops keep very young girls for the purposes
of prostitution ; in my district decidedly all of them do so."

He was asked whether, generally speaking, he thought
that drunkenness was the great source of crime among
the poorer classes of the people ? His answer was, " I am
satisfied that it is much more so than the Legislature have
the least idea of.   I am sure that the judges who, ever
since the time of Lord Bacon and Sir Matthew Hale
down to this day, have proclaimed the monster effect of
drinking upon crime, have stated it within the mark:
Lord Bacon said four-fifths; Sir Matthew Hale said
four-fifths ; and the present judges, even on the last
circuits, have said that four-fifths of the crime committed
in England is attributable, either directly or indirectly,
to drunkenness, or to the drinking usages of society."

The clergyman who had been acting chaplain of Wor-
cester gaol for twenty-eight years deposed that he had
found beer-shops in general " schools for crime." He had
found them the resort of all sorts of thieves, young and old,
and places where the young find ready instruction in crime.

There was a good deal of evidence given to the Committee indicating that magistrates were frequently neg-

lectful of their duty in respect to public-houses and beer-houses. The chief constable of the county of Hants made the following complaint (Evidence, 491) :—

" There was a case occurred at the last licensing day in the Fareham division, on which occasion I went down specially to request that the magistrates would not renew the licences to certain public-houses at Gosport: the keepers of those houses we had convicted of harbouring prostitutes, who assembled there, dressed in the most indecent manner, I might say almost undressed. Dancing and music is carried on in these houses at all hours of the night. I requested the magistrates to suspend the licences of four or five of these houses, and in one or two instances to take them away entirely. They conceded the point in one instance ; they took away one man's licence. To my astonishment, a week or two afterwards the super-intendent of the division reported that the brewer to whom the house belonged had attended for the purpose of applying for a renewal of the licence to another party. I went again to Fareham, to urge the magistrates not to renew the licence ; I said that the brewer was unworthy of confidence ; that he had made such bad selections in his tenants that he was not worthy to be trusted in select-ing a fit and proper person to keep a public-house. The magistrates would not listen to my suggestion, but renewed the licence to a party whom I have since con-victed of keeping a disorderly house ; I have likewise indicted the same party at the last sessions for keeping a house of ill-fame.

" (492.) Are those the borough magistrates ? No ; I am sorry to say that it was the county magistrates who renewed this licence. Gosport is a seaport town in the Fare-ham division ; and nothing can exceed the disgraceful way in which the public-houses are conducted in that town."

The Chief Commissioner of Excise (Examination, 5th March, 1850) says that his Board is powerless with regard to the regranting of Excise licences to beer-shop-keepers who have misconducted themselves, unless they have a statement from the convicting justices of their desire that the effect of a second conviction shall be a deprivation of the licence. The Board has no notice whatever—no knowledge of any convictions—unless the justices choose to send them; and they do not choose. " I have seen," said Mr. John Wood, " several justices in the country on the subject, and I have stated to them that they never send us the ' adjudications;' and they have said that they considered, generally speaking, that the conviction was sufficient, and they did not choose to add to it a cumulative penalty, which would disqualify the party, if they were so to certify, from holding a licence again for two years. I do not say this in the way of complaint, but as a statement of fact."

The reform necessary in respect to public-houses and beer-shops is impeded by a too superstitious or a too sordid dread of the pecuniary loss which would result from suppressing the vice connected with them. The magistrates might indeed shut up a house which they know to be a sink of iniquity, and a concentration of all that is abominable; but when they reflect that this would destroy property to the extent of some hundreds a-year, a sympathy is called into action, more powerful than any other sympathy they possess. They have not the heart to pass a decree which costs the public-house owner so dearly. The chief constable of Hampshire says (512)—

" With regard to the public-houses at Gosport, it frequently occurs that there are a dozen common prostitutes connected with the house, who form a part of the establishment; they lodge in rear of the house, but are in

communication with it; some of the rooms are over the
tap-room of the house where these women live, and where
men cohabit with them, sometimes two or three at a time,
and the most horrible scenes that one can conceive are
carried on in these places.   I have done everything in my
power to get rid of these houses altogether; and I concluded that, after the magistrates had once taken away the
licence from one of them, they would not again renew it;
but they seem to be under the impression that it will
injure the property of the brewer to take away licences
from their houses.   A house which would, perhaps, be
worth 800*l.*, if you take away the licence would not, perhaps, be worth more than 400*l.* : and I think it was under
that impression that the magistrates renewed the licence
in the case which I mentioned just now.   The man who
lost the licence never left the house; he still remains;
but the brewer procured a female to keep the house, and
the licence is granted in her name."

And again the same witness states,—" At one time I
sent notice to the various public-houses in Gosport, point-
ing out that if they were caught tripping against the
tenor of their licence I would lay an information, and get
their licence withdrawn.   This had an extraordinary
effect for about a fortnight; a great many of the women
left those houses, and the houses were much better conducted.   At last a publican called upon one of the
magistrates residing in Gosport, and said, ' We shall be
ruined if this goes on:' the answer from the magistrate
was, ' Well, Captain Harris must come to us after all;
and I recommend you to go on as you did before.'   And
they commenced again from that time.   I directed the
superintendent to lay informations against those houses,
but the magistrates would not look at them."

This is a mode of "indifferently ministering justice,"

which it is to be hoped is not very general in England.
There is, however, reason to suspect that, somewhere
or other, the public-house and beer-shop abominations
meet with more favour than could be awarded them by
those who were heartily indignant at the vice which they
promote, and the profligacy which they encourage. The
" brewery interest" is perhaps more powerful in England
than it is quite desirable it should be. It is, however, to
be observed that the same gentleman who gives the account above quoted of the conduct of some magistrates in
Hampshire says, that, having regard to the good order
and morals of the county, he would think it desirable that
beer-houses should be done away with altogether; but,
at all events, the granting of licences should be taken out
of the hands of the Excise, and be vested in the magistrates only. He continues, " I look upon them as a great
evil in their present condition; they exceedingly demo-
ralise the people." Here it is grammatically doubtful
whether the witness is condemning the beer-houses or the
magistrates; and perhaps it may be what Dr. Johnson
calls a happy ambiguity of phrase.

Mr. Johnson, a coalowner of Lancashire, who says he
employs a thousand people, speaks in very strong terms of
the injury to the peace, happiness, and decency of the
families of the working classes from drinking habits. The
following is part of his evidence :—

" What is the result of your observations as to the
operation of the Beer Act upon those classes ?—It has
been most injurious : the beer-houses are indescribably
injurious.

" As contrasted with the licensed houses ?—As contrasted with the licensed houses ; inasmuch as the beer-
houses take in persons whom respectable victuallers
would not ; and not unfrequently, when the public-houses

have been closed, those persons, when turned out of public-houses, have been received into beer-houses.

"Are you able to speak of the state of things before the Beer Act?—I think that there was infinitely less depravity and drunkenness among the poor than there is now, and I think less crime.

"Do you find that these places are sources of attraction, particularly to the younger classes?—To the younger classes they are very much so. Great allurements are held out in the shape of music; there are itinerant musicians, and young persons are engaged there in games, and in many attractions. I know, from observation, as well as from what I have heard from the police authorities, that young persons of both sexes have been attracted there for purposes highly improper."

This gentleman suggests the providing of amusements for the people out of doors to wean them away from drinking habits. He is also an advocate for the use of " edifying books." But he is of opinion that "a better class of society" than the present is rising up. He thinks that the formation of subscription and endowed schools will, in the course of a few years, give us a very different class of society.

Mr. Tremenheere, the commissioner for inspecting mines, in his last Report to the Secretary of State, says, that the great number of beer-houses and public-houses in the mining districts is considered by nearly all the persons who adverted to it as " a fruitful source of much of the demoralization which prevails." He adds that it is earnestly to be desired that some further restrictions could be placed on the Act for the sale of beer, &c.; "an Act which, according to almost universal testimony, has exercised a most demoralizing influence upon the labouring population of this country."

In London and other large towns, where the concourse of customers gives the retail beer-seller quite enough to do in his own legitimate trade, the mischief of beer-shops is less striking. At all events, they are not an unmixed evil, and many of them are so conducted as to be a considerable convenience to their respective neighbourhoods. I shall extract some portion of the evidence of a certain Mr. Benjamin Bouch, a London beer-seller, not only for the sake of the information it affords on this particular subject, but as an illustration of a blunt Englishman in an humble way of life, whose sturdy common sense conducts him by the shortest road into just conclusions. Observe the pithy brevity of many of his answers.

" You keep a beer-house ?—I do.

" You have kept one for some years ?—I have kept a beer-house for 17 years.

" From the first establishment of beer-houses ?—Very nearly.

" Have you always lived in the same house ?—I have.

" Where is it ?—48, Crescent-street, Euston-square.

" What is the rating of your house ?—About 25l. a-year.

" You began with small means ?—I began with one shilling ; I had not paid for my beer at the time when I commenced.

" And you have gradually increased ?—I stand most pre-eminent in the beer-trade ; I believe that I am more interested in the beer-trade, as a beer-retailer, than any other individual in London—in the world, I may say.

" Have you any objection to state the number of barrels that you sell ?—We sell about 48 barrels per month. We do not allow any swearing ; we do not allow any smoking before two o'clock at the front of the bar ; we do not serve any drunkards ; if they come in intoxicated they go out as they came ; we do not serve them.   We do not allow any individuals to remain to get drunk on the premises ; although it says 'licensed to be drunk on the premises,' we do not allow it.*

" Do you find that your business is a profitable one ?—Most profitable.

" Do you brew yourself ?—I do not.

" Is the house in which you live your own house ?—I hold it on lease.

" You are at liberty to deal with any brewer you think proper ?—Yes.

" Have you any causes of complaint against the present system of selling beer ?—Certainly not ; the contrary. The working class fetch their beer from my house because we sell it good ; we do not mix it up as many do—as the trade in general do.   Upon the sale of a large quantity we get a small profit ; yet we get a large one in consequence of selling so much.

" Is yours a ready-money business ?—Yes."

He then explains, in a variety of answers, that, though to some slight extent he allows people to drink their glass of beer in his shop, his great trade is in selling beer to those who carry it away to their own homes ; and this, he says, is far the best plan for all parties.   The noble Lords who examined endeavoured to lead the man into condemning beer-houses of a low class, which they explained to mean beer-houses which persons without property had set up.   Blunt Benjamin, however, would not be drawn into condemnation of that poverty from which he had himself risen.   " I entered the trade myself," he says, " with a

---

* It is odd enough that the common jocular interpretation of " licensed to be drunk on the premises " appears to be taken in serious earnest by the witness, and the Committee let it pass in silence.

single shilling and a good character, which I have endeavoured to retain, and I have done so." He thinks
that, if persons are inclined to do wrong in his trade, the
infliction of penalties would not make much difference:
" An evil-disposed person is an evil-disposed person, and
the law itself will never cure him." He is then asked,
does he think the penalties are of no value ? To which he
answers, " I have never been fined myself; but I should
think that persons who transgress, and are convicted
of an offence, will endeavour to avoid the fine in future."
It is clear this practical philosopher spoke, in the first
instance, of the inner nature of man, which, if it be evil,
the law, however penal, will not make good ; but in the
second instance he admits that the penalty, though it will
not cure a man's bad dispositions, may make him, for his
pocket's sake, avoid the offence. I confess—though it
may seem fanciful—that the examination of this man leads
me to think how astonishingly true to nature Shakspeare
was, even when he is generally considered to be merely
grotesque ; *e. g.*—

" *Touchstone.* Hast thou any philosophy in thee, shep-
herd ?

" *Corin.* No more but that I know the more one sickens
the less at ease he is ; and that he that wants money,
means, and content, is without three good friends ; that
the property of rain is to wet, and fire to burn ; that good
pasture makes fat sheep, and that a great cause of the
night is lack of the sun ; that he that hath learned no wit
by nature nor art, may complain of good breeding, or
comes of a very dull kindred.

" *Touchstone.* Such a one is a natural philosopher."

Mr. Benjamin Bouch, being a man of simple good sense
and observation, is, in his way, a Protectionist :—

" Do you find that beer-houses increase in London ?—

I suppose they do in some measure : they cannot increase them on Lord Southampton's estate, for his Lordship prohibits more beer-houses than the number that is licensed by him.   His Lordship grants a licence to the houses licensed by the Excise, but no more.

" You find that an advantage ?—Yes, his Lordship protects us in our trade.

" That assists in maintaining the character of the trade? —Yes.

" If you were exposed to having a number of houses opened close by you, you would not have the same comfort ?—There might be the same comfort, and there might be a better article by force of competition ; and perhaps they would ruin themselves in the end by competition.

" In the mean while they would ruin the others ?—One would ruin another ; I cannot say which would be ruined first.

" But you have the benefits where you live of a kind of protection ?—Yes."

The witness deposes that his son has the best beer-house in London, taking about 30l. a-week.   " We sell about sixty barrels a-month.   They have no accommodation to sit down there except in front of the bar.   If all the beer-houses were conducted in a similar way to ours, I think there would be no complaint.   I have a sister that is provided for by the beer trade in one of my houses, and a niece in another : the houses are all conducted on one principle, and I find them to answer."   In the midst of his satisfaction, however, as usual, *surgit amari aliquid.* He has not a spirit licence, and he says—

" All well-conducted houses ought to receive the benefit of a spirit-licence.   I think there ought to be an investigation as to the character of persons keeping beer-houses, and not to condemn the evil and the good altogether.

" In whose hands would you place that examination as to character ? "

To most men this would have been a *poser*, but the witness gets out of the difficulty by simplicity and directness of mind. He answers,

" It is not for me to say ; I am ignorant of such matters ; I should say disinterested persons. It must not be the friend of the publican, and it must not be the enemy of the well-conducted beer-house keeper.

" You think it of great importance that there should be some security for the character of those who keep houses of entertainment ?—I have explained that in my opinion good conduct is the best rule that you can go by ; and so far I consider that the free-and-easy, and places of that sort, are not suitable houses to be licensed for the sale of spirits ; I have always set my face against them. There are hundreds of others in London who have conducted their houses as well as myself, and are fit to be trusted as much as I am ; and they ought to be well considered in the Committee as far as regards the property of those who are doing well.

" Is there not a Licensed Victuallers' Association ?— There is.

" Are beerhouse-keepers admitted into it ?—We have a Protection Society for ourselves.

" Is there a friendly feeling between the two ?—Yes, very much so.

" Do they draw together ?—Not quite.

" But there is no rivalry between the two ?—Not the least; publicans and well-conducted beerhouse-keepers are all on a par, except in the spirit-licence.

" Why did not you become a publican ?—What I have said will answer that question. A person with a single shilling cannot well become a publican ; and if he does well, and his beer-house is well conducted, he is satisfied with doing well.

" You would be glad to have a spirit-licence ?—I should have no objection to that change at all.

" You think that inquiry as to character is necessary ? —It is quite requisite : *that is the only safe rule, a good character.*"

The last answer given by Mr. Benjamin Bouch is a pleasing climax to the little history which his evidence develops :—

" I am going," he says, " to leave off business next year ; I shall have five shillings a-day coming in. We pay our brewers about 270*l.* a-month. The profits are not immense, but sufficient, during seventeen years, to enable us to live in a little cottage in the country where there are no ill-conducted beer-houses. My great object is to take care of my son and his family." *Exit* Mr· Benjamin Bouch, and the curtain drops. This evidence was given on the 20th of July, 1849, and, at its close, the Committee adjourned for the session, and no doubt anticipated the worthy witness by retiring into the country without delay.

The Committee met again on the 28th of February, 1850, and the first witness they examined was Robert Crossman, Esq., a great brewer in the Mile End-road. The following extract from his evidence will show the moral distinction subsisting between this *gentleman* and plain Benjamin Bouch :—

" When you engage to supply beer do you take any pains to ascertain the *character* of the person whom you are about to supply ?—Invariably, *unless they pay ready money ;* and if they do *that*, it is a proof that they can pay their way.

" As to the scale of house which you require, in order

to supply it, do you make any rule not to supply any house that is rated below a certain amount?—We will supply any person that comes to us, provided he has a licence.

" Any person who is entitled to get a licence you would supply with beer?—Yes.

" But you make inquiry as to his character?—*Before we give him any credit.*

" Simply as to his pecuniary means?—Yes.

" Not as to his moral character?—*We have nothing to do with his moral character.* When I speak of a man being *respectable in business,* I mean that he can *pay his way;* if they are bad characters they soon show themselves." This admirable judge of respectability of character gave in a list to the Committee of fifty-six beer-houses which his brewery supplied. Three of the houses of Benjamin Bouch figure in the list.

A Mr. Samuel Millis, a London retail beer-seller, gives a most flattering account of the respectability of beer-shops in the metropolis. He says " respectable people," who would not go into public-houses, come into the beer-shps : " they are in reality what the old public-houses were of the respectable sort."

Mr. James Bishop tells their Lordships a fact to illustrate the fair play which subsists in respect to licensing. A very successful beer-seller, having made 2000*l.*, built with it a house, intended for a public-house, on the bank of the Thames opposite Greenwich. He tried for several years to get a licence, but could not succeed. At last he had to sell it. A brewer bought it, and the first year after he had bought it *he* obtained a licence !

The Clerk of the Petty Sessions at Swindon stated that nearly two-thirds of the cases that come before the bench are to be traced, from some cause or another, to the beer-

houses. Mr. Grindall, a licensed victualler of Birmingham, thinks the Beer Bill has been productive of a great
deal of convenience to the public generally. " Birmingham," he says, " is an ale-drinking town, and the respectable portion of the inhabitants frequent the parlours
and drink ale, and they indiscriminately visit a beer-
house and a public-house." It appears, from one of the
questions put, that in the " Birmingham district " the
number of licensed victuallers is 1027, the beer-sellers
1022, besides 799 who brew their own beer. Mr. Grindall is, however, of opinion that drunkenness is on the
decline in Birmingham, and that there is an "intellectual
improvement in the rising generation." This may be
true ; but it is not so obvious from the evidence as that
other proposition of his—that Birmingham is " an ale-
drinking town." Another witness from the same town, who
is a beer-seller but not a publican, and who laments that
drinking in his house is put an end to by the police at
eleven o'clock at night, says there are plenty of licensed
victuallers in Birmingham that keep houses open for the
reception of thieves, rogues, and everything you may
name, and who do it with impunity because there is no
restriction placed upon them. When he turns out his
customers from his house at eleven o'clock at night, they
turn in to the spirit-vaults at the very next door, and
there they get drink till one, or two, or three o'clock in
the morning ! It is to be supposed that these are old
stagers who do not share in " the intellectual improvement of the rising generation."

   In March, 1850, the Chairman of the Board of Inland
Revenue, Mr. John Wood, was examined for the second
time by the Committee, and he furnished them with a
great deal of statistical information, which I shall proceed
to abridge and condense within as brief limits as I can.

They who have attended to the history of public finance in modern times will remember that the Duke of Wellington's Government, in 1830, without any urgency upon the subject, and merely because they had more money than they wanted at the time, gave up the whole of the beer-tax, which brought in about three millions a-year. The tax was taken off on the 10th October, 1830, and in the very next month the Government was beaten in the House of Commons upon a financial question, and resigned. Mr. Wood states the amounts of the last three complete years of beer-duty :—

1827	3,200,905
1828	3,294,697
1829	2,989,602

In the ten years 1821-30, the average quantity of malt charged with duty per year in England and Wales was 26,813,938 bushels, the duty 2s. 7d. per bushel, and the average annual receipt 3,463,467l.

In the ten years 1831-40 the duty was the same, the average yearly quantity was 34,414,354 bushels, and the average annual receipt 4,445,186l.

In the nine years 1841-49 the duty was 2s. 7d. and 5 per cent. additional, the average quantity charged was 31,779,179 bushels, and the amount of duty averaged 4,310,051l.

Thus the addition to the rate of duty was attended with a diminution of receipt.

In the year 1829 the number of publicans' beer-licences in the United Kingdom was 88,930, and the amount received on this account was 130,741l. In the year 1839 the licences had increased to 94,097, and the sum received was 139,346l. The very next year the number dropped to what it had been twelve years before. In 1843 the number of publicans' licences was 86,393.

In 1849 the number was 88,496, and the amount received 146,298*l.* The following is an account of beer-shop licences:—

Years.	Number of Licences issued at £2. 2s.		Amount of Duty.
			£.
1830 . .	24,342		51,118
1831 . .	30,978		65,053
1832 . .	33,515		70,381
1833 . .	34,976		73,449
1834 . .	21,975		46,147
	To be drunk on the Premises, at £3. 3s.	Not to be drunk on the premises, at £1. 1s.	
1834 . .	13,654	1,752	44,849
1835 . .	35,563	4,118	116,262
1836 . .	39,100	5,030	128,446
1837 . .	39,902	5,291	131,246
1838 . .	39,865	5,852	131,719
1839 . .	38,789	5,940	128,422
	(at 5 per cent.	additional.)	
1840 . .	36,871	5,743	125,623
1841 . .	32,715	4,954	113,657
1842 . .	31,307	7,372	108,359
1843 . .	31,212	4,195	107,850
1844 . .	31,745	3,945	109,337
1845 . .	32,624	3,687	111,961
1846 . .	33,941	3,528	116,140
1847 . .	34,967	3,508	119,512
1848 . .	34,551	3,324	117,933
1849 . .	34,900	3,300	119,300

Here we perceive a steady increase of the tippling houses, or places licensed for people to drink beer in, and an equally regular diminution of the beer-shops which merely sell beer to be consumed at the homes of the buyers or elsewhere. Every person applying for a licence to sell beer to be drunk on the premises was required by the Beer Act to deposit with the Commissioners of Excise a certificate of good character signed by six rated inhabitants of the parish, and certified by one of the overseers. Then came Sir J. Pakington's Act (3 & 4 Vict. c. 61), providing that a licence be not granted to any but " the real resident occupier in respect of any house rated at less than 15*l. per annum* within the Bills of Mortality or in towns containing 10,000 inhabitants, nor less than 11*l. per annum* in places exceeding 2500 inhabitants, nor less than 8*l. per annum* in places situated elsewhere."

In the year 1829 the number of brewers' licences in the United Kingdom was 28,594, and the amount of licence-duty 55,973*l.* The highest number since then was in 1838, when it reached 49,265. The number of licences in 1849 was 43,269, and the duty 76,505*l.* The brewer's licence varies from one to seventy-five guineas according to the quantity brewed. Until the quantity exceeds 40,000 barrels a-year, sixty guineas will pay the licence.

It has been seen that in the nine years 1840-49 the consumption of malt has diminished. Mr. John Wood attributes that diminution to the altered habits of the population, and the increased consumption of coffee, tea, and cocoa. He handed in a paper which, in a brief compass, gives much information as to the drink-consuming habits of the people   (See next page.)

The consumption of these commodities, taking them year by year, appears to be curiously irregular. Of the fifteen years from 1835 to 1850 the year 1847 shows considerably the largest general consumption of drinks of various kinds. Tea appears to be the only one of these articles in the consumption of which there has been for the last ten years an uninterrupted progress of increase :*—

---

* The slight decrease in 1848 from the preceding year can scarcely be considered an exception.

An Account of the Quantities of Coffee, Tea, Cocoa, Foreign and British Spirits, Beer, Malt, and Wine, respectively retained for Home Consumption in the United Kingdom in the following years:—

Year ended January 5.	COFFEE.	TEA.	COCOA.	RUM.	Other Foreign and Colonial Spirits.	BRITISH SPIRITS.	BEER (calculated on the quantities of Malt and Sugar used by Licensed Brewers, and deducting the Beer exported).	MALT.	WINE.
	Lbs.	Lbs.	Lbs.	Gallons.	Gallons.	Gallons.	Barrels.	Bushels.	Gallons.
1836 · ·	23,295,046	36,574,004	1,084,170	3,416,966	1,348,740	24,710,208	16,330,010	42,892,054	6,420,342
1837 · ·	24,947,690	49,142,236	1,130,168	3,324,749	1,292,271	26,745,300	17,018,429	44,387,719	6,809,212
1838 · ·	26,346,961 admitted at 5 per cent. ad valorem	30,625,206	1,416,613	3,184,255	1,240,210	24,493,539	15,988,035	40,551,049	6,391,531
1839 · ·	25,765,673	32,351,593	1,601,787	3,135,651	1,232,574	26,486,543	16,039,597	40,505,566	6,990,271
1840 · ·	26,789,945 admitted at 5 per cent. ad valorem	35,127,287	1,606,800	2,830,263	1,195,154	25,190,843	15,883,311	39,930,941	7,000,486
1841 · ·	28,664,341	32,252,628	2,041,678	2,512,960	1,131,450	21,859,337	15,769,434	42,456,862	6,553,922
1842 · ·	28,370,857	36,675,667	1,928,847	2,277,970	1,186,104	20,642,333	14,537,266	36,164,448	6,184,960
1843 · ·	28,519,646	37,355,911	2,246,569	2,097,747	1,103,268	18,841,890	14,284,646	35,851,394	4,815,222
1844 · ·	29,979,404	40,293,393	2,547,934	2,103,715	1,055,242	18,864,332	14,122,191	35,693,890	6,068,987
1845 · ·	31,352,382	41,363,770	2,589,977	2,198,592	1,044,014	20,608,525	14,624,854	37,187,186	6,838,684
1846 · ·	34,293,190	44,193,433	2,579,497	2,469,135	1,080,754	23,122,588	14,925,113	36,545,990	6,736,131
1847 · ·	35,754,554	46,740,344	2,951,206	2,683,701	1,561,629	24,106,697	16,283,298	42,097,085	6,740,316
1848 · ·	37,441,873	46,314,821	3,079,198	3,328,985	1,574,068	20,639,797	14,515,391	35,307,813	6,053,847
1849 · ·	37,077,546	48,734,789	2,919,591	2,986,979	1,648,384	22,302,450	14,555,010	37,546,157	6,136,547
1850 · ·	34,431,074	50,024,688	3,233,372	3,044,758	2,224,709	22,962,012	15,243,681	38,935,460	6,247,689

Since 1845 the import-duty on coffee has been $4\frac{1}{5}d$. on the produce of British possessions, and $6\frac{3}{10}d$. on foreign, per lb.

On cocoa it has been $1\frac{1}{20}d$. per lb. on the produce of British possessions, and $2\frac{1}{10}d$. on foreign.

Since 1849 the duty on rum has been, in England, 8s. 2d. per gallon; in Scotland, 4s.; in Ireland, 3s.

Since 1847 the duty on all other foreign spirits has been 15s. per gallon.

Since 1844 the duty on British spirits has been, in England, 7s. 10d. per gallon; in Scotland, 3s. 8d.; in Ireland, 2s. 8d.

Since 1841 the duty on malt has been 2s. 7d. per bushel, with 5 per cent. additional.

Since 1849 the duty on wine of the Cape of Good Hope has been $2s.\ 10\frac{13}{20}d$. per gallon; on wine of any other British possession, 2s. 9d.; all other sorts, $5s.\ 9\frac{3}{10}d$. per gallon.

So much for the statistics of drinks. The aggregate amount derived from the tax upon them has been already noticed in the paper upon Public Revenue.

CHAPTER XXXIV.

NATIONAL AND PRIVATE INDEBTEDNESS.

POLITICAL philosophers have much differed in opinion as to the amount of good or evil resulting from the system so extensively adopted by the governments of modern times, of borrowing large sums for present purposes, and mortgaging future revenues for the payment of the interest. The truth seems to be, that to resort to the borrowing system is a very excellent and very just expedient under peculiarly pressing circumstances, but it is one which is exceedingly liable to be abused, and therefore it is undoubtedly very dangerous. If financial ministers were always wise, prudent, and just, nothing could be better than to give them a power of raising sums which present times could scarcely afford, by distributing the burden over times in advance; but if they are careless and extravagant, and more ready to foster existing follies, than to provide for the future welfare of the nation, the borrowing system too often affords a fatal facility of indulging in expense which sorely presses upon the industry of after times. It has, moreover, a double tendency to deceive. The people are not practically conscious of the vast expenses to which their government has gone, when they have only to pay the interest on the capital expended. If they had to pay the full sum at once, the reasonableness of the expenditure would be more carefully inquired into. Again, the owners of wealth are deceived by reckoning that they possess not only the substantial riches of the country in their full amount, but also the riches which are registered under the name of stock, annuities, and so forth, but which have no intrinsic value in them, except in so far as they give a claim upon a part or the whole of the substantial riches before reckoned upon. For example, suppose all the houses and lands, mines, quarries, and so forth, in England and Wales, which financiers call " real property," to be worth 90,000,000*l.* a-year, or, in one capital sum, 2,800,000,000*l.*, the owners of that property think they are owners of that amount of wealth. But of national debt, funded and unfunded, that is, of government stocks and annuities of all kinds, and of Exchequer bills, there are holders to the amount of nearly 800,000,000*l.*, who suppose themselves equally rich to that extent. These two classes of real-property owners, and of government-stock owners, imagine that between them they have 3,600,000,000*l.* But this is delusion. The 800,000,000*l.* of one of the classes constitute a claim or mortgage upon the 2,800,000,000*l.* of the other, though, in fact, it is the annual industry of the country which pays the annual income to both classes. But if a settlement of account were to come, there would be no 3,600,000,000*l.* but only the 2,800,000,000*l.* of real property, of which 800,000,000*l.* should be transferred to the fundholders, leaving the others with only a clear 2,000,000,000*l.*, or *minus* nearly a third of their wealth.

The same sort of thing, or something like it, may be observed every day in private affairs. My Lord This, and Sir something That, hold estates which are worth perhaps 40,000*l.* a-year, and they persuade themselves they are proprietors to that extent, when, in fact, a variety of engagements to various members of their families, or interest on debts of their own, contracted before they came

into the property, run away with half the income.   They
are really worth 20,000*l*. a-year, and not 40,000*l*., as their
nominal ownership of lands, &c., would seem to imply.
The difference, however, between the action of private
debt and public debt upon the property of the country is
important in this respect, that, whereas in respect of private debt the possessor of the property; which is the security for it, must pay the interest, in the case of public
debt the interest is thrown upon the whole mass of the
people who pay taxes.   The property of the country is
the security for the principal, but it does not exclusively
pay the interest.

As if to prove that there is nothing absolutely uniform
in this world, and that even a political economist can
apply the dictates of plain good sense to important practical matters, Mr. M'Culloch has given a chapter on the
advantages and disadvantages of the funding system, in
which both sides of the question are stated with admirable
clearness and impartiality.*   He says, and I think with
truth and justice, that, "despite the dangerous nature of
the borrowing system, and its all but irresistible temptations to abuse, it is not unfrequently a most valuable
resource.   Thus, if a country engaged in war, be so
situated that the imposition of the taxes required to carry
it on would give any serious shock to industry, loans
should certainly be negotiated, if not for the whole, at
least for a portion of the extraordinary expense.   Political considerations may also make recourse to loans indispensable.   An increase of taxation is always unpopular,
and a weak or insecure government might not have power
to levy any considerable amount of taxes, however able
the country might be to bear such increase.   The rise of

---

* 'Treatise on Taxation and the Funding System,' Part III. Chap. I.

the funding system in Great Britain was mainly ascribable to such circumstances."

This concluding remark has reference to the kind and disinterested interference of a Dutch Prince, to enable us to conduct our affairs in 1688. When we were honoured with his arrival amongst us, our national debt amounted to only 664,000*l.*, but his Highness soon changed all that, and at his death, in thirteen years afterwards, it had reached the more respectable amount of 16,394,702*l.* The system, once begun, went on with wondrous rapidity, and the ministers of Queen Anne showed themselves twice as clever as the ministers of her predecessor had been in augmenting the national debt. Mr. M‘Culloch, though he follows the ordinary pleasantry of calling Prince William " our great deliverer," honestly confesses that the revolutionary government stood on such terms with the people at large, that it did not dare to attempt obtaining the sums it required by the ordinary course of taxation. The government was too " weak and insecure " for that. " Funding was the only means of raising supplies to which government could then resort." So says Mr. M‘Culloch; but he adds that " we are in a very high degree indebted to the aid which it afforded to the revolutionary leaders (honest words those) for the establishment of our free institutions, and, consequently, for the wealth and greatness to which we have since attained." No question the funding system has been a fine thing for wealth and greatness; but Mr. M‘Culloch, as I have shown in another place, is well aware that wealth, extravagance, and luxury, in certain classes, may advance concurrently with the depression of the great mass of the working people. For that mass what has the funding system done, or the " free institutions " which our considerate Dutch friend * of

* Mr. M‘Culloch does not believe it to be true that William the

1688 was so obliging as to patronize ?   " No one," says
Mr. M'Culloch, " can doubt that it is the bounden duty
of the legislature to adopt every safe and practicable
measure for eradicating or countervailing the causes of
poverty among the mass of the people, and for adding to
their comforts and enjoyments.   But of these causes none
seem to be more prolific of mischief than oppressive and
ill-contrived taxes."   But what is it that has, more than
anything else, made heavy taxation inevitable ?   What
is it that we are told makes it impossible to remove the
malt-tax, the tea-tax, the sugar-tax, the soap-tax, and all
the other taxes which enhance the price of commodities
consumed by the poor ?   It is that we must pay the interest upon that national debt which the weakness of an
unpopular foreign ruler first caused to rise into a formidable amount, and which has since been accumulated so
enormously, because owners of wealth preferred a perpetual tax upon industry to yielding up a larger portion
of their vast possessions for national purposes.

The account (on next page) of the gradual increase of
the national debt, and of the charge thereon, is taken from
Mr. M'Culloch's book.   He says it has been compiled
principally from Dr. Hamilton's work on the national
debt, and from the annual finance accounts.   He admits
there may be errors in it, but he feels pretty confident
that they are immaterial.

It will be observed that in the earlier periods the annual
charge created is enormous in proportion to the amount
of principal debt.   Mr. M'Culloch says that, " no doubt

Stadtholder " purposely involved us in debt and difficulties that the Hol-
landers might have the better chance of surpassing us in manufactures
and commerce."   He thinks the going into debt was a matter not of
choice, but of necessity, on account of the weakness and unstable foundation of the new government.

Account of the gradual Increase of the National Debt, and of the Charge thereon.

	Principal, Funded and Unfunded.	Interest and Management.
	£.	£.
Debt at the Revolution in 1689 . .	664,263	39,855
Excess of debt contracted during the reign of William III., above debt paid off .	15,730,439	1,271,087
Debt at the accession of Queen Anne in 1702	16,394,702	1,310,942
Debt contracted during the reign of Queen Anne	37,750,661	2,048,416
Debt at the accession of George I. in 1714	54,145,363	3,351,358
Debt paid off during the reign of George I., above debt contracted . . .	2,053,125	1,133,807
Debt at the accession of George II. in 1727	52,092,238	2,217,551
Debt contracted between the accession of George II. and the peace of Paris in 1763, three years after the accession of George III., above debt paid off .	86,773,192	2,634,500
Debt in 1763	138,865,430	4,852,051
Debt paid off from 1763 to 1775 . .	10,281,795	380,480
Debt at the commencement of the American war in 1775	128,583,635	4,471,571
Debt contracted during the American war	121,267,993	5,395,794
Debt after conclusion of the American war, 1786	249,851,628	9,867,365
Paid during peace, from 1786 to 1793 .	5,411,322	243,277
Debt at commencement of French war in 1793	244,440,306	9,624,088
Debt contracted during French war .	603,842,171	22,829,696
Debt at the consolidation of the English and Irish Exchequers at the commencement of 1817	848,282,477	32,453,784
Debt cancelled from 1817 to 5th January, 1844	55,942,584	3,184,624
Debt on 5th January, 1844, and charge thereon during preceding year . .	792,339,893	29,269,160

on account of the supposed instability of the government,
the terms on which loans were contracted during the
reigns of William III., Anne, and George I., were most
unfavourable." He consoles himself, however, with the
reflection that by means of them immense political advantages were gained. These advantages are doubtful, but
there can be no doubt of the great advantage to the
money-owners, who, because the government was unstable,
obtained for a small sum a large lien upon the fruits of
the future industry of the people.

But throughout the progress of this enormous structure
of debt, the grossest improvidence has been displayed by
those who managed the proceedings. It seemed as though
repayment of the sums borrowed was never contemplated,
for financial ministers only considered the amount of interest they engaged to pay, and did not hesitate to create
amounts of capital stock exceeding, by 80 per cent. or
more, the amount of the money they received. For a
very large portion of the original three per cent. stock,
the government did not receive more than 60l. in the
100l., and now it cannot be paid off or bought in, without
paying 66 per cent. more than was received. Going no
further back than the commencement of the great French
war, the loss in this way has been immense, as will be
seen by the table (next page), showing the amount of money
obtained, and the stock created in order to obtain it.

Thus it appears that, for the accommodation of
584,000,000l. in cash (with government security), the
country gave its bonds for 879,000,000l., of which
576,000,000l. remain still outstanding, and 303,000,000l.
have been discharged by means of the sinking fund.
Such improvident bargaining resembles more the heedless
conduct of a spendthrift heir, than that of a prudent
nation. Nor is this all : our government first gave
879,000,000l. in stock for 584,000,000l. in paper money,

Years ending the 1st of February.	Loans contracted in each Year.	Amount of Stock created.	Annual Charge created.	Portion paid to Sinking-Fund.
	£.	£.	£.	£.
1794	4,500,000	6,250,000	187,500	1,630,615
1795	12,907,451	15,676,526	599,118	1,872,200
1796	42,090,646	55,539,031	2,132,369	2,143,596
1797	42,756,196	56,945,569	2,274,528	2,639,724
1798	14,620,000	29,019,300	935,579	3,361,753
1799	18,000,000	35,624,250	1,105,602	3,984,253
1800	12,500,000	21,875,000	656,250	4,288,209
1801	18,500,000	29,045,000	871,350	4,620,479
1802	34,410,450	55,954,312	1,775,530	5,117,723
1803	23,000,000	30,351,375	910,541	5,685,542
1804	10,000,000	16,000,000	512,083	6,018,179
1805	10,000,000	18,200,000	546,000	6,521,394
1806	21,526,700	39,543,126	1,140,632	7,181,482
1807	18,000,000	29,880,000	896,400	7,829,589
1808	12,200,000	18,373.200	577,060	8,908,674
1809	12,000,000	13,693,253	587,744	9,555,854
1810	19,532,100	22,173,645	947,312	10,170,105
1811	16,311,000	19,811,107	763,955	10,813,017
1812	24,000,000	29,244,712	1,191,736	11,543,881
1813	27,871,325	40,743,031	1,486,272	12,439,632
1814	58,763,100	93,731,523	3,230,600	14,181,006
1815	18,500,000	24,694,830	851,833	12,748,232
1816	45,135,589	70,888,403	2,577,820	11,902,051
1817	3,000,000	3,000,000	90,000	11,491,670
	520,124,577	776,257,193	26,849,814	176,648,860
Loans raised on account of Ireland in Great Britain	64,750,000	103,032,750	3,324,550	11,873,490
Total sum raised	584,874,557	879,289,943	30,174,364	188,522,350
Deduct sums raised on account of Sinking-Fund	188,522,350	302,911,955	9,168,232	
Balance . £	396,352,207	576,377,988	21,006,132	

and then the legislature made a change in the law which
gave to the whole of the outstanding stock the value of
gold money. Thus the 576,000,000*l.* of outstanding
stock was enhanced from 30 to 40 per cent., or, in other
words, in return for 396,352,207*l.*, the net sum received
from loans from 1794 to 1817, the nation is now bound
in a sum equal to 768,000,000*l.* of the money in which
those loans were contracted ! Very excellent all this for

the fraternity of money-lenders, but a very grievous weight upon the industry of the country, and a monstrous injustice to those who are obliged to spend a very large proportion of their hard-earned incomes in heavily taxed commodities.

The official accounts, dated January 5, 1850, represent the total capital debt of the United Kingdom to be 775,734,579*l.* 18*s.* 3¾*d.*, of which 2,566,263*l.* 0*s.* 5*d.* have been transferred to the Commissioners for the reduction of the debt. The total "unredeemed debt," therefore, upon which the nation has to pay interest (independently of Exchequer bills) is 773,168,316*l.* 17*s.* 10¾*d.* The particulars of this debt are as follows :—

	CAPITALS UNREDEEMED.		
GREAT BRITAIN	£.	s.	d.
Debt due to the South Sea Company, at 3 per cent.	3,662,784	8	6½
Old South Sea Annuities , ,	3,195,194	4	5
New South Sea Annuities , ,	2,195,670	6	9
South Sea Annuities, 1751 , ,	494,780	11	9
Debt due to the Bank of England . , ,	11,015,100	0	0
Bank Annuities, 1726 . , ,	744,961	16	0
Consolidated Annuities. , ,	374,215,203	0	7¼
Reduced Annuities , ,	121,276,462	0	9
Total, at 3 per cent. .	516,800,156	8	9¾
Annuities at 3¼ per cent.	215,249,670	12	8
New 5 per cent. Annuities .	429,951	8	2
Total, Great Britain	732,479,778	9	7¾
IRELAND.			
Irish Consolidated Annuities, at 3 per cent.	5,361,597	15	11
Irish Reduced Annuities . , ,	115,475	1	2
Annuities at 3¼ per cent.	32,577,522	15	4
Debt due to the Bank of Ireland, at 3¼ per cent.	2,630,769	4	8
New 5 per cent. Annuities .	3,173	11	2
Total, Ireland	40,688,538	8	3
Total, United Kingdom, on January 5, 1850 .	773,168,316	17	10¾

The official statement of the annual charge upon the above debt of 773,168,316*l.* is as follows:—

CHARGE.

	IN GREAT BRITAIN.			IN IRELAND.		
	£.	s.	d.	£.	s.	d.
Due to the Public Creditor:—						
Annual Interest on Unredeemed Capital . . . . }	22,521,116	11	2	1,315,317	5	6
Long Annuities, expire 1860 . .	1,247,500	12	0	46,024	18	10
Annuities, per 4 Geo. IV. c. 22, expire 1867 . . . . }	585,740	0	0	. .		
Annuities for a limited term of years, per 59 Geo. III. c. 34, 10 Geo. IV. c. 24, and 3 Will. IV. c. 14, which expire at various periods, viz :						
£. s. d.						
Granted up to 5 Jan. 1850 . } 1,692,432 2 0						
Deduct Expired and Unclaimed up to ditto, including 106,100*l.* Waterloo Annuities, 59 Geo. III. c. 34 . . . . } 776,569 4 2						
	915,862 17 10	viz. 866,112	17	10	49,750	0	0
Payable at the National Debt Office.						
Life Annuities, per 48 Geo. III. c. 142, 10 Geo. IV. c. 24, and 3 Will. IV. c. 14, viz :						
£. s. d.						
Granted up to 5 Jan. 1850 } 2,294,261 8 6						
Deduct, Expired and Unclaimed up to ditto . . } 1,392,855 6 0						
	901,406	2	6	. .		
Tontine and other Life Annuities, per various Acts } English	17,809	13	1			
Irish .	34,230	8	7	6,524	2	3
	26,173,916	5	2	1,417,616	6	7
Management	94,925	19	3	. .		
Total Annual Charge, exclusive of 86,032*l.* 10*s.* 7¼*d.*, the Annual Charge on Capitals and Long Annuities, and Annuities for Terms of Years, per 10 Geo. IV. c. 24, standing in the names of the Commissioners on account of Stock Unclaimed 10 years or upwards, and of Unclaimed Dividends, and also on account of Donations and Bequests . . . . . . }	26,268,842	4	5	1,417,616	6	7

Total Annual Charge for the United Kingdom   .   £27,686,458 11 0

Mr. M'Culloch furnishes a table, by which it appears that, if no more interest on debt had to be paid than that which existed in 1793, the country might have expended all that it did expend upon internal government and foreign war from that time to 1816, and have incurred only 151,327,007*l.* of new debt, instead of 573,377,988*l.* In fact, the total expenditure of the country, on account of internal government, colonies, the war, and the debt *contracted previously to* 1793, from that year to 1816, both inclusive, was only 151,327,007*l.* greater than the revenue actually derived from taxes during that period. It was the profuse system of borrowing, and the interest and premiums paid for borrowed money, which rendered necessary the immense loans with the burden of which the nation is still loaded.   Such is the pressure of that load in our present currency, that one can scarcely contemplate any considerable addition in any shape to the National Debt; but if the necessities of the State should ever again make it necessary to throw forward a part of the weight of present expenses upon future years, it is to be hoped it will be managed as the Government now manages its *advances* for the purposes of drainage and other local improvements.   This is done, not by creating a perpetual annuity in the form of interest, till the principal sum is paid off, but by receiving an annuity which pays off both principal and interest in thirty years.   This seems to be as far forward as we can reasonably distribute the pecuniary pressure of present times.   It is rather too much that in the reign of Queen Victoria we should be paying for the wars of Queen Anne.   Even the battle of Waterloo ought to be remembered at this day for the glory which it cast upon British valour rather than for the amount of tax still paid, on account of the expense of it, by hard-working men who were unborn when it was fought.

During the reigns of the Dutch Prince and of Queen
Anne the ability of government financiers was confined to
the contracting of debt. In the time of George I. they
bethought them of paying off and reducing the annual
charge, and in the reign of subsequent sovereigns the
operations both of contracting and paying off debt, or
reducing the interest, have been largely attended to.
The first reduction of interest was in 1716, when, by
bringing it down to 5 per cent., a reduction of about 20
per cent. was effected in the annual charge. In 1727 the
5 per cent. was brought drown to 4 on the greater portion
of the debt. In 1737, as Mr. M‘Culloch relates, the 3
per cents. rose to 107, the highest they have ever been,
but Sir Robert Walpole would not avail himself of the
opportunity thus afforded to reduce the 4 per cents. interest to 3. This, however, was effected in 1749 by Mr.
Pelham. There was then a long interval of seventy-
three years before any further measure of a similar kind
was attempted. In 1822 the Navy 5 per cents.,
149,627,825l., were converted into new 4 per cents.,
157,109,218l. In 1826 the old 4 per cents., 70,105,403l.,
were converted into the same sum of 3½ per cents. reduced.
In 1830 the new 4 per cents., 151,021,728l., were converted into 150,344,051l. new 3½ per cents., and 474,374l.
new 5 per cents. In 1834 the 4 per cents. of 1826,
10,622,911l., were converted into new 3½ per cents. of
the same amount. In 1844 the new 3½ per cents.,
157,329,286l., were converted into new 3¼ per cents. of
the same amount, with a provision that the interest should
be further reduced to 3 per cent. in October, 1854, and
should not then be redeemable for twenty years more.
The result of all these operations was to increase the
capital of the debt by the sum of 7,278,090l., and to
decrease the annual charge or interest by the sum of
2,749,169

So much for the affairs of our public or National Debt, which to the cursory reader will doubtless seem a very dry subject, but I really think it will not be found to be so by those who will take the trouble to study the matter with some attention.   Any one who feels a call of the spirit in this direction cannot do better than read diligently and repeatedly the third part of Mr. M'Culloch's book on Taxation and the Funding System.   There is very little dogmatic theorizing in it, and a great deal of information.

Something, however, is yet to be said of debts other than those in the care of the Chancellor of the Exchequer.

The amount of private debt in the United Kingdom of Great Britain and Ireland has frequently been estimated, or rather guessed at, and conjecture seems to range between the amounts of 1,000,000,000*l.* and 3,000,000,000*l.* To most persons this will probably seem—at all events at the first glance—an incredible magnitude of debt; but I think they who place the amount somewhere between 1,500,000,000*l.* and 2,000,000,000*l.* do not make an extravagant estimate.   The amount of fixed property— such as lands, houses, mines, quarries, canals, railways, &c.—is actually returned to the Property-Tax Commissioners at about 90,000,000*l.* a-year, which does not include Ireland.   But suppose we take the income from fixed property at 100,000,000*l.* a-year, I believe it is not going too far to say that one-half of it is tied up by mortgages, settlements, or incumbrances of one kind or another ; or, in other words, the nominal proprietors of the property worth 100,000,000*l.* a-year have to pay away one-half, in the shape of interest, or of annuities, to persons to whom they are, in some form or another, indebted.   In this country a proprietor, until absolutely

compelled by the pressure of circumstances, rarely trans-
fers any part of his estate to those to whom he is indebted,
or to the children or other relatives whom he may desire
to endow with fortunes. He leaves his estate nominally
the same, but charges it with heavy sums of money which
remain as debt, and upon which an annual interest or
equivalent annuity is paid.   Now if half the income from
fixed property be thus disposed of, this 50,000,000*l*. a-
year may be considered to represent 1,500,000,000*l*. of
debt or incumbrance, to say nothing of the large amounts
which are lent upon personal credit, upon stock in trade,
upon goods *in transitu*, and in all the various transactions of a great commercial country. I exclude credits
from week to week, or day to day, such as are adjusted
by millions at the banker's "clearing-house" in London;
but, referring only to those various debts, whether upon
fixed or floating security, which pay interest, I apprehend
it is not an exaggeration to estimate them at nearer
2,000,000,000*l*. than 1,500,000,000*l*.   When we add
this to the National Debt, we shall find an enormous
sum of indebtedness of *a fixed amount of money*, from
which we may infer the extreme importance to this
country of any change in the currency.

Although they who took a principal part in the great
Currency change of 1819 did not contemplate an appreciation of more than 4 per cent., yet the result was an
increase in the value of money of not less than 33 per
cent.; and, supposing the private debt of that period to
have been 1,600,000,000*l*., the National Debt being half
as much more, the effect of the change of 1819 was to
add to the actual amount of then existing incumbrance,
public and private, an amount equivalent to the whole
National Debt, although the nominal amount was unal-
tered It has been sometimes argued that it matters

not much what is done with the currency, for if people
choose to agree among themselves that a counter repre-
sents a shilling or a guinea, so long as all start on equal
terms, no injustice is done.   But when we take into
account debts or fixed engagements of any kind, a change
in the currency must disturb the balance of justice ; and,
when the change is such as to increase the value of money,
it is a severe measure of oppression upon the weaker or
indebted class, while an undue advantage is given to those
who are least in need of it.

CHAPTER XXXV.

LOCAL OR PAROCHIAL TAXATION.

The local or parochial taxation of England and Wales is a subject of very great importance, and one which appears to stand very much in need of better regulation; yet, seeing that it has grown into what it is by local habits, good or bad, it would be rash to suppose that any very sweeping change could be carried into effect without producing much inconvenience and some results not conformable with justice. For example, though it cannot be denied that local taxation is most unequal, and that poor parishes are in many cases taxed much more highly than rich ones, yet, if we sought to remedy this by applying a general rate to all parishes, we should then oblige those whose local affairs were managed with economy, care, and skill to pay for others whose affairs are managed with slovenliness or extravagance. And as there is—I believe —more favouritism and artifice, or what is technically called *jobbing*, in the outlay of local taxation than of any other, the general diffusion of these local charges is the more to be objected to. But there are evils on both sides of the question, and certainly the *inequality* of local taxation in England is one of the most striking features of the whole subject. From a paper laid before a Committee of the House of Lords on the 6th of June, 1850, and compiled by Mr. G. L. Hutchinson from a Parliamentary Return of 1848, it appeared that there were

13,304 parishes in England, and 1016 in Wales, rated to the relief of the poor. Of these the number rated from

$\frac{1}{4}$*d.* in the pound to 6*d.* in the pound was			1,650
6*d.* ,,	1*s.* ,,		3,327
1*s.* ,,	2*s.* ,,		5,540
2*s.* ,,	3*s.* ,,		2,542
3*s.* ,,	5*s.* ,,		1,104
Above 5*s.* in the pound			157
			14,320

The same gentleman also gave in an account of the twenty parishes in England and Wales which in 1847 paid the highest rates, and the twenty parishes which paid the lowest. These are the parishes which had the honour of being rated highest:—

NAMES OF PARISHES.	Annual Value of Property Rated to the Poor's Rate in 1847.	Amount of Rate in the Pound paid in 1847.
	£.	*s.* *d.*
Livermere (Suffolk)	828	13 10
Nether Hoyland (York, West Riding)	799	12 4
Winterton (Norfolk)	517	12 4
Peterstone-super-Ely (Glamorgan)	100	11 9$\frac{1}{2}$
South Cockerington (Lincoln)	189	11 2$\frac{3}{4}$
Hindon (Wilts)	1,052	9 3
Duckenfield (Southampton)	226	9 2$\frac{1}{2}$
Weston-in-Gordano (Somerset)	347	8 9$\frac{1}{4}$
North Shields (Northumberland)	6,666	8 8
Newborough, St. Peter's (Anglesey)	814	8 6$\frac{1}{4}$
Stonesfield (Oxford)	888	8 5$\frac{1}{2}$
Fittleworth (Sussex)	1,111	8 1$\frac{3}{4}$
Brackley, St. James (Northampton)	1,379	7 8$\frac{1}{2}$
Colchester, St. Mary Magdalen (Essex)	512	7 8$\frac{1}{4}$
Lower Llansamlet (Glamorgan)	1,916	7 7$\frac{1}{2}$
Hastings (Holy Trinity)	293	7 7
Fernhurst	1,592	7 4$\frac{1}{4}$
Queenborough (Kent)	1,415	6 11$\frac{3}{4}$
Llanwchaeron (Cardigan)	533	6 11$\frac{3}{4}$
Crawley (Oxford)	781	6 11
Average, £1,097	21,958	..
Average of Twenty of the highest-rated Parishes	..	9 0

The following are the twenty parishes which were rated lowest in 1847 for the relief of the poor:—

NAMES OF PARISHES.	Annual Value of Property Rated to the Poor's Rate in 1847.	Amount of Rate in the Pound paid in 1847.
	£.	d.
Grove (Bucks)	1,316	¼
Barton Blount (Derby) . . .	1,800	¼
Drakelow (ditto)	1,933	¼
Bently Hungry (ditto) . . .	1,473	¼
Stillington (Durham)	1,285	¼
Syde (Gloucester)	750	¼
Laughton (Lincoln)	1,413	¼
Kingerby (ditto)	1,796	¼
Newball (ditto)	1,163	¼
Willoughby Scott (ditto) . . .	778	¼
Witchister (Northumberland) . .	859	¼
Bavington, Great (ditto) . . .	1,252	¼
Burton, West (Nottingham) . .	1,672	¼
Wardley (Rutland)	939	¼
Forscote (Somerset)	708	¼
Litchfield (Southampton) . . .	1,390	¼
Cold Norton (Stafford)	1,293	¼
St. Mary-Bulverhithe, Hastings (Sussex)	577	¼
Orleton (Worcester)	862	¼
Whitwood (York, West Riding) . .	4,038	¼
	27,297	
Average	1,364	

"Thus an annual value of property of 21,958*l.* paid in 1847 for Poor's Rate 932 times greater in amount than similar property the annual value of which was 27,297*l.*!"*

The parishes, however, in which the amount of property is very great, do not appear to figure either among the highest rated or the lowest. When a return states that a place is rated at so much for the "relief of the poor," it is not certain whether it means the relief of the poor merely, or the poor, police, and county rates, which are generally put together and collected in one sum. The local rates generally consist of poor, police, and county together; church rate; highway rate; paving, cleansing,

* *Sic.*; in House of Lords' Report.

and lighting (if in or near a town); sewer rate; burial-ground rate: and then there are separate borough rates and county rates in some instances. In the evidence of Mr. G. C. Lewis, M.P., to the Committee of the Lords, 28th of May, 1850, he gives some particulars of the larger and richer parishes as well as the smaller. The following is extracted from the evidence:—

" In what manner have you calculated the amount of assessments upon rural parishes?

" I will read one or two statements to the Committee. These facts were obtained about six or seven years ago; they are not very recent, but they were quite accurate at the time they were obtained, and for the purpose of comparison they still hold good. In the parish of St. Mary, Whitechapel, the poor rate and county and police rates were 2s. 10d., the church rate 1d., the paving rate 1s. 3d., the cleansing, lighting, and highway rate 8d., the sewer rate 2d.; making in the whole 5s. In Christchurch, Spitalfields, 5s. 7d. was the amount of the different rates; in St. George's, Hanover-square, they were only 2s. 3d., that being a rich parish. In St. Mary, Lambeth, the rates were 4s. 7½d.; in St. Mary Magdalen, Bermondsey, the rates were 5s. 10d.; and in Faversham borough 5s. 5d. I have here some rural parishes: in the parish of Graveney, in Kent, the whole rates were 1s. 6d.; Goodnestone, 2s.; Bromley, 3s. 3d., that contains a town; Farnborough, 3s. 10d.; the parish of Orpington, 3s. 6d. In St. James's, Dover, the rates are 2s. 3d. only. On looking through all the different parishes, it appears to me, as far as I can form a judgment from those figures, that the rural parishes pay a somewhat smaller poundage than the town parishes.

" In that account you have given of the metropolitan parishes, is there not likewise a heavy charge for police rates?

" I include all local rates.

" Which are assessed nearest to the net annual value, the metropolitan parishes or the rural parishes?

" I cannot answer that question."

Local taxation does not depend upon any fixed or regular basis. The whole sum required for each parish depends upon its local circumstances—the number of its pauper population—the management of the parish so as to provide work for the population—and a variety of other things. The pressure upon each owner of property depends not only on the gross sum required, but on the aggregate amount of property liable to be taxed, and on the judgment or the caprice of the valuator. In Mr. John Hyde's evidence to the Lords, 6th of June, 1850, he said,—

" This is a printed table of the valuation of the parishes. I was requested to test the valuation, and I carefully did so, with another gentleman ; we found that the first parish examined, which was a small one, was valued at upwards of 1300*l.*, and the real value of the parish, according to its rental, and it was a rental without any beneficial holdings, was also upwards of 1300*l.* ; there was only a few pounds difference. We went into the parish nearly adjoining, and found that it was valued by the same valuer at upwards of 1400*l.* ; but the *bonâ fide* rental of the parish was upwards of 2400*l.* We went into another parish, on the other side, which, with the exception of one, adjoins, and we found that the value placed by the valuer for the county rate was upwards of 4400*l.*, but the *bonâ fide* rental of the parish was upwards of 6400*l.* We went into another part of the county, and the first parish that we took we found was valued at something more than 2000*l.*, and the rentals were above 3000*l.* We went into the adjoining parish to that, a very valuable parish, with some good houses, as well as various descriptions of property, and we found that the value placed by the valuer was 3500*l.*, but the rental of the parish was 4500*l.* That is the case throughout the whole country."

Yet it is upon such uncertain valuations that the local tax is distributed upon the individuals who hold property in each parish. The same witness stated that in his own parish there was a railway, and also the most important canal in the kingdom, both of the same length; the canal is rated at 90*l.*, and the railroad at 4500*l.*! Railroads in some parishes he found assessed at a certain sum per mile, and in other places at 1000*l.* per mile more. In the same parish he found the railway assessment fixed at 1500*l.*, and afterwards raised to 4000*l.* Mr. G. L. Hutchinson stated to the same Committee (6th of June, 1850), that the assessment of the annual value of the property of England and Wales for the relief of the poor was 67,320,587*l.* The valuation for the property tax, which includes nearly the same descriptions of property (though some by construction of law are omitted in the assessment for the poor), was returned in 1843 at 85,802,735*l.*, and is now computed at 91,000,000*l.*

As to parochial expenses, take by way of specimen the following "little account" from the parish of St. Mary, Lambeth, a very extensive parish stretching several miles to the south of Westminster Bridge, and including both town and country. This is a *half-year's* account :—

PARISH OF ST. MARY, LAMBETH.

Expenditure of the Churchwardens and Overseers, from Michaelmas, 1849, *to Lady-day,* 1850.

		£.	s.	d.
Treasurer of the guardians of the poor	.	26,780	0	0
County rate	.	4,916	1	7
Carried forward . .		£31,696	1	7

Brought forward . . £31,696	1	7
Police rate	7,976	6	11
Collectors' poundage	1,163	3	3
Brokers' commission	361	15	2
Printing borough lists, as per barrister's order .	118	12	6
County lists	17	15	6
Jury lists	105	15	9
Expenses marking off for election of guardians .	9	3	0
Solicitor's account	64	17	3
Assistant overseer, 6 months to Lady-day . .	100	0	0
Fire rewards	70	7	0
Housing and care of engine and fire-escape, 6 months	6	11	0
Stamps for September and January rates . .	20	19	0
Visiting lunatics and chaise-hire	9	5	0
Printing	47	8	11
Stationery	60	4	9
Overseers' expenses (surveying) . . .	39	3	1
Gas for committee-room	14	2	7
Water rate, three-quarters to Lady-day . .	2	5	0
Sessions fees, allowance of rates, 10s.; poll-clerks, 2l. 2s.	2	12	0
Posting notices	1	19	0
Chaise-hire	11	8	0
Expenses for perambulation	16	5	8
Stone-mason, boundary posts . . .	87	15	0
Coals, 14l. 11s.; ditto, 6l. 10s. . . .	21	1	0
Fire-engine, 7s. 6d.; screens, 8s. . . .	0	15	6
Carpenter's work, poling	0	15	4
Constable's expenses	16	10	0
Disallowances to officers of 1839 and 1840 . .	150	0	0
Firemen, working engine, 6s. 6d.; Acts of Parliament, 3l. 9s. 11d.	3	16	5
	£42,196	**15**	**2**

J. B. CLARK, *Vestry Clerk.*

Vestry Hall, May 8, 1850.

I have not found in the official documents that have come under my observation a statement of the aggregate amount of local taxation in England and Wales. I think it has been assumed to be, in some Parliamentary statements, 12,000,000*l.* a-year for the United Kingdom. It appears by the Report of the Poor Law Commissioners presented to Parliament 'in 1850, that the assessment of England and Wales for what is commonly called poor rate for one year to Lady-Day, 1849, was 7,674,146*l.*, of which 5,792,962*l.* were expended for relief of the poor, the balance being applied to various other local charges, among which church rate and highway rate are not enumerated. The particulars were these :—

Relief of the poor	£5,792,962
Law charges, parochial and union	70,251
Proceedings before magistrates (expense of) . .	62,776
Fees to vaccinators	29,374
Payments for registration, under the Registration Act .	57,200
Payments for surveys, valuations under Assessment Act	15,282
Payments towards the county, borough, or police rate .	1,381,131
Costs of voters, burgess, and jury lists . . .	28,564
Expenses of parish property	5,817
For all other purposes	267,255

To pay all this there was a sum of nearly 200,000*l.* received from " other sources " in aid of the poor rate, as well as the sum levied by assessment. The expenditure for medical relief, 211,180*l.*, is not set down as having been defrayed out of the parochial rates. Mr. Cornewall Lewis, M.P., says in his evidence to the Lords (24th of June, 1850), that *half* the payment to the medical officers has been transferred to the Consolidated Fund, but the Report of the Poor Law Commissioners keeps the whole sum separate from the parochial charge, or at least does not state that the sums set down are only part of the expense of medical relief.

As some of the local rates are not included in the poor rate collection already mentioned of 7,674,146*l.*, and as that return relates only to England and Wales, it is very probable that the whole local rates of the United Kingdom are not short of 12,000,000*l.*

Mr. Spackman enumerates the "direct and local" taxation of all the counties in England and Wales leviable in respect of property, and makes the total sum 15,857,244*l.*, of which he says 12,012,410*l.* are paid by the landed interest and 3,844,834*l.* by the manufacturing interest. This sum, however, appears to include much more than local taxation, namely land tax, tithes, property tax on land, poor and county rates, highway rates, church rates, turnpike trusts, and property tax on dwelling houses and other property not being land.

Of late years certain sums have been granted by Parliament out of the general taxes of the country, in aid of the county rate and the rate for the relief of the poor, but the amount is inconsiderable compared with the whole amount of these rates. The county rate, Mr. Cornewall Lewis says (evidence to Lords' Committee, 27th of May, 1850), is only 859,000*l.* for all England: on the 24th of June he gives a statement of the sums voted by Parliament in aid of the county rate from 1835 to 1848.

1835, half year	£35,184
1836, whole year	82,944
1837 ,, ...	91,429
1838 ,, ...	94,855
1839 ,, ...	101,837
1840 ,, ...	115,663
1841 ,, ...	115,380
1842 ,, ...	134,566
1843 ,, ...	133,700
1844 ,, ...	118,669
1845 ,, ...	98,415
1846 ,, ...	125,482
1847 ,, ...	230,384
1848 ,, ...	248,688

I do not find any explanation of the great increase in the last two years, but I believe it arises from some arrangement made in 1846 as to the expense of criminal prosecutions, which were considered to be a national rather than a local concern, and therefore the expense was undertaken by the general government.

The aid granted to the poor-rate in 1848 and 1849 was as follows :—

Year ended Lady-day.	Medical Officers.			Schoolmasters and Schoolmistresses.			District Auditors.	Total.		
	£.	s.	d.	£.	s.	d.	£.	£.	s.	d.
1848 . .	77,891	18	0	18,362	8	9	13,000	109,254	6	9
1849 . .	78,424	16	7	20,529	0	4	13,000	111,953	16	11

The great object of the Committee of the Lords upon the laws relating to parochial assessments, which sat in 1850, appears to have been to investigate the question, whether a more general rating as to property, and a more uniform rating as to the various localities of the kingdom, were not desirable? The Earl of Malmesbury appears to have been the active advocate of a change, while Mr. Cornewall Lewis, M.P., Secretary of the Treasury, and formerly a Poor-law Commissioner, who was examined at great length on three different occasions, seems to have very elaborately supported the other side. The whole law regarding liability to assessment was laid down by him in detail on his first examination. The pith of the discourse is, however, to be found in the following extract:

" Will you state, as far as you recollect, what property is assessable to the poor-rate under the Act of Elizabeth? —I do not know that I can answer the question better than by reading the material words out of the Act of the forty-third of Elizabeth, upon which the whole of the law of rating, with respect to the poor-rate (and consequently most of the other local rates), turns. These are the words of the Act of the forty-third of Elizabeth : ' And they (*i. e.* the churchwardens and overseers of the poor), or the greater part of them, shall take order from time to time, by and with the consent of two or more such justices of peace as is aforesaid, to raise weekly, or otherwise (by taxation of every inhabitant, parson, vicar, and other, and of every occupier of lands, houses, tithes impropriate, propriations of tithes, coal-mines, or saleable underwoods in the said parish, in such competent sum and sums of money as they shall think fit), a convenient stock of flax, hemp, wool, thread, iron, and other necessary ware and stuff to set the poor on work, and also *competent sums of money* for and towards the necessary relief of the lame, &c., to be gathered out of the same parish, *according to the ability of the same parish.*' Those are the words of the Act of Elizabeth by which the poor-rate, the county-rate, and, with some few exceptions, the highway-rate, the church-rate, and all other minor local rates, are imposed. The Act expressly mentions ' occupiers of lands, houses, and tithes.' It further specifies ' coal-mines ;' and the express mention of coal-mines has been construed to exclude mineral mines ; it also specifies 'saleable underwoods ;' and the express mention of saleable underwoods has been construed to exclude timber. This is the general description of real property which is made expressly liable to the poor-rate. It is also said in general terms, that the inhabitants are to pay ' competent sums of money,' which are ' to be gathered out of the same parish according to the ability of the same parish.' Now those words certainly, in their general sense, might be construed to include all species of property, both personal and real. It is not said that each inhabitant is to be taxed according to his ability, but it is said that ' sums of money are to be gathered out of the parish, according to the ability of the parish.' The language is rather ambiguous, but *still it may be under-*

stood *in its generality to include personal as well as real property.* Now, that being the case, we have to look to the practice which has grown up under the words of the Act of Elizabeth. The practice has been to rate *the occupiers of lands and houses, and the tithe owners;* but it has *not* been the practice to rate any person *in respect of personal property.*"

This practice the Earl of Malmesbury desires to reform, and stated his plan in the following letter, which was given in as evidence, to the Committee of the Lords on the 24th of June, 1850 :—

"*Whitehall Gardens, June* 3, 1850.

"My Lord,—As a Committee of our House is now sitting to consider 'The Laws relating to Parochial Assessments,' I trust that the following suggestions, which I venture to present to your Lordship, will not be deemed illtimed or irrelevant.

" I assume that the injustice of assessing all local rates exclusively upon *real* property is admitted.

"I also assume that the anomaly of our parochial system is acknowledged, its most glaring defects being that the proprietors of close rural parishes can, and do, transfer their poor population to a neighbouring parish, thereby reaping all the advantage of their labour when efficient, without the responsibility of their maintenance when impotent; and that, in London, the rich western parishes, by their building improvements, are gradually driving the pauper population from their own courts and alleys into the eastern parishes, which, although possessing less property, must meet the increased charge. Thus the fundamental injustice of the law of assessment is rendered still more unfair in the details of rating.

" To any change in this system a strong opposition may be expected from the powerful and numerous body of persons who are comparatively exempt from local rating, such as capitalists of every kind, pensioners, annuitants, mortgagees, and receivers of fines, &c. They have always met any proposition in Parliament to charge them with an *equal* share of the local assessments (not by a direct assumption of privilege) but by objecting to the difficulty of reforming the various kinds of ratings, and by arguing that, if these rates were charged upon the consolidated fund, poor consumers would have to bear a new burden, and that the rates exciting no individual or personal interest would increase *ad libitum.* By also mixing up the various local imposts into one category, they have a great advantage in a debate, and also throw confusion upon the whole subject in a discussion.

" It appears to me, therefore, that our first step in legislating upon these imposts should be to take the *poor-rate* separately and *per se,* and that we ought to handle this subject as entirely distinct in its policy and moral obligations from the county, church, and highway rates.

" The virtue of the law of Elizabeth once admitted, it must be difficult for a man to affirm that any peculiar description of property should, by any vested and inherent privilege, be exempt from paying its proportionate quota to the maintenance of the poor, and if he said so there would be an irresistible argument *ad verecundiam* against him.

1. " Fully agreeing with the reasons usually set forth against charging the consolidated fund with the poor-rate, I prefer recommending a national tax, and would call it the Poor-tax.

2. " I propose that it should be assessed and levied on the same principle, and by the same officers, as the present income and property tax, assisted (if advisable) by the overseers.

3. " It appears that the average of the poor-rate expended for the five years from 1844 to 1848, in England and Wales, amounts to 5,289,930*l.* per annum, which is as nearly as possible the result of the *income* and *property tax* (5,408,159*l.*).   The poundage of this tax is 7*d.* ; but as it does not touch incomes below 150*l.* a-year (which would, of course, be liable to the poor-tax which I recommend), I calculate that about 5*d.* in the pound would be sufficient to raise the 5,400,000*l.* per annum lately expended on the poor of England and Wales.

4. " I propose that this poor-tax should be voted for a period not less than ten years, but that the assessments should be taken annually, so as to be adapted to the variability of income.

5. " From this fund each parish should be allowed the *average* sum expended by it on the poor during the last *five* years, which is ascertainable from returns already made to Parliament.

6. " To meet the probable and just apprehension that such a plan might induce carelessness in the local management, and increase the rates even more rapidly than under the present law, I propose that, if any parish should exceed this allowance so granted, it should be compelled to make up the difference by a *rate in aid*, raised *as it is now* on the *real* property of the said parish.

7. " The commissioners and their assistants would watch the changing circumstances of parishes, so that at the end of the ten years an equitable revision of the necessary allowance may be made.

8. " It is evident that this revision should not be too frequent (I think not oftener than *ten* years), because the *longer* the term the more careful the parish would be not to exceed the fixed allowance.

9. " Should a parish improve in its circumstances during

the period, and not expend the annual sum granted, I
propose that the guardians report each year to the Commissioners accordingly, and that these should be empowered to employ the surplus in aiding local emigration,
regard being first had to the analogous requirements of
that parish.

10. " The present average poundage upon *real* property
is 1*s*. 10*d*., or 9*l*. per cent. upon 67,320,507*l*.   Under the
system which I suggest, *personal* property (*which now pays
nothing*) would contribute a direct tax *of* 5*d*. in the pound
(and no more) for ten years.   The *land* would pay 5*d*. on
the rent and 2½*d*. on the tenants' profits, *i. e.* 7½*d*. in the
pound ; the whole of this being paid by the occupier, as it
is now, and a portion of the rate assessed on the rent
being deducted from mortgagees, jointures, and annuitants on the estate.

" Under the present system 822 parishes pay *below*, and
13,498 parishes *above* 5*d*. in the pound ; so that under
mine the ratepayers of the latter would be more or less
relieved.

" This plan would alter no present arrangement of staff,
and would incur no new expense.   It would interest a
large class of men of business and intelligence in the expenditure of the parish allowance, about which (from paying little or nothing) they are now careless.   It does not
shake the present principle asserted by Mr. Cobden, that
land is the best and natural security to the pauper for his
maintenance ; because, if the personal property of this
country gradually diminished, the poundage would increase
on what remained, and also upon *real* property ; and if
personal property altogether vanished in England, *real*
property would have to bear the full burden of the poor's
tax, and remain, as now, the great and last security of
the pauper.

" I believe that the security I propose against lavish expenditure would be more efficient than at present, when we find that poor-rates have increased 1,400,000*l.* in eleven years, from 1836 to 1847.

" A reform of other rates seems to me a more difficult matter, as they are hampered with the magisterial system. Their increase in some counties to *triple* the sum at which they stood eleven years ago, certainly requires reform. I believe, however, that the building and maintenance of the gaols, lunatic asylums, and police, should and could be, without any opposition from the public, charged on the consolidated fund, for all men are equally liable to insanity and robbery, and *personal* property is more exposed to depredation than *real.*

" I have the honour to remain
" Your Lordship's obedient servant,
" Malmesbury."

Since this letter was circulated the noble Lord says he has been made aware that money in the public funds was advanced to the country upon the express condition that it should not be subject to local rating. He must, therefore, increase his 5*d.* rate upon all other property to 5½*d.* The abstract justice of this plan can scarcely be disputed, or its conformity with the spirit of the law of Elizabeth's reign ; but there is undoubtedly this great objection to it, that it would equalize the burden where particular circumstances would rather justify an unequal pressure. In some parishes great pains are taken and sacrifices are made to prevent pauperism, and to cause all but the sick and aged to be supported by the wages of labour. In other parishes the owners and occupiers of property are stupidly inattentive to this matter, or wilfully reckless. It would be a great hardship, with reference to such cases, that well and ill conducted parishes should be equally taxed to the relief of the poor.

The Committee of the Lords reported that " the relief of the poor is a national object, towards which every description of property *ought justly to be called upon to contribute*, and that the Act of 43rd Eliz. c. 2, contemplated such contribution according to the ability of every inhabitant." Their Lordships reported also that " the substitution of a special tax, to be assessed and levied in the manner of an income tax, instead of all parochial rates incurred for the relief of the poor, but still under local supervision, has been ably enforced by the Earl of Malmesbury in his evidence, wherein he suggests some securities against any increase of expenditure which might result from such plan, upon which the Committee are not prepared, without further inquiry, to offer any opinion."

Thus, then, the question of local tax reform rests for the present; but as local taxation becomes year by year more oppressive from various projects of improvement, such as boards of health, sewage commissions, extramural interments, and the like, it seems impossible that the basis of such taxation should remain as it is. It has continued so long, because the land had privileges for which it was reasonable the land should pay. The legislature, having swept away such privileges as conferred a pecuniary advantage, must lay its account with having, ere long, to adjust the basis of local taxation accordingly; and with having to make all forms of wealth pay a certain proportion to the poor as well as houses and lands.

CHAPTER XXXVI.

SANITARY CONDITION OF THE PEOPLE.

In former times it was considered that the English were a cleanly people. I am very much inclined to hold to that opinion still, notwithstanding all the nauseous details with which every report upon the health of the people is filled, and which, taken by themselves, might lead to a different judgment. These reports all agree in assuming the great cause of disease, especially of epidemic disease, to be filth, and its poisonous exhalations. This cause of disease, misery, and death, is of course immensely aggravated by the growth of towns, and the increasing habit of gathering the people together in masses, for the greater convenience of manufacturing and money-making. Country villages, we are told, are no less badly provided with what promotes household cleanliness than towns are, but still the pure air has access to them, and dilutes or blows away the poison ; while, in the streets and courts of the towns, the fatal gases are confined, and inhaled by the unfortunate inhabitants. Every one who takes up a Sanitary Report must prepare himself for details of a character almost more disgusting than those of crime. For my part, I think a sense of decency should restrict and modify the publication of such statements of what is most loathsome and degrading in connexion with humanity. Such foul and hideous circumstances ought certainly to be attended

to and remedied, but this might be done without the
minute descriptions of them which are put into the official
records, and printed for public information. But the
persons who have undertaken the examination of these
subjects seem to have a kind of morbid satisfaction in
giving the most intensely disgusting particulars; and
though I have no doubt that the reality of the case is very
bad, and requires all the energy of plain, honest reform
that can be applied to it, yet I am persuaded that there
is a great deal of loose statement, and even of downright
exaggeration, in the printed accounts of these matters,
together with the most pedantic parade of scientific terms
and signs. Take as an example the following extract
regarding the Metropolis, from the Third Report of the
Sanitary Commissioners, which is republished in the
Report of the General Board of Health for 1849 :—

" At the last census, in 1841, there were 270,859
houses in the metropolis. *It is known* that there is
scarcely a house without a cesspool under it, and that a
large number have two, three, four, and more, under
them, so that the number of such receptacles in the
metropolis may be taken at 300,000. The exposed surface of each cesspool measures on an average 9 feet, and
the mean depth of the whole is about $6\frac{1}{2}$ feet; so that
each contains $58\frac{1}{2}$ cubic feet of fermenting filth of the
most poisonous, noisome, and disgusting nature. The
exhaling surface of all the cesspools $(300,000 \times 9) =$
2,700,000 feet, or equal to 62 acres nearly; and the
total quantity of foul matter contained within them
$(300,000 \times 58\frac{1}{2}) = 17,550,000$ cubic feet; or equal to
one enormous elongated stagnant cesspool 50 feet in
width, 6 feet 6 inches in depth, and extending through
London from the Broadway at Hammersmith to Bow
Bridge, a length of 10 miles."

" This," say the Metropolitan Sanitary Commissioners,
"there is reason to believe, is an under estimate. The
cesspool, however, in general forms but one-fourth of the
evaporating surface : the house-drain forms half or two-
fourths, and the sewer one ; but, connected as the sewers
and house-drains mutually are, and acted upon by the
winds and barometric conditions, the miasma from the
house-drains and sewers of one district may be carried
up to another. We cannot be absolutely certain that
part of the stench experienced in the Dean's Yard may
not have been due to the contents of the sewers from the
drains of the House of Commons, or at some time from
Duck-lane or Pye-street ; and, according to the evidence
of Mr. Batterbury, who met a strong current of air coming
from the extended cesspools near the school, the miasma
from that place would have been carried through the
common sewers, and from them into the streets and houses
of other neighbourhoods."

One cannot contradict a specific official statement of
this kind, and affirm that it is not so ; but I shall venture
to say, with all due deference, that I, for one, cannot
believe it. Nay, there is official evidence to prove that it
is at least an exaggeration, for in the Ninth Annual Report of the Registrar-General, dated August 1, 1848, the
state of the great metropolitan parish of Marylebone, in
respect to this very matter, is specially alluded to. After
stating that the parish contained in 1841 the vast number
of 14,169 inhabited houses, and 138,164 inhabitants, and
that the annual value of the property rated for the relief
of the poor was 815,279*l.*, the Registrar adds, " Yet a
considerable part of the parish is without sewers, or any
direct open communications with the sewers. *It is said*,
though the information on this head is imperfect, that
half the houses in the parish have cesspools, many of

which remain unemptied from year to year." Let this be compared with the report just quoted, asserting that there is scarcely a house without a cesspool under it. The *calculation* with which the assertion is accompanied seems to me too nauseous an absurdity to be examined. Immediately following this unsavoury account of London, there is in the Report of the Board of Health an allusion to Paris. The public are informed that in the French capital, "besides bad drainage, there is overcrowding to an extent of which some conception may be formed from the fact that a population of nearly 1,000,000 souls is crowded into little more than 40,000 houses, whilst the 2,000,000 people in London are distributed amongst upwards of 280,000 houses; the average number of persons in each house being in Paris 25, and in London 7." This is certainly a notable specimen of the information afforded in statistical tracts! The writer of the comparative statement seems to think that a house is a house, and that one is as capable of accommodating a given number of persons as another. Surely he ought to have remembered the difference between the street architecture of Paris and of London. Two or three of the Paris houses afford as much room for living and breathing in, as a whole street of the mean and confined dwellings which, in considerable districts of London, are called houses.

In the year 1839 the government, in compliance with an address of the House of Lords, directed the Poor Law Commissioners to make a general inquiry into the extent and cause of disease among the lower orders of the people. The result of this inquiry was a great mass of reports, which Mr. Chadwick, the Secretary of the Poor Law Board, condensed into one general report of his own. This was presented to Parliament in July, 1842. It forms a closely printed book of between four and five

hundred pages, very pedantic and painful, and very interesting in spite of some of its disgusting details.   The
philosophy extracted by Mr. Chadwick out of the whole
subject may be found in the following summary of his
conclusions, drawn up by himself :—

" First, as to the extent and operation of the evils
which are the subject of the inquiry :—

" That the various forms of epidemic, endemic, and
other disease caused, or aggravated, or propagated, chiefly
amongst the labouring classes, by *atmospheric impurities,
produced by decomposing animal and vegetable substances,
by damp and filth, and close and overcrowded dwellings,*
prevail amongst the population in every part of the kingdom, whether dwelling in separate houses, in rural villages, in small towns, in the larger towns—as they have
been found to prevail in the lowest districts of the metropolis.*

" That such disease, wherever its attacks are frequent,
is always found in connexion with the physical circumstances above specified ; and that, where those circumstances are removed by drainage, proper cleansing, better
ventilation, and other means of diminishing atmospheric
impurity, the frequency and intensity of such disease is
abated ; and where the removal of the noxious agencies
appears to be complete, such disease almost entirely dis-
appears.

" That high prosperity in respect to employment and

---

* " The population of Surrey exceeded that of Manchester, yet in seven
years 16,000 persons died in Manchester over and above the deaths in
Surrey."—*Registrar-General, 9th Report.*

" The great fact remains that the deaths (from cholera) were nearly
twice as numerous in ill-constructed towns, where the poison is concentrated, as in the country, where it is diluted and destroyed by the fresh
air."—*Ibid.*

wages, and various and abundant food, have afforded to
the labouring classes no exemptions from attacks of epidemic disease, which have been as frequent and as fatal
in periods of commercial and manufacturing prosperity as
in any others.

" That the formation of all habits of cleanliness is ob-
structed by defective supplies of water.

" That the annual loss of life from filth and bad ventilation is greater than the loss from death or wounds in
any wars in which the country has been engaged in modern
times.

" That of the 43,000 cases of widowhood, and 112,000
cases of destitute orphanage, relieved from the poor's-
rates in England and Wales alone, it appears that the
greatest proportion of deaths of the heads of families
occurred from the above specified and other removable
causes ; that their ages were under forty-five years ; that
is to say, thirteen years below the natural probabilities of
life, as shown by the experience of the whole population
of Sweden.

" That the public loss from the premature deaths of
the heads of families is greater than can be represented
by any enumeration of the pecuniary burdens consequent
upon their sickness and death.

" That, measuring the loss of working ability amongst
large classes by the instances of gain, even from incomplete arrangements for the removal of noxious influences
from places of work or from abodes, this loss cannot be
less than eight or ten years.

" That the ravages of epidemics and other diseases do
not diminish, but tend to increase, *the pressure of population.*

" That in the districts where the mortality is the
greatest, the births are not only sufficient to replace

the numbers removed by death, but to add to the population.

" That the younger population, bred up under noxious physical agencies, is inferior in physical organization and general health to a population preserved from the presence of such agencies.

" That the population so exposed is less susceptible of moral influences, and the effects of education are more transient, than with a healthy population.

" That these adverse circumstances tend to produce an adult population short-lived, improvident, reckless, and intemperate, and with habitual avidity for sensual gratifications.

" That these habits lead to the abandonment of all the conveniences and decencies of life, and especially lead to the overcrowding of their homes, which is destructive to the morality, as well as to the health, of large classes of both sexes.

" That defective town cleansing fosters habits of the most abject degradation, and tends to the demoralization of large numbers of human beings, who subsist by means of what they find amidst the noxious filth accumulated in neglected streets and bye places.

" That the expense of local public works is in general unequally and unfairly assessed, oppressively and unecomically collected by separate collections, wastefully expended in separate and inefficient operations by unskilled and practically irresponsible officers.

" That the existing law for the protection of the public health, and the constitutional machinery for reclaiming its execution, such as the courts leet, have fallen into desuetude, and are in the state indicated by the prevalence of the evils they were intended to prevent.

" Secondly. As to the means by which the present

sanitary condition of the labouring classes may be improved :—,

" The primary and most important measures, and at the same time the most practicable, and within the recognised province of public administration, are drainage, the removal of all refuse of habitations, streets, and roads, and the improvement of the supplies of water.

" That the chief obstacles to the immediate removal of decomposing refuse of towns and habitations have been the expense and annoyance of the hand labour and cartage requisite for the purpose.

" That this expense may be reduced to one-twentieth, or to one-thirtieth, or rendered inconsiderable, by the use of water and self-acting means of removal by improved and cheaper sewers and drains.

" That refuse when thus held in suspension in water may be most cheaply and innoxiously conveyed to any distance out of towns, and also in the best form for productive use, and that the loss and injury by the pollution of natural streams may be avoided.

" That for all these purposes, as well as for domestic use, better supplies of water are absolutely necessary.

" That for successful and economical drainage the adoption of geological areas, as the basis of operations, is requisite.

" That appropriate scientific arrangements for public drainage would afford important facilities for private land-drainage, which is important for the health as well as sustenance of the labouring classes.

" That the expense of public drainage, of supplies of water laid on in houses, and of means of improved cleansing, would be a pecuniary gain, by diminishing the existing charges attendant on sickness and premature mortality.

" That for the protection of the labouring classes and of the ratepayers against inefficiency and waste in all new structural arrangements for the protection of the public health, and to ensure public confidence that the expenditure will be beneficial, securities should be taken that all new local public works are devised and conducted by responsible officers, qualified by the possession of the science and skill of civil engineers.

" That the oppressiveness and injustice of levies for the whole immediate outlay on such works, upon persons who have only short interests in the benefits, may be avoided by care in spreading the expense over periods coincident with the benefits.

" That, by appropriate arrangements, ten or fifteen per cent. on the ordinary outlay for drainage might be saved, which, on an estimate of the expense of the necessary structural alterations of one-third only of the existing tenements, would be a saving of one million and a half sterling, besides the reduction of the future expenses of management.

" That, for the prevention of the disease occasioned by defective ventilation and other causes of impurity in places of work and other places where large numbers are assembled, and for the general promotion of the means necessary to prevent disease, it would be good economy to appoint a district medical officer independent of private practice, and with the securities of special qualifications and responsibilities, to initiate sanitary measures and reclaim the execution of the law.

" That, by the combinations of all these arrangements, it is probable that the full insurable period of life indicated by the Swedish tables—that is, an increase of thirteen years at least—may be extended to the whole of the labouring classes.

" That the attainment of these and other collateral advantages of reducing existing charges and expenditure are within the power of the legislature, and are dependent mainly on the securities taken for the application of practical science, skill, and economy in the direction of local public works.

" And that the removal of noxious physical circumstances, and the promotion of civil, household, and personal cleanliness, are necessary to the improvement of the moral condition of the population; for that sound morality and refinement in manners and health are not long found co-existent with filthy habits amongst any class of the community."

The first part of these conclusions seem to me to be nothing but a high-sounding and scientifically-expressed assertion of a self-evident truth. No one requires elaborate demonstration of the evils of filthiness, nor can any one of the least observation doubt that between dirt and depravity there is a close connexion. Grossness or deadness, or in some cases perversion, of the moral sense leads to neglect of cleanliness and decency, and then, in conformity with Nature's ordinary principles of production and reproduction, squalor and filth beget reckless and debased moral habits. It is a grave practical complaint against the discipline or tendency of the Roman Catholic religion, that, somehow or another, it is not at all so inimical as it ought to be to nastiness of living. In Ireland and in Switzerland the contrast between people of the same position in life, but professing the one the Roman Catholic, and the other the Presbyterian form of faith and worship, is very striking. The one seems to sanction the notion that dirt and physical discomfort are rather conformable with religious sentiment than averse from it; the other (more wisely and justly) appears to countenance the opinion that purity of mind should be marked by purity of body and cleanly habits. It is indeed very true that cleanliness, like the use of outward ornaments, very often arises from mere pride or vanity, and that dirtiness also frequently arises from a sense of abasement, as if people felt they were not worthy the trouble of making themselves and the things around them clean. But these are only additional illustrations of what every one knows, that in moral as well as in material things we constantly find the spurious mixed up with the genuine—that vanity does the work which ought to have its root and origin in virtue, and that humility, the sublimest of Christian graces, may be aped by that filthy moral debasement which most degrades humanity and brings it nearest to a level with brute nature.

But, to return to Mr. Chadwick's conclusions, what need of all the parade of words which they contain? Is it not enough that towns are generally filthy, that filth engenders disease, and measures of government, both general and local, ought to be resorted to in order to remedy the evil? That was, however, by no means sufficient for those appointed to inquire into the subject of dirt; they were resolved to magnify their office and to show off their science and philosophy. Moreover, it appears that the Chief Reporter had a favourite theory to bring forward, namely, that of liquifying all the dirt of towns by large supplies of water, and thus causing the deleterious matters, so noxious in towns, to run off into places where they might be made serviceable to the fields. Now this is a very excellent theory to be handled in treatises, and to be experimentally tried where there are means and opportunities of doing so, but it is as yet by no means certain that towns are best cleansed upon this principle, and very doubtful whether, in general, liquid manure is nearly so serviceable for agricultural purposes as solid manure. There are practical men who maintain that the shovel and the broom and the dry pit, well closed up, are far better, as well as more generally-applicable means of cleansing, than artificially conducted supplies of water; and that, as to the value of the refuse collected and compressed, it is incomparably greater than that of the refuse diluted so that it may run off in pipes and be lifted by pumps. But, besides this, there is the great practical consideration, that, even if it were quite true that, upon a wide national estimate, it would be cheaper to cleanse towns by conveying to them large supplies of water, yet still, as this expense is very great at the beginning, and as people are apt to be deterred by great and expensive plans, it might be far more beneficial practically to recommend measures more easy of adoption, and therefore more likely to be adopted. Had a shovel, broom, and cart establishment been recommended for immediate remedy in every town, subjecting the local authorities to penalties if cleanliness were not thus attended to, it is probable that some important good would have been really and immediately done. But something too grand and " scientific" having been projected, nothing was done; and when the frightful epidemic came a few years afterwards, and swept away thousands, the filthiness of towns was found to be every whit as bad as before the Commissioners had made their inquiries and Mr. Chadwick had published his Report.

The Reports of the Sanitary Commissioners in 1844 and 1845, the Ninth Annual Report of the Registrar-General, published in 1848, and the Report of the General Board of Health, presented to Parliament in 1849, are all of them full of the most shocking representations as to the filthy condition of certain parts of the metropolis, and of provincial towns and villages. In the metropolitan parish of Marylebone, we are told, that, while " the vestry, under the local Act, is empowered to nominate persons to carry out the dust, dirt, cinders, or ashes, yet no effectual arrangements are made for the removal of decaying animal and vegetable matters—the filth and noxious matters which are really prejudicial to health. The contracts only apply specifically to ashes, which are innoxious."   There is in this, as in so many other practical affairs in England, a curious slavery to the word and letter of statutes and legal agreements, which hinders the progress of business.   What ought to be done is left undone, because the nets and entanglements of legislation or of law—the difficulty of exactly defining the legal responsibility applicable to the case—stand between the desire to do what is needful and the execution of the work.   In the Report of the General Board of Health, published the year after the passing of the Public Health Act, they relate that a clergyman, the incumbent of Christ Church, Regent's Park, wrote to the Board for information as to " what he should do in order to effect the cleansing and draining of his parish ? "   But they, the guardians of the public health, instead of giving him a plain answer to his plain question, only showed him that it was impossible such an answer could be given ! They wrote him a letter, from which the following is an extract, copied from their own Report :—

" The number, condition, and action of the bodies constituted by the local Acts is one object of investigation by the Metropolitan Sanitary Commissioners, and they have been hitherto unable to complete that inquiry.

" There appear to be upwards of 120 local Acts for the more dense portions of the metropolis, for the management of upwards of eighty distinct local jurisdictions, many of which coincide neither with parish, nor union, nor police district, nor any other recognised division. When a householder, who gives his address in a particular street, applies to know how he may proceed—if the local Act be sought out, and the provision in relation to the matter in question be also sought out—he cannot always be safely answered, inasmuch as streets are frequently divided, sometimes longitudinally, and paved and cleansed at different times, under different jurisdictions. At present no public maps are known to exist by which the area of the jurisdiction could in any such cases be ascertained correctly.

" In the parish of St. Pancras, where you reside, there are no less than sixteen separate Paving Boards, acting under twenty-nine Acts of Parliament, which would require to be consulted before an opinion could be safely pronounced as to what it might be practicable to do for the effectual cleansing of the parish as a whole.

" The General Board of Health can only state, in answer to such applications, that the information sought can be obtained by no other means than local inquiry; and they hope that this will be done on behalf of house-holders, by the Parochial Board acting under the general directions of the Board of Health now issued."

When we read such a statement as this, we may rest assured that tedious and perplexed Acts of Parliament, attempting to define everything, and to give effect to scientific theories, are not the remedies proper for the case. Well-guarded, but still discretionary, power should be given to some person or persons to cause to be done, as expeditiously as may be, that which the circumstances of the case require. If these circumstances must wait till voluminous and perplexed legislation can be propounded and understood, and new systems on a great scale can be organized, the reform will come too late, and will probably be neglected altogether. I think this should be plain enough to any one of common sense, and yet the Board of Health is so full of the idea of accomplishing a grand "scientific" revolution in respect to sanitary improvement, that they put forth such a paragraph as the following in their Report :—

" In the local works which it is necessary to execute for the sanitary improvement of towns, it is to be recollected that *an entirely new system of sewerage must be combined with a new system of house drainage, with a new system of water supply, and with a new system of removing and of applying the refuse of towns to agricultural production.* All the improvements in these works are founded on the demonstration of actual trials and established precedents, but the instances are distant and widely scattered, and may be out of the reach of any one engineer or person whom the local authorities could employ, and to these authorities themselves they will generally be utterly unknown."

Who does not see that this is to attempt a great deal too much ? It may be very well to lay down such rules for towns yet to be built, or for the additions to those in existence, but to think of carrying into effect all these new systems in the old streets of the old towns is dreamy extravagance. Some more rapid remedy for existing evils must be resorted to. The Report of the Registrar-General (December, 1846) says that " the population of the district of St. George, Manchester, is to a great extent composed of the lower order of Irish, who live and lodge together in great numbers in the same house. In one part of the district called *Angel Meadow* it is not uncommon to find twenty or thirty persons living in one house, where there is not accommodation for one-third of

that number, especially if health is to be in the least considered. During the last two or three months large
numbers of the poor from Ireland have crowded themselves in the district, droves of them rambling about the
streets seeking lodgings, and no doubt being exposed to
the severe and inclement weather. Many of the poor
creatures have died from cold, producing fever and other
diseases. It cannot be surprising that, while such a state
of things exists, the mortality should be great." Certainly
not; but what will " entirely new systems of sewerage
or house drainage " do for such evils, even if it were
possible to carry these systems into effect? It is evident
that for such a case altogether a different sort of remedy
is required. The passport system should exist in respect
to vessels carrying this class of passengers, and these
miserable crowds should not be allowed to come over
without previous inquiry as to their means of existence
for a limited time after they arrive, and as to the accommodation which could be provided for lodging them.
There should be powers of police, as well to protect
public health, as to protect private property.

In the year 1848, six years after the elaborate Report
upon the sanitary condition of England had been made,
several Acts of Parliament were passed under the pressure
of an alarm which existed about epidemic disease. The
Nuisances Removal and Diseases Prevention Act was for
immediate use, but the grand *Magna Charta* of the sani-
tarians is the Public Health Act, 11 and 12 Vic., cap. 63,
passed on the 31st of August in that year. It appears
at first surprising that, in a free country, it should be
possible to pass an Act which sets aside all constitutional
principle as this does—which gives unlimited powers of
taxation to local bodies, which sets at nought the old
principle that an Englishman's house is his castle that he

may hold against the world, and which gives the Privy
Council power to *make law* upon matters regarding public
health for all towns or other localities not previously
governed under the provisions of some local Act of Parliament ; but the public was alarmed, the Public Health
Act was passed late in the session, and, in short, none,
save the framers of it, took any interest in its details.

The Act applies to all England and Wales, *except*
London and Westminster, but the whole area for twelve
miles round St. Paul's Cathedral, in the City of London,
is subjected to an equally tedious and tyrannical measure,
passed in the same session, and called the Metropolitan
Sewers Act.   Under the Public Health Act the General
Board of Health is constituted.   It is to consist of the
Chief Commissioner of the Woods and Forests for the
time being, together with two other persons to be appointed
by Her Majesty,* and this Board is of course to have its
establishment of secretary, clerks, servants, &c., for which
establishment the Treasury is empowered to pay, together
with a staff of inspectors, whose allowance is not to *exceed*
three guineas a-day to each, besides travelling expenses !
It is then enacted, that upon the petition of not less than
one-tenth of the rated inhabitants of any city, town,
borough, parish, or place, having a known or defined
boundary, not being less than thirty in the whole ; or
where the number of annual deaths in any place shall
have exceeded the average number of twenty-three to the
thousand ; a superintending inspector may be directed to
make a visitation and inquiry, and to examine witnesses,
for the purpose of enabling him to report on its sanitary
condition.   Various minute provisions are introduced,

---

* A fourth member of the board (with a suitable salary) is constituted
by the Public Cemeteries Act, 1850.

commanding the publicity of all the proceedings of the inspector, and an interval of one month is ordered to take place from the publication of his report, within which statements may be forwarded to the General Board of Health respecting this report.

If, after these preliminaries have been gone through, the General Board of Health think fit to apply the Act to the place in question, and if there be no local Act of Parliament in force for paving, lighting, and cleansing the place, they shall make their report to her Majesty in Council, and her Majesty, with the advice of her Privy Council, may order the Act to be put in force ; but if an Act of Parliament be already in force, then the General Board of Health shall make a " Provisional Order," with such provisions, regulations, and restrictions as they may think necessary, and such provisional order shall be published and officially deposited in the place to which it is to be applied ; " *and* in case it shall be enacted by any Act of Parliament hereafter to be passed that the whole or part of any provisional order or orders of the General Board of Health shall be confirmed and be absolute, such orders, or so much of them as shall be so confirmed, shall be as binding and of the like force as if the same had been expressly enacted by Parliament, and every such Act shall be deemed a public general Act." These " provisional orders" may *repeal*, alter, or extend any existing Act ; and the practical effect is, that a number of these provisional orders, prepared in a public office, relating to various towns, are lumped together, and the consent of Parliament has in the last two sessions been obtained as a matter of course. Practically, the local law, oversetting former Acts of Parliament, is made in the office of the General Board of Health, and not in Parliament. Though there is ample provision in the general Act, the

operation of which I am now considering, for full publicity
of all the preliminary proceedings, there is no provision
that Parliament shall satisfy itself of these things having
been done before giving to " provisional orders" the force
of law ; and it was complained, by petition to the House
of Lords in the session of 1850, that the preliminary proceedings commanded by the 11 & 12 Vic. c. 63, had not
in fact taken place in respect to certain towns included in
the " provisional orders." The Minister, however, who had
charge of the bills which gave these " provisional orders"
the force of law did not heed the petitions—nor did the
House, for it was near the close of the session—nor did
the public ; for neither the petitions, nor the scarcely
audible conversational discussions of them, found a place
in the newspapers.

The costs of preliminary inquiries are, with the consent
of the Treasury, to become a charge upon the general
district rates leviable under the Act. The local Boards of
Health are to consist of the town councils, or of a selection of persons qualified to be town councillors, and made
partly by the municipality and partly by the owners of
property and ratepayers. The rules of election are laid
down with the usual minuteness and unintelligibleness of
Acts of Parliament. They occupy about ten folio pages
of print. The expenses of such elections are to be defrayed out of the general district rates. The local boards
may appoint such servants, at such salaries, as they think
proper, subject to the approbation of the General Board ;
the expense to be defrayed out of the rates. The local
boards may also appoint a medical practitioner as " officer
of health." They may also have maps and plans made
at the expense of the ratepayers. The sewers become
vested in the local boards, to deal with them as they think
proper. No drains are to be made into " the sewers of

the local Board of Health" without their consent; and
any one who builds any vault under the street without
consent of the local board may be fined. No new house
is to be built without proper drains; and if a house be
without a proper drain, the local board may order it to
be made, and if the order be not obeyed they may cause
it to be made, and compel the owner to pay the cost. The
same enactments are made with respect to certain in-door
conveniences; and if any one complain that anything of
the kind in any one's house is a nuisance, and injurious
to health, the local board may, after twenty-four hours'
notice to the occupier, enter such house, with or without
assistants, and open the ground and make examination,
and give notice to the owner *or occupier* to do what is
considered needful, and fine him for every day the work
is left undone; or the board may cause the work to be
done, and compel the owner to pay the expense. The
board shall take charge of surface cleansing of all streets,
&c., and they may erect and maintain public conveniences, which the 57th section more particularly describes. They may cover up offensive drains and ditches,
and the owner or occupier of premises " whereon the same
exist" may be made to pay the expense. If, upon the
certificate of any officer of health, it appear to the local
board that any one's house is in a dirty condition, and
wants cleansing or whitewashing, the board may order
it to be done by the owner or occupier, or do it, and
compel the owner or occupier to pay the cost. In short,
except providing a man's dinner for him, or paying his
bills for such things as he may presume to order on his
own account, it is hard to say what the local Board of
Health may not undertake to do in household arrangements. And, besides all these things, lands may be
entered upon, moneys may be borrowed, rates may be

mortgaged, and rates may be made either for expenses past, or expenses present, or expenses contemplated at some future time. This pleasing enactment is to be found in section 89. The Act contains, from beginning to end, no less than 152 sections; and if it were possible for largeness and minuteness of authority, "regardless of expense," to arrange everything upon the most salubrious footing that Swift's "nice men"—that is, "men of nasty ideas"—could possibly have devised, one might expect such a result from this Act. But it is easier to plan than to execute. To make Acts of Parliament, and to appoint commissioners, and even to provide them with salaries out of the public taxes, are much easier achievements than to make such a complicated piece of machinery as the Public Health Act *work*. Hitherto it has produced a great deal of party strife in towns, and, it is said, some not very creditable official proceedings at head-quarters; but it is to be feared that as yet very little, if indeed anything, has been done to make the atmosphere of crowded neighbourhoods more wholesome, and to give that part of the population which lives in the worst and most decayed parts of towns, more favourable opportunities for obtaining clean water and pure air. And even this would not be enough; for though I am unwilling to bring any charge against the poor and the hard-working, yet it must be owned that, without some kind of compulsion, the miscellaneous, and often degraded, population of towns would be but too slow to take advantage of opportunities afforded them, however much for their own ultimate advantage.

The Report of the General Board of Health (1849) frankly confesses that a great dread of the expense of what the new Act requires, constitutes the main objection to it on the part of the people. To me this seems both a

natural and a reasonable dread.   The General Board of
Health, however, thinks that, under the new system,
works would be so much more economically executed
than they have ever been before, that there is no good
ground for apprehension on the score of expense.   They
rely upon the *estimates* made by the inspectors, which
strongly contrast with the experience of the local authorities, insomuch that these functionaries *incredulously*
exclaim that such works cannot be carried out for such
sums as those mentioned in the Reports.   For my part, I
think it a very discreet incredulity which distrusts official
estimates, and holds past experience to be a better guide.
The General Board says that

   " The reports of the inspectors show, almost invariably,
that the chief works required will (if properly executed)
be largely in reduction of existing direct charges ; as, for
example, that the house-drains and the apparatus, with
the water supply, in substitution of the cesspool, will not
be half the annual expense of cleansing the latter. Similar
works, where there had been any executed under the un-
controlled direction of the local boards, had, as we shall
show, been far from inspiring confidence either in their
efficiency or their economy of construction ; while the
dread of heavy immediate outlays was frequently sufficient to preclude a fair hearing, or a consideration of the
means provided in the Act to avoid them, through facilities for raising money on loan, and by arrangements for
repayment by equal annual instalments of principal and
interest, proportioned to the benefits conferred, and distributed over periods of time.

   " The persons interested in the lower class of houses
commonly demanded that securities should be given that
the expense of the works should not exceed the estimates,
and that they should be efficient ; and they frequently

asked that the inspector, as an engineer, should be made responsible for the works.   At Totness, and Launceston, and several other places, this was anxiously expressed; and it was mentioned at Durham and elsewhere, as a desirable advantage, even by professional men.

" The steps required by the Act, of the local publication of the recommendations of the inspector as to the works proposed to be executed, the provision for sending in and considering objections, denote the intention of the Legislature that the ratepayers should be satisfied in respect to the fairness and advantage of the future expenditure; and, undoubtedly, the examination of past works continues to confirm the apprehensions expressed, both as to the efficiency of the works and as to the reasonableness of the expenditure and the justness of the assessments."

It may easily be believed that the *intention* of the Legislature was that everything necessary for the health of the people should be done upon pure public grounds, and with all the economy that is consistent with efficiency. And we may rest satisfied also that the General Board of Health has no other object than to improve the sanitary condition of the places with the present local government of which it interferes.   But when we come to consider local parties and their mutual animosities, the case is very different; and the General Board should take great care that their officers do not become partisans of one side in these local feuds, and that they strictly comply with " the steps required by the Act which denote the intention of the Legislature."   In this respect there is certainly room for improvement, and some vigilance in high quarters will be requisite to prevent the measures, ostensibly for the improvement of the health of towns, becoming really the elements of strife and the instruments of oppression.

People of experience know that this result is by no means guarded against by making the local authority elective. Popular elections, as they are commonly conducted in England, do not tend to quell bad passions, nor to soothe discordant feelings. Neither is it usual in towns of considerable size for the sense of the majority to be fairly attained in this way. There are such things as surprises, and canvassings before the matter is understood, and various manœuvres, more distinguished for dexterity than justice, by which matters of this kind are often managed. Above all, there is in England the great difficulty of inducing those classes whose judgment ought to have great weight to take the trouble necessary for success in matters determined by popular election. Indolence or disdain, or pre-occupation with their own affairs, or disgust of being brought into conflict with a rough and ill-mannered crowd, throw popular elections very often into the power of those not only least qualified to judge with knowledge and discretion, but determined, so far as they can, to do mischief with the means put into their hands to do good.

The Board of Health itself complains of its want of power to compel popular bodies to do what is necessary in cases of emergency. It complains that guardians of the poor (elected by the ratepayers), although in a state of ignorance as to the course which such occasions require, refuse to be guided by the larger experience which they have no means of acquiring of themselves, and instances are pointed out in which by their mismanagement and delay—as alleged—a great loss of life has occurred.

A measure has been passed in the session of 1850 giving power to the Board of Health to forbid interments of the dead within certain localities, and to provide public cemeteries and all the usual establishments therewith connected. It is intended that these establishments should support themselves by means of interment-fees—a power, however, is given to levy a rate-in-aid of a penny in the pound annually upon the property assessed to the relief of the poor.

It is unquestionable that of late years much stir has been made in various ways regarding public cleanliness and public health; but I suppose all the practical operations are, as yet, only in their preliminary stage; for, up to the present time, I have not heard of much having been actually done, except in respect to public baths, or rather baths and washhouses, at a cheap rate, for the poor; and also lodging-houses for persons of moderate means, on an economical scale. These, however, are all the result of private speculation or associated benevolence, and do not spring from any measures of the legislature or of the Board of Health.

CHAPTER XXXVII.

THE ENGLISH POOR LAW.

A FRENCH Commission reported of our Poor Law some twenty years ago that it was *la plaie politique la plus dévorante de l'Angleterre.* About the same period, or shortly afterwards, very strong statements were made about it in Parliament, leading to a public belief, or alarm, that the real property of England was likely to be swallowed up altogether by the charge for relief of the poor, unless something were done to check the progress of so large an expense. A change of the law—intended for reform and improvement—took place in 1834. The total amount of money, however, raised as poor rate for England and Wales, was at its *maximum* in 1818, when it reached 9,320,440*l.* In 1824 it had fallen to 6,836,505*l.*, and in 1833 it had gone up to 8,606,501*l.* In 1837, three years after the change of the law, the sum levied as poor rate was 5,294,566*l.*, and the amount " expended for the relief of the poor " reached the *minimum* of 4,044,741*l.* ; in 1818 the sum *expended* was 7,870,801*l.* It has been noticed in a previous paper that the money collected as poor rate includes several charges as well as that of maintaining or relieving paupers. In 1848 the poor rate collected amounted to 7,817,430*l.*, and the sum expended for relief of the poor was 6,180,764*l.* In 1849 the sum was nearly 400,000*l.* less. The difference of expenditure between 1834 and 1848 was trifling. It was indeed found

that the strictness of the law of 1834 could not be maintained.   The habits of certain large classes in England
had been so formed to the system of obtaining help from
the poor rates, without becoming absolute paupers, that
it was found impracticable to maintain a different system,
which in theory recognises no right to relief except as an
inmate of the poorhouse or pauper asylum.   The expenses, therefore, which rapidly declined after the passing
of the law of 1834, and while the system of what is called
" out-door relief" was considerably checked, grew up
again as that check, in obedience to public opinion, was
relaxed.

Whether the poor law of England be abstractedly an
evil or a good, is a question of great difficulty ; but even
if the question could be determined, we are not in a
position to act upon any decision directly and largely
adverse to the existing system.   The habits and circumstances of the nation are such that, without a system of
large relief of the indigent, society would not be safe.
If we had never had a poor law, there certainly would be
very good reason to hesitate before adopting a system,
liable at all events to some serious objections, which costs
five or six millions a-year ; but the prudent politician
must consider circumstances as they are, and content
himself with the best arrangement of which they will
admit.   It has been matter of complaint against the spirit
of the present time, that, whereas we once thought it our
duty to relieve poverty and suffering, whenever we could,
we now think it our duty to criticise and sit in judgment
rather than relieve.   I am not indisposed to sympathise
with this complaint, but I feel very much the difficulty
of determining whether the poor-law system, in the extent
to which it has gone, has been more a good or an evil to
the great body of the people who live by labour.   It is

by that principle, and by that principle alone, that I
would try the system. If the legal provision for the poor
has a tendency to produce, and does in fact produce, a
very large amount of pauperism that otherwise would be
struggled against and avoided, then it is, for so far, an
evil. If it operates against carefulness and thrift, or if
it induces people to submit to an unjustly low rate of
remuneration, relying upon the poor rate for that assistance in times of difficulty which even the working man
ought to be able to provide out of his own surplus in
periods of full work, then it is for so far a mischief, and
not a good.

From what we have seen, in a preceding chapter, of the
remuneration of the peasantry, and the difficulty which is
found in eking out a bare subsistence from the wages of
agricultural labour in many counties, it seems as if the
rates of payment were really too low, leaving the poor
rate as the only available provision for age or sickness,
or any other incapacity for work. On the other hand, it
is found that, where wages are very good, as in mines, or
in some kinds of manufacture, there exist habits of the
most reckless waste, as if the English workman had no
sense of a future to be provided for—no thought beyond
that of pampering his present appetite while he has the
means. Upon this point there are some statements in
Mr. Tremenheere's "Blue Book" for 1850 upon the
mining districts, more startling than anything of the kind
I ever read before. Speaking of South Staffordshire, he
gives much credit to the clergy for having effected a considerable softening of the formerly fierce manners of the
people ; but in other respects the picture he gives is very
deplorable. The cruel and brutalising sports to which
the population were formerly addicted have greatly de-
creased. The incumbent of Wednesbury informed him

that twenty-two years ago he had seen brought in one
day to the "baiting-place" of that town seven bulls,
three bears, and a badger, besides dogs and cocks for
fighting. With the decline of those exhibitions of cruelty,
the manners and language of the lower classes have improved, as have also the external aspects of cleanliness
and comfort. Many matters affecting the health and
self-respect of the mass of the population, which were
formerly overlooked, now attract attention, but the dark
part of the picture is yet to come :—

" Nevertheless, in recognising with satisfaction the
advance already effected, and the more cheering prospects
of the future, we must not be led away from a steady
contemplation of the actual state of society in this district.
Its distinguishing feature at the present moment unquestionably is, that, as regards the labouring classes, *the half-
savage manners of the last generation have been exchanged
for a deep and almost universally pervading sensuality.*
The people employed at some of the works towards the
outskirt of the district, and a portion of those towards its
centre who have had the benefit of resident masters or
more careful superintendence, may be somewhat raised
above the rest in this respect; but the unvarying testimony of all the most competent observers, residing or
engaged among them, is, that the above is the prevailing
characteristic of the present habits of the mass of the
population.

" The means of ministering abundantly to gratifications
of this kind are seldom long out of the reach of the
labouring classes in this district, especially of those employed in the iron-works, whose great earnings in good
times (perhaps 50*s.* a-week on an average) are well
known. Even in times of depression, as of late, the
colliers and miners seldom earn less than 16*s.*, and might

usually earn more if they would consent to work six days
in the week.   When trade is in a good state, the earnings
of the ' thick-coal collier ' are from 20s. to 30s. per week,
and those of his family often 10s. to 20s. in addition ;
the earnings of the ' thin-coal colliers ' being at the same
time from 20s. to 24s. per week.   The recklessness and
extravagance with which these sums are spent have been
commented on in all the Reports on the habits of the
mining population yet published.   Poultry, especially
geese and ducks ; the earliest and choicest vegetables
(e.g. asparagus, green peas, and new potatoes, when they
first appear in the market) ; occasionally even port wine,
drunk out of tumblers and basins ; beer and spirits in
great quantities ;   meat in abundance, extravagantly
cooked ; excursions in carts and cars, gambling, &c., are
the well-known objects upon which their money is squan-
dered.   The universal tenor of the evidence collected by
me on my recent inquiry justifies the assertion of only
a very partial improvement in these respects : and this,
more, I fear, under the pressure of the recent presence of
the cholera, and of comparatively low wages, than as the
result of any higher motive.

" The causes that have encouraged this devotion to
mere animal indulgences have been so often pointed out
that they need scarcely be repeated.   This vast crowd of
men has been gathered together within a narrow space,
without any adequate means being provided to arm them
against the increased temptations which such agglomera-
tion, accompanied by high wages, brought with it.   The
external circumstances with which they are surrounded,—
the smoke that darkens the face of nature, the surface of
the ground either occupied by or marked with the adjuncts
of mining or manufacturing labour, the dirt of the streets
and lanes, the frequent absence of drainage, the common

want of a sufficient supply of water for purposes of cleanliness, personal and domestic, the crowded houses, the
absence of privacy, the ignorance of the wife of household duties,—these causes, added to the vacancy of mind
arising from want of culture, and the slight restraints
imposed by their religious convictions, place every kind
of recreation but those connected with the lowest appetites,
almost out of the question for the great majority, and
combine to sink the labouring man below the level at
which it is either safe or creditable that he should be.

" But, in addition to the discredit of such a state of
things to the wealth and intelligence of the most important iron-producing district in England, the practical
inconveniences and pecuniary losses resulting from it have
long since forced themselves on the attention of all the
principal persons who have embarked their capital in the
great enterprises with which that county abounds. The
ignorance which obstructs all appeals to a man's reason
and sound judgment; the sensuality which debases his
character and renders him inaccessible to any arguments
except the grosser ones of the lowest and most short-
sighted self-interest; the absence of due domestic control
in the bringing up of children, which renders all after-
discipline the more difficult ; the few ties of any kind that
bind man to man in this district ; the insulation and
independence which so many circumstances in their daily
life tend to foster and exaggerate, have aided in producing a spirit of insubordination, as much out of harmony with a satisfactory state of society, as it is injurious,
even under the most purely commercial point of view, to
all parties concerned.

" This spirit of insubordination shows itself under
various aspects.   In its effects it amounts practically to a

claim, that, in relation to the application of capital, the servant is to govern and not the master."

It certainly is matter of regret that people who behave in this way—even allowing something for exaggeration of statement—should have a claim upon the rates for support, when they are unable otherwise to live. Education is said to afford the best ground for expecting improvement, but the Commissioner says that parents take away their children from school as soon as they can earn anything, in order that there may be more to spend in gross indulgence. The following are points of evidence :—

" A leading minister of a Dissenting congregation said,—

" ' I have long been well acquainted with the mining people of this neighbourhood, and have frequent occasion to visit them in their houses. They are sadly given to sensual and self-indulgent habits. They spend their money as fast as they get it in "feasts and fasts." Men who are getting a pound a-week, and might get more, will let their wives and daughters work upon the pit bank, and you may see them on their return home, filthy and dirty, set about cooking their husband's or father's dinner, and with no ideas of how to make a home respectable.'

" A contractor, who also held prayer meetings in his pits, as a local preacher, said,—

" The conduct of the men in good times was very bad ; sabbath-breaking, gambling, drunkenness, and neglecting their families, are their common practices ; and a great many have said lately that the bad times and the cholera were sent to punish them.'

" The Rev. Mr. Davis, whose experience had been longest of the Dissenting ministers stationed at the large town of Bilston, informed me,—

" ' That he regretted to say, that, according to his own observation, the women were quite as much given to self-indulgence in their habits as the men. He knew instances of men earning 2*l.* a-week, who, to add to their means of extravagance, allowed their wives or daughters to work on the pit banks, or anywhere ; and that numbers who were earning a pound a-week did so.'

" A large employer, also a Dissenter, stated,—

" ' *After the wages are received on the Saturday night, plenty of the men go into a cook's-shop with their wives and spend nearly every farthing they have.*'

" Another contractor, in the employ of one of the principal proprietors of the district, stated,—

" ' The efforts of the Wesleyans have been very great in doing what they could for the religious instruction of the people. I am a Wesleyan myself, but my apprentices attend the church. I have been a "butty" for many years, and do what I can to discourage bad habits in the men, especially drunkenness. But they will bring their families clear to ruin for drink. Plenty of them go to chapel and attend prayer meetings, but they take very little heed of what goes on, and plenty cannot understand what they hear either in church or chapel. The butties are doing all they can to set the best example ; but all the prayer-meetings and preachings will not keep the men from drink or from their other bad habits, and they spend every farthing they can upon themselves, and care little what becomes of their families.'

" It is superfluous to add that the account given to me by the clergy and by all persons best capable of observing the real moral condition of the labouring classes in this district was to the same effect in every respect as above."

If these statements be true, or anything like the truth, it is no wonder that pauperism and want should abound in bad times. The most striking illustration of the improvidence of certain classes of the English working-people is, however, yet to be given :—

"It is both interesting and instructive to compare the conduct of English workmen with that of foreigners under similar circumstances. In the Appendix to my Report on Mining Inspection in France and Belgium (1848) I described the habits and manners of the French colliers and miners, especially those at the large iron and coal works in the coal-field near Valenciennes, and I was compelled, by the force of unexceptionable evidence, to show how superior they were in every respect, except that of mere animal power, to the generality of the mining population in this country. I mentioned the fact that at the large iron-works at Denain, employing about 4000 people, there were 30 Englishmen from Staffordshire. These men were earning about one-third more wages than the French labourers ; *but they spent all they earned* in eating and drinking, were frequently drunk, and in their manners were coarse, quarrelsome, disrespectful, and insubordinate. The very respectable English manager, who had held for many years responsible situations under some of the leading iron-masters in Staffordshire, stated to me with regret that so different and so superior were the intelligence and the civilized habits and conduct of the French, that, if any thirty Frenchmen from these works were to go to work in Staffordshire, ' they would be so disgusted, they would not stay ; they would think they had got among a savage race.' By a somewhat singular coincidence there have been lately 40 Frenchmen employed at one of the large manufactories in Staffordshire, by the Messrs. Chance, at their extensive and well-known glass-works, in the parish of West Bromwich, in the immediate neighbourhood of some of the great iron-works. I thought it desirable to endeavour to ascertain from Mr. Chance what had been the character of these men while in his employ. Mr. Chance informed me as follows :—

" 'A few years ago we brought over 40 Frenchmen to teach our men a particular process in our manufacture. They have now nearly all returned. We found them very steady, quiet, temperate men. They earned good wages, and saved while they were with us a good deal of money. We have had as much as 1500*l.* at a time in our hands belonging to these men, which we transmitted to France for them. One of them, who sometimes earns as much as 7*l.* a-week, has saved in our service not much short of 4000*l.** He is with us now. He is a glass-blower. We have about 1400 men in our employ (in the glass-blowing and alkali works) when trade is in a good state. I am sorry to say that the contrast between them and the Frenchmen was very marked in many respects, *especially in that of forethought and economy.* I do not think that, while we had in our hands the large sum mentioned above as the savings of the Frenchmen at one time, we have had at the same time 5*l.* belonging to our own people. They generally spend their money as fast as they get it.'

" I should hope it would be scarcely possible for any one in any rank of life connected with South Staffordshire to read this statement without a feeling of humiliation. Forty French labourers come over, and by honest industry, reasonable economy, and conduct becoming them as men and as Christians, save in a few years what may place them in circumstances of comfort for the rest of their lives. During the same time 1400 Englishmen by

---

* This seems rather an incredible sum ; perhaps it should be four hundred.

their side, earning high wages, live a life of sensuality, and are as poor and discontented at the end of that period as at the beginning. I conversed with a few of the Frenchmen remaining, whom I saw at their work; their manner and mode of expressing themselves formed a contrast with those of the generality of English labourers, and, judging from the expressions of one of them, their appreciation of the state of society around them in their own class was such as might be expected from men who felt themselves above it."

These are very striking facts; and though I cannot help feeling a little incredulous about the extent of the Frenchmen's savings, yet I have no doubt that in general they are more thrifty, more sober, and more provident than English workmen are. Whether the legal provision for the poor have, or have not, anything to do with this absence of saving habits on the part of English workpeople, it is certain that it interposes a shield between these spendthrifts and that absolute destitution, the dread of which would perhaps make them more careful. A recent writer on the comparative state of the working people abroad and at home, has put forward the theory that the British workman is improvident from want of opportunity to become an independent proprietor by means of his savings. I do not think the effect is produced so much by want of opportunity as want of ambition or taste for proprietorship. The Frenchman or German certainly has that ambition, and practises great self-denial (for which he deserves great praise) to attain his object. What might be the result of making land more easily purchaseable in small quantities, I cannot pretend to determine; but at present not one English labourer in a thousand, or one skilled handicraftsman in fifty, ever dreams of proprietorship. To live on wages, and to eat and drink of

the best these wages will afford, is all the personal independence to which he aspires. He is so accustomed to
look up to proprietorship upon a grand scale, that his feeling with regard to small proprietorship is not that of envy,
but of contempt. This is fortunate for employers ; and
perhaps among the many causes which conspire to make
England so great in manufactures and commerce, not one
of the least is the patience and willingness with which
multitudes of men, from their early years to their old age,
go on working for various masters, without the ambition
to be proprietors, or to work only for themselves.

The last complete return presented to Parliament of
the expense of maintaining and relieving the poor of England and Wales, was for the year ending Lady-day,
1849 :—

For that year the sum expended in maintenance was	£1,052,515
Out-relief	3,359,269
Other expenses immediately connected with relief .	1,381,177
	£5,792,961
The total amount levied by assessment as poor-rate was	£7,674,146
The amount expended in law charges was . . .	£70,251
Further charges for proceedings before magistrates, &c.	62,776
Paid to vaccinators	29,375
Paid for medical relief	211,181

By an account presented to Parliament towards the
close of the Session of 1850, it appeared that the number
of *adult able-bodied* paupers of both sexes receiving relief
in England and Wales on the 1st July, 1849, and 1st
July, 1850, were as follows :—

	In-door.	Out-door.
July 1, 1849 :—England, 563 unions . .	16,726	136,658
,, Wales, 42 unions . .	539	10,636
Total . . .	17,265	147,294

Of those receiving out-door relief upwards of 50,000 were widows:—

	In-door.	Out-door.
July 1, 1850 :—England, 563 unions . .	13,834 ··	114,224
,, Wales, 42 unions . .	393 ··	10,124
Total . . .	14,227 ··	124,348*

Of those receiving out-door relief upwards of 51,000 were widows.

Taking the totals of the 605 unions in England and Wales, the numbers of able-bodied receiving relief on 1st July, 1849, were 164,559; and on the 1st July, 1850, 138,575, showing a decrease of 25,984. In every county in England, save Kent, Northumberland, and Westmoreland, there appears to have been a decrease of the pauperism of the able-bodied. In Kent the increase is 1, in Northumberland 117, and in Westmoreland 12. In Wales there was an increase in Brecon, Cardigan, Merioneth, and Pembroke ; in the other counties a decrease.

The following is the detailed return of the paupers of all classes, including children, in the different counties of England and Wales, at the dates already mentioned :—

---

* A letter from Mr. George Frederick Young, published in the *Times* newspaper of Sept. 4, 1850, charges this return with being disingenuous, and complains that it, as well as other poor-law returns, have been made up with a view of supporting the case of those who advocate what is called Free Trade. Mr. Young asserts that "an examination of the period that has elapsed since the withdrawal of protection will, with the single exception of 1847 (during which year wheat absolutely reached at one time the price of 120s. per quarter), exhibit the ascending scale of expenditure for the relief of the poor, measured in wheat, as follows:—

To Lady-day, 1846	1,860,738 quarters.
,, 1847	1,797,894 ,,
,, 1848	1,916,516 ,,
,, 1849	2,877,438 ,,
,, 1850	2,523,761 ,,

NAMES OF COUNTIES.	Number of Unions.	Population in 1841.	Relieved on 1st July,	
			1849.	1850.
ENGLAND:				
Bedford	6	112,379	7,366	6,899
Berks	12	190,367	12,369	12,046
Buckingham . . .	7	138,255	11,060	10,927
Cambridge	9	171,848	14,496	13,268
Chester	9	344,860	13,768	13,408
Cornwall	13	340,728	21,076	18,688
Cumberland . . .	9	177,912	8,213	8,123
Derby	9	242,786	8,176	7,129
Devon	17	430,221	34,418	31,388
Dorset	12	167,874	15,972	14,762
Durham	14	326,055	19,335	17,760
Essex	17	320,818	24,268	23,830
Gloucester	16	330,562	22,030	20,769
Hereford	8	110,675	8,061	8,028
Hertford	13	176,173	12,135	10,551
Huntingdon	3	55,573	3,723	3,662
Kent	27	534,882	31,289	31,721
Lancaster	28	1,719,306	91,731	81,482
Leicester	11	220,232	14,993	12,363
Lincoln	14	356,347	18,415	18,482
Middlesex	22	846,207	43,881	40,399
Monmouth	6	150,222	9,133	8,526
Norfolk	21	343,277	27,469	27,669
Northampton . . .	12	199,104	13,383	12,929
Northumberland . . .	12	265,988	16,975	17,712
Nottingham	9	270,719	11,729	11,272
Oxford	8	143,510	11,123	10,991
Rutland	2	23,150	1,020	1,052
Salop	13	191,052	9,665	9,631
Somerset	17	454,446	36,763	35,537
Southampton . . .	23	268,989	21,961	21,190
Stafford	16	443,982	17,725	17,898
Suffolk	17	314,722	24,131	24,468
Surrey	19	523,238	29,524	26,525
Sussex.	20	223,623	17,425	16,960
Warwick	12	358,244	22,368	14,350
Westmoreland . . .	3	56,469	2,968	2,999
Wilts	17	223,246	20,459	19,931
Worcester	13	336,108	17,256	16,675
York, East Riding . .	10	221,847	10,819	10,729
York, North Riding . .	15	180,643	8,645	8,481
York, West Riding . .	22	917,033	48,207	39,877
TOTALS of 563 unions in England . . . }	563	13,423,672	815,523	761,087

NAMES OF COUNTIES.	Number of Unions.	Population in 1849.	Relieved on 1st July,	
			1849.	1850.
Brought forward . .	563	13,423,672	815,523	761,087
WALES.				
Anglesey	1	38,105	3,729	4,621
Brecon	4	55,399	3,277	3,350
Cardigan	5	75,136	5,943	5,818
Carmarthen	5	110,404	7,256	7,219
Carnarvon	4	86,728	8,304	8,196
Denbigh	3	68,483	4,889	4,562
Flint	2	64,355	5,504	5,365
Glamorgan	5	178,041	12,500	11,397
Merioneth	4	50,696	4,771	4,908
Montgomery . . .	3	58,709	6,724	5,794
Pembroke	3	78,563	5,300	5,497
Radnor	3	19,554	2,017	1,894
Totals of 42 unions in Wales	42	884,173	70,214	68,621
Totals of 605 Unions in England and Wales . }	605	14,307,845	885,737	829,708

Thus in Kent, Lincoln, Norfolk, Northumberland, Rutland, Stafford, Suffolk, Westmoreland, Anglesey, Brecon, Merioneth, and Pembroke, there has been an increase of general pauperism between July, 1849, and July, 1850; but in all the other counties of England and Wales a decrease. Upon the whole the balance shows a decrease of 56,029 upon the gross number of 1849, which was 885,737. While, however, the returns from 605 unions of parishes in England and Wales showed an amount of but 829,708 persons of all classes receiving relief on the 1st July, 1850, the return (in p. 165 of the last Report of the Poor Law Commissioners) from 590 unions and single parishes, states the number receiving relief on the 1st Jan, 1850, to have been 881,206. It is probable that the season of the year makes a considerable difference in the amount of pauperism, and that the date of the 1st July is precisely that when the accounts would present the smallest number receiving relief. It is worthy of remark, that Staffordshire, the scene of that reckless extravagance of the working miners, noted in Mr. Tremenheere's " Blue Book," is one of the counties in which an increase of pauperism has taken place. Might not a wise and watchful Government attend to such indications as these, and try whether a little wholesome discipline might not be permitted by the Legislature to check the ruinous habits of these people, and to make them take better care of their own interests? In Ireland the experiment has been tried of giving large and increasing doses of political liberty for the cure of social recklessness, but it has not been attended with very distinguished success. Might it not be worth while to try a somewhat different plan in those parts of England and Wales in which the population seem to invite their own degradation and ruin?

A gentleman who, as a guardian of the poor in a large union of one of the Metropolitan counties, has considerable opportunities of observing the working of the present Poor Law system, writes to me as follows :—" The old Poor Law was designed to encourage the growth of population. Abuses grew to such a height under its administration that a reform became indispensable ; but change was substituted instead. Upon the same principle that a man can manage his own affairs for himself better than his neighbour can manage them for him, a parish can do the like for itself; and the machinery was already in existence. Each parish had its own workhouse ; and if the law had forbidden relief in aid of wages, and had made the clergyman of the parish *ex officio* chairman of the guardians of the poor, with full instructions as to the intentions of the Legislature, and individual responsibility for carrying out those instructions, the old parochial system might have been retained with greater economy to the rate-payers, and greater satisfaction both to them and the paupers. All the parish workhouses have now been abandoned, and union-houses built in their stead. A number of parishes—in the country from ten to twenty generally – are grouped into a union, which is usually built in the largest of the market-town parishes. The union has a master and matron and staff of officers, so that a very considerable proportion of the whole amount of the poor-rate of the kingdom is absorbed in establishment-charges—that is, it is not spent directly in the sustentation or aid of paupers at all. Each parish pays for its own paupers, whether in the union-house or receiving out-door relief, and also pays towards the establishment expenses a quota proportionate to what it pays to its paupers.

" The paupers in the union-house seem so much better fed and kept, than the class of labouring poor who support themselves, that one wonders at first why all the poor do not betake themselves to the workhouse— but practically there is little or no enjoyment of life there, and the great mass would rather be half-starved out of doors than fatten in the union-house. On the other hand, the dissolute and profligate *do* use the union-house for their home, leaving it when fairs, or races, or any other circumstance leads them to do so, and demanding readmittance whenever it suits their purpose to return. The provisions of the law are such that these persons—and especially abandoned women—can set the guardians at defiance. They go when they please, and come when they please, and make a mere convenience and a foundling hospital of the union-house. The expenditure of

the union to which I belong, and which embraces twelve
parishes, is about 300*l.* per week, including out, as well
as in-door relief; and the guardians all believe that the
expenditure would be less if each parish had its own poor
in its own workhouse.   Character goes for little when a
pauper comes before the board of guardians, because to
the great bulk of them the pauper is of course an utter
stranger.   So generally, however, is misconduct of some
sort the cause of the pauperism, that whenever a case of
mere misfortune, not brought on by ill desert, is plainly
proved before the board, it is hailed with a burst of sympathy as a rare and deplorable case.   Two relieving-
officers have the duty of attending to all cases of destitution, from whatever cause, from week to week.   On the
weekly day of meeting these cases come before the board
itself.   The paupers appear in person, if not prevented
by illness or inability, and the relieving-officer reports
verbally all that he knows, or has been able to ascertain,
of the particulars as to character and means of the applicant, and also what he has already done in the way of
relief.   Every parishioner of every parish in the union has
the right of demanding from the relieving-officer an order
of admission to the house ; but this is a last resort : what
is usually sought is temporary out-of-door relief during
sickness, or while out of work.   After long trial we have
abandoned in despair the attempt to find in the workhouse
any profitable, or even any unpleasant, form of work for
the able-bodied poor, whom we want to deter from
throwing themselves upon the union-house for support.
Compulsory idleness—such as requiring men to sit all
day upon a bench with their arms folded—has been
gravely proposed as a remedy.

" The general arrangements in-doors are just like
those of any large hospital—large well-ventilated wards

with a multitude of beds, and all kept scrupulously clean
—but with an absence of any air of home or comfort.
There are similar wards, without beds, for day-rooms.
The sexes are separated; and the old, the able-bodied,
and the children, kept apart in three several departments
to each sex. Both women and men can depart when they
please, and return when they please, in defiance of the
master and guardians, who may not make a prison of the
union-house, nor may they deny admission to any applicant pleading destitution. Women who are known to be
prostitutes, undisguisedly employ the union-house as a
means of defraying their domestic expenses, more especially in cases of child-birth. They go forth at their
own pleasure to follow their calling, and return when it
better suits their convenience, from ill-health, or pregnancy,
or any other cause, to take to the union-house, where they
have always a numerous companionship of women like
themselves, to lessen the irksomeness of idleness and clean
living.

" The cost of maintaining an adult pauper varies of
course at different times and in different places. The
present weekly average with us is from 3s. 6d. to 3s. 10d.,
not including establishment charges."

This account of the pauper-union system I give as it
has been given to me. I do not agree in the opinion that
it would be well to place the clergyman of the parish at
the head of the parochial establishment for the support of
the poor. I would have the clergyman to be as little as
possible the administrator of civil government, and to
have as little as possible to do with secular affairs. The
harshness of legal authority is better placed elsewhere.
The clergyman serves a higher Master than the highest
of those who make human laws, and I would not willingly
see him mixed up with the painful details of business.

which poor-law administrators, who do their duty to the public, must constantly encounter. The picture, however, which has been given, shows, I think, sufficiently that the existing system for relief of the poor is greatly abused ; and while it is, I believe, true that very many suffer the most awful severities of destitution without any relief at all, it is no less true that hundreds, or perhaps thousands, of audacious profligates, live upon the funds which are collected from the people in order to succour the unfortunate.

The Report of the Poor-Law Board presented to Parliament in the last Session, indicates the great pains taken to regulate the very important business of providing for the poor, so far as general rules of administration can be made effectual.   But, in truth, the details of indigence throughout every parish in the kingdom form too vast a subject for the cognizance of central authority.   In every distinct locality peculiarities of circumstances exist, and the same rules which are salutary in one place, are found to be productive of abuses in another.   No one, without reading the Report, would imagine the variety of matters over and above the leading object of providing sustenance and shelter for paupers, to which the attention of the governing body is given.   The measures to be taken for the education of pauper children, and the providing more suitable and healthful accommodation for those of the metropolitan parishes and unions, appear to occupy much attention.   It is to be feared the contrast is very great in this respect between the children left to the public care as paupers and those of the working classes who support themselves.   In all that regards school education and training, pauper children have a very decided advantage. And yet one cannot feel that this compensates for the other circumstances of their condition.   Nay, there is something in the uniformity of their appearance and behaviour, produced by this very training, which one contemplates with pain. I thought it an ingenious and touching observation of an anonymous writer respecting a long procession of charity children—" Altogether it is a depressing sight—so many living things, and so little life." * The spirit of Charles Lamb was in that remark.

The relief of vagrants, or wandering poor, appears to be one of the most difficult points connected with poor-law administration, and the precautions taken with respect to this class of applicants, open some curious views of the life of a large number of persons in England. The Poor-Law Board issued, in August, 1848, a minute which is much referred to in the Reports of the District Inspectors as having been productive of useful results. The minute urged on boards of guardians the necessity of discriminating between real and simulated destitution, in order to stay, if it were possible, the rapid increase of vagrancy. The recommendations of the minute were very generally adopted, and a considerable decrease has taken place in the number of vagrants applying for relief. The number relieved on the 1st of July, 1848, was 13,714, and on the 1st of July, 1849, only 5662. It is, however, to be observed that general distress and difficulty of living were much more marked in 1848 than in 1849. Mr. Grenville Pigott, an inspector of the metropolitan counties, says that much greater vigilance has been exercised since the issuing of the minute, and proceeds with the following statement :—

" Two opposite courses, with reference to vagrants, were pursued in unions in 1848 and in 1849. In the former of these years, every casual applicant for admission

---

* *Spectator* newspaper, July 7, 1849.

to a workhouse was admitted, as a matter of course, receiving at least two meals in the workhouse ; whereas,
in the latter, it became a general practice to admit none
but those who were suffering under sickness, or evident
destitution, or women with young children. The result
of these different courses seems to confirm the truth of
an opinion generally entertained by those who have to
deal with this class of paupers, that, independently of the
great aggregates or professional rogues and vagabonds of
which London and other large towns are the homes and
centres, there existed, in each rural district, *a certain
number of idle and dissolute persons, many of them brought
up in workhouses, who systematically passed the summer
months in wandering from union to union, within a limited
circuit, begging and committing petty depredations ; and
finding each night certain food and shelter in the adjacent
workhouse.* So long as masters of workhouses believed
that they were bound to admit all applicants, a great
encouragement was afforded to idle persons to lead a
vagabond life rather than to apply themselves to regular
labour, and many young boys have no doubt been thus
encouraged to run away from their masters or families.

" It does not appear that any injury has been inflicted
upon the poor by the more stringent administration of
this species of relief. On the contrary, *bonâ fide* way-
farers, poor persons going from one place to another for
a legitimate object, if destitute, are now better treated
than before was possible, when, from the numbers demanding admission after nightfall, no discrimination could
be made, and thus persons of good character had often to
pass the night in crowded wards with the most filthy and
worthless of the community."

These, indeed, are painful " annals of the poor," or
rather of the profligate, who, in England, avail them-

selves to so considerable an extent of the provision made
for the poor. In the Report of Mr. Andrew Doyle, Inspector of the North-Western District of England and
Wales, there is a still more graphic account of pauper
vagrancy and its shifts :—

" In compliance with the instructions of the Board,
that I should communicate the result of any measures
adopted in this district for the repression of vagrancy, I
have the honour to inform you, that immediately after
the Circular of August 4, 1848, was issued, I took occasion to bring it under the consideration of the Guardians
of the different Unions comprised in this district. By
many of those Unions the increasing pressure of vagrancy
was then severely felt, and I found amongst the Guardians a general disposition to avail themselves of the
remedies suggested in the circular of the Board.

" Of a number of communications received by me in
reply to inquiries which I made immediately after the
circular had been issued, I select the following letter from
Mr. Kemp, the master of Wrexham Workhouse, as containing, I think, a not exaggerated statement of the character of the evil which had attracted the attention of
the Board :—

" For a length of time we were in the practice of giving
the tramps their supper and lodgings without any return
being asked in the shape of work ; but the breakfast in
the morning was withheld until some little was done in
the way of acknowledgment. At some times, they had
the option of going away without any breakfast, if they
preferred that to working. The number of vagrants continuing to increase, the Board of Guardians passed a
resolution, embodying a labour test, by which the tramps
were to have their breakfast at the usual hour (at the
same time as the other inmates of the house), and be

detained for three hours and a half thereafter to work at
the mill or break stones.   When this alteration became
known *on the road*, it for a short time operated in reducing
the number, but not until gang after gang had been sent
to gaol for refusing to work.   The magistrates in their
places at the Board complained of the expense to the
county of those wholesale committals ; and as this resist-
ance to the labour test on the part of the tramps appeared
more to arise from the fact of their being turned out on
the road in the middle of the day, and with a comparatively empty stomach, having had their breakfast four
hours previous, than to the mere labour test itself, it was
ordered that they be put to work immediately after rising,
and have their breakfast three hours and a half after, so
that they thus left the house about ten o'clock A.M.,
having just had a tolerable meal, and were in a comfortable plight for the day.   The consequence of the above
alteration was, as you will readily conceive, an almost
immediate increase in the number of tramps.   In about
three weeks the number rose from about 70 to 120 per
week.   On this becoming apparent, the matter was again
reported to the Board, who instantly placed the order on
its original footing, viz., that they (the tramps) be set to
work three hours and a half *after breakfast*.   This was,
as before, resisted ; but on the parties finding that the
Bench and the Board were both determined to carry it
out, they submitted, and for months we had no trouble on
account of their refusing to work.   As these parties
appeared, as it were, to have taken our terms, and their
numbers began again to increase, the Board again took
the whole question into full consideration, and after due
deliberation, it was determined to refuse all relief to the
systematic vagrant ; at the same time, the officers were
instructed to use their best discretion to prevent any *casual*

poor person from suffering, and hence, acting on this order in the spirit of good faith, while we (I mean the paid officers) have refused relief to any of the vagrant fraternity (for a fraternity they are, and are easily distinguished as such), we have given relief as usual to the other poor travellers who appeared to be on a *bonâ fide* errand.

" I then, sir, as a matter of opinion, hold, that the last course above referred to is the best, and decidedly think that vagrants, as a class, deserve but little pity, and ought rather to be *under the cognizance of the police than the poor-law officer*. They are, for the most part, if not criminals, at least on the verge of crime. The greater portion of them have never done a week's work consecutively in their lives, and, if they can help it, never intend to do one. From many who have been taken ill on their journey, and had, for a time, to remain in the house, I have ascertained that they have, since shortly after the passing of the New Poor Law, passed their time circling from Union to Union, and either begged or stole to eke out an existence. On one I found a written list of all the workhouses for several counties round, and had those marked off for more frequent visitation which he deemed the best. I have personally examined many who began a life of vagrancy at about twelve years of age, and from the facilities afforded by workhouse relief, have continued ever since in the same pursuit, *outcasts from society, knowing no home, counting all men their enemies, and thus educating themselves for the most flagrant crimes*, and are ready on a day's notice, without remorse, to concentrate themselves for mischief in any part of the country.

" About three months ago, two, who had passed the night at this Union, were committed for setting fire to a stack of hay, and another for the same offence last week. One, who has often visited here, was lately committed for an attempt at highway robbery, and another is now lying in Ruthin gaol, under a sentence of transportation for theft.

" In giving these parties relief then, in the way we have done, I really think we were aiding them in their criminal career, as it afforded them a comfortable leisure to mature their plans, and go, without the care of providing for themselves, in quest of adventures. By the refusal of relief they are only put a little more to their shifts, and must either betake themselves to honest pursuits, or show themselves in their true colours, and, consequently, *be absorbed through the law.*

" The statements of Mr. Kemp were corroborated, generally, by the officers of other Unions, and I therefore adopt his letter as exhibiting fairly enough the character of the evil with which the Guardians of several Unions of this district had to contend.

" The measures adopted by the different Unions in this district for the repression of this evil were generally in strict accordance with the suggestions contained in the Circular of the 4th of August, 1848."

Mr. Kemp is perhaps a little too keen against the wandering poor, and his notion of having vagrants " absorbed " through the law, is a touch of workhouse " science " surpassing the ordinary intellectual flights of those localities. It is, however, unquestionable that a very large amount of low and gross imposture is continually practised by these wandering beggars or " tramps," and Mr. Kemp says, very justly, that they ought rather to be under the cognizance of the Police than of the Poor Law officer. These profligate idlers are practically the greatest enemies of the really distressed and unfortunate, for they cast such suspicion upon every case of alleged destitution, that they prevent actual misery from meeting with the ready relief from the affluent, which frequently it would meet with, if there were no doubt of its genuineness.

In the evidence of Mr. Cornewall Lewis, M.P., on Parochial Assessments, June 24, 1850, he gave the following statement of the number and salaries of Poor-Law Officers :—

					Salary.
Clerks	.	.	.	590	£59,431
Chaplains	.	.	.	415	19,140
Medical officers	.	.	.	2,680	124,532
Relieving officers	.	.	1,259	103,881
Masters and matrons	.	.	1,238	44,369
Schoolmasters	.	.	.	284	7,423
Schoolmistresses	.	.	.	423	7,009
Porters	.	.	.	347	6,340
Nurses	.	.	.	171	2,161
Taskmasters	.	.	.	20	936
Collectors or assistant overseers	.		499	23,026
Treasurers	.	.	.	52	973
Other officers	.	.	.	264	7,447
				8,240	406,968
District auditors	.	.		50	12,933
Total	.	.	.	8,290	£419,901

The Table on next page, showing the financial history of the Poor Law, since its alteration in 1834, is given in the Appendix to the last Report of the Poor Law Board.

Enough has now been brought forward to give, I trust, a tolerably accurate general view of that remarkable system existing in England for the sustentation of the destitute at the expense of all who own or who occupy houses or lands. It is, indeed, a very condensed statement, but I have endeavoured to represent plainly the leading facts, and to bring forward some of the more striking particulars of a complicated and repulsive subject. If it be asked how it is that, notwithstanding this extensive provision for the relief of distress, so many cases of frightful and totally

TABLE showing the estimated Population, the Amount of Money Levied for Poor Rates, the Amount Expended for the Relief and Maintenance of the Poor in England and Wales, in the years ended at Lady-day, 1834 to 1849, both inclusive; with the Rate per head of the Amount Levied and Expended for Relief to the Poor, on the estimated Population, the Rate in the Pound of Expenditure for Relief to the Poor on Annual Value of Rateable Property in 1847, and the Average Price of Wheat per Quarter in each year.

Years ended at Lady-day.	Population estimated according to the Ratio of Increase which prevailed between 1831 and 1841.	Amount of Money levied for Poor Rates.	Total expended in Relief and Maintenance of the Poor.	Rate per head of Amount Levied and Expended in Relief to the Poor on the Estimated Population.				Rate in the Pound of Expenditure for Relief to the Poor in each Year, calculated on the Annual Value of Rateable Property, in 1847.		* Average price of Wheat per Quarter.	
				Levy.		Relief to the Poor.					
		£.	£.	s.	d.	s.	d.	s.	d.	s.	d.
†1834	14,372,000	8,338,079	6,317,255	11	7¼	8	9½	1	10½	51	11
1835	14,564,000	7,373,807	5,526,418	10	1½	7	7	1	7¾	44	2
1836	14,758,000	6,354,538	4,717,630	8	7½	6	4¾	1	4¾	39	5
1837	14,955,000	5,294,566	4,044,741	7	0¾	5	5	1	2½	52	6
1838	15,155,000	5,186,389	4,123,604	6	10¼	5	5¼	1	2¾	55	3
1839	15,357,000	5,613,939	4,406,907	7	3¾	5	8¾	1	3¾	69	4
1840	15,562,000	6,014,605	4,576,965	7	8¾	5	10½	1	4¼	68	6
1841	15,770,000	6,351,828	4,760,929	8	0¾	6	0½	1	5	65	3
1842	15,981,000	6,552,890	4,911,498	8	2½	6	1¾	1	5½	64	0
1843	16,194,000	7,085,595	5,208,027	8	9	6	5¼	1	6½	54	4
1844	16,410,000	6,847,205	4,976,093	8	4¼	6	0¾	1	5¾	51	5
1845	16,629,000	6,791,006	5,039,703	8	2	6	0¾	1	6	49	2
1846	16,851,000	6,800,623	4,954,204	8	0¾	5	10½	1	5¾	53	3
1847	17,076,000	6,964,825	5,298,787	8	2	6	2½	1	7	59	0
1848	17,304,000	7,817,430	6,180,764	9	0½	7	1¾	1	10	64	6
1849	17,534,000	7,674,146	5,792,963	8	8	6	6½	1	8¾	49	1

NOTE.—The annual value of rateable property in 1847 was 67,320,587*l.*

* The average price of Wheat per quarter was obtained from the Comptroller of Corn Returns.

† The year 1834 was the last parochial year prior to the passing of the Poor Law Amendment Act.

unaided destitution are brought under public notice from time to time in Police reports, and reports of Coroners' Inquests? I can only answer that sometimes there are technical legal impediments to the claims of destitute persons upon the authorities of the parish or union in which they happen to be resident; and, yet more frequently, the indolence of despair, or the dread of something even more horrible than starvation, prevents the requisite application from being made to those who would officially afford relief.

The Poor Law originated in the reign of Elizabeth, shortly after the ecclesiastical establishments of England had been robbed of those great endowments which were devoted, in part at least, to the assistance of the poor and needy. Civil government has perhaps done what it could, but it can do but imperfectly the work of Christian charity. The parish overseer, or union relieving officer, can scarcely be regarded as doing the office of the good Samaritan. The best relief of the poor is, and must ever be, that which springs from a right sense of Christian duty—from a heartfelt sense of Christian brotherhood, as deducible from the authority—" Inasmuch as ye have done it unto one of the least of these my brethren, ye have done it unto ME."

(355)

INDEX.

A.

ABERCORN, Marquis of, his Irish
farms, ii. 223.
Advertisements in newspapers, i. 235.
Advocacy, professional, ii. 148 to 168.
——— its variety, ii. 158 to 161.
Age, the present, character of, i. 161,
214, 217; ii. 131, 132.
Agriculturists and manufacturers,
i. 22, 24.
Agriculturists, their alleged ignorance, i. 299, 332.
——— must begin to work early in
life, i. 329, 330, 333.
Albert, H. R. H. Prince, on University Commission, ii. 114.
Alison, A., on condition of the people, i. 81, 84, 137.
Allotments and small farms, ii. 213,
to 238.
——— ii. 227 to 235.
——— report of Commissioners
upon, ii. 227.
——— Bishop of Bath and Wells'
experiment, ii. 228.
——— proper size of, ii. 233.
Animals, import of, i. 55.
——— sale of, at Smithfield, ii.
240 to 244.
Archbishops, their jurisdiction, ii. 57.
Archdeacons, ii. 64.
Arches, court of, ii. 58.
Aristocratic sentiment in England
universal, i. 348, 349.
Aristocrats, i. 347, 348.
Arnold, Dr., on English scenery, i. 5.
——— on condition of the people,
i. 91.
——— on Church of England, ii. 1
to 3.
——— on Church ordinances, ii. 20.

Arnold, Dr., on Christian union, ii.
43.
——— on Church property, ii. 45.
Aspect, rural, of England, i. 1.
Attorneys, ii. 169 to 176.
Austin, Mrs., on education, i. 289.

B.

Bacon, Lord, i. 163.
Bamford on English scenery, i. 7.
Barristers, ii. 148 to 168.
——— their number, ii. 149.
——— their duty, ii. 153 to 160.
——— their practice, ii. 158 to 161.
——— their cruelty, ii. 161.
Bath and Wells, late Bishop of, his
allotments of land, ii. 228.
Beer-shops, ii. 247 to 268.
——— their evil tendency, ii. 248,
250, 255.
——— disappointment respecting
them, ii. 248.
——— increase of them, ii. 249.
——— advantages of, ii. 250.
——— in London, ii. 256.
——— licences of, ii. 264.
Beer, consumption of, 1836 to 1850,
ii. 267.
Beer duty, ii. 264.
Belgium, agriculture of, ii. 215, 221.
Belgian farmers, ii. 225.
Benefices, number of, ii 24, 25, 48.
——— value of, ii. 25.
Bennett, Rev. W. J. E., on crime
and education, i. 139, 299, 323.
Birmingham, drinking habits, ii. 263.
Births, i. 149, 151, 152, 156.
——— illegitimate, i. 157.
Bishops not aristocratic, ii. 28.
——— incomes, ii. 35 to 37, 50, 53.
——— proposed increase of number,
ii. 42, 43.

THE END.

PRINTED BY W. CLOWES AND SONS, STAMFORD STREET.